THE CUBS OF '69 ★

Recollections of the Team That Should Have Been

RICK TALLEY

CB

CONTEMPORARY
BOOKS

CHICAGO · NEW YORK

Library of Congress Cataloging-in-Publication Data

Talley, Rick.
  The Cubs of '69.

  Includes index.
  1. Chicago Cubs (Baseball team)—History.   I. Title.
GV875.C6T35   1989   796.357'64'0977311   88-35189
ISBN 0-8092-4501-9

Published by Contemporary Books, Inc.
180 North Michigan Avenue, Chicago, Illinois 60601
Manufactured in the United States of America
Library of Congress Catalog Card Number: 88-35189
International Standard Book Number: 0-8092-4501-9

Published simultaneously in Canada by Beaverbooks, Ltd.
195 Allstate Parkway, Valleywood Business Park
Markham, Ontario L3R 4T8 Canada

To my father, Virgil,
who dug southern Illinois coal,
fished, threw a fork ball,
and took his 11-year-old son on a bus
to old Sportsman's Park in St. Louis
to see the Cubs play the Cardinals.
The year was 1945.

Contents

Acknowledgments

Thanks and appreciation to players and supporting cast of the 1969 Cubs who consented to be interviewed for this book.

Thanks, too, to those who helped locate people, verify anecdotal material, and provide support. Namely, Bob Hertzel, Joe Gilmartin, John McGrath, Steve Nidetz, Larry Casey, Gordon Verrell, Bob Ibach, Cubs publicist Ned Colletti and staff, Jim Dunegan, Pat Bourque, Jim Armstrong, Herman Franks, *Chicago Tribune* Library staff, Vicki Johnson of the Dodger publicity staff, Manny Mota, Joe Resnick, Paul Jensen, Mark Belanger of the Major League Baseball Players Association, Mike and Cathy Corey, George and Carolyn Casanave, Jack Rosenberg, Bob Ottowell, and Mert Letofsky.

Special thanks to family members—Jane, Wendy, Scott, and Jennifer—who endured my curmudgeon work personality; to companion George, my bassett hound, who listened to my ideas and occasionally offered negative rebuttal; and to Shari Lesser Wenk, who edited the same way. She is the best in her business.

Author's Note

I am not a behavioral scientist or even a very good amateur psychologist, but it has occurred to me nevertheless that the Chicago Cubs' 20 consecutive second-division finishes, 1947–1966, a major league record, may have affected my personality. At the time, from the ages of 13 to 32, it seemed wholly natural to argue about and defend the wretched baseball team that represented the Chicago franchise in the National League. My first Cubs hero was Dominic Dallesandro, who stood only 5′6″; my second was Roy Smalley, who threw baseballs into Section 5, Row 6.

Therefore, when the 1967 and 1968 teams blossomed and the 1969 Cubs raised partisans to unprecedented heights of joy, only to drop them like so many crumpled Old Style cups, there was impact.

It was a season, I am convinced, that Cubs fans have not forgotten, perhaps have even perversely cherished, as its memory far overshadows subsequent historical events such as a 23–22 game, a 600-foot home run by a jerk, and a ground ball rolling through a first baseman's legs.

The men who played on that '69 team haven't forgotten

either. Twenty years later, from venues of other successes and failures, they reflect on the dramatic 1969 season that in many ways fused them together as one.

Ken Holtzman, 43, born the year the Cubs last won a pennant, talks about the unique fellowship that develops among professional athletes: "Somebody likened it to combat without the blood. You do things and say things together that you would never share with other people. In a baseball clubhouse you're fully exposed, all of your weaknesses, your whole life. Everything becomes a common struggle."

Cubs fans know a little about struggle.

At the conclusion of the 1969 season, a reviewer of a book about the New York Mets wrote, "After eight books on the Mets, isn't it about time someone gave us a book about the team that lost?"

The time has come. I even considered concocting an ending in which the Cubs sweep through September of 1969 with victory after victory.

But Cubs fans, for whom this book was written, know better.

—Rick Talley
February 1989

THE CUBS OF '69 ★

trauma—a disordered psychic or behavioral state resulting from mental or emotional stress or physical injury.
—*Webster's Ninth New Collegiate Dictionary*

You may glory in a team triumphant, but you fall in love with a team in defeat.
—Roger Kahn,
The Boys of Summer

APRIL 30

East	W	L	GB
Chicago	16	7	—
Pittsburgh	13	8	2
New York	9	11	5½
St. Louis	9	12	6
Philadelphia	8	11	6
Montreal	7	13	7½

MAY 31

East	W	L	GB
Chicago	32	16	—
Pittsburgh	24	23	7½
New York	21	23	9
St. Louis	21	25	10
Philadelphia	18	24	11
Montreal	11	32	18½

JUNE 30

East	W	L	GB
Chicago	49	27	—
New York	40	32	7
Pittsburgh	38	38	11
St. Louis	35	41	14
Philadelphia	33	39	14
Montreal	21	52	26½

OPENING DAY LINEUP

Don Kessinger	SS
Glenn Beckert	2B
Billy Williams	LF
Ron Santo	3B
Ernie Banks	1B
Randy Hundley	C
Jim Hickman	RF
Don Young	CF
Fergie Jenkins	P

1
In the Beginning

"We knew that this was the season
we were going to win."
—Ron Santo

It was the summer man first stepped onto the moon. Actress Sharon Tate was found dead in Los Angeles, and Charles Manson was found guilty. Senator Edward Kennedy drove off a bridge at Chappaquiddick Island, Massachusetts, killing Mary Jo Kopechne. Heavyweight champion Rocky Marciano perished in a plane crash near Newton, Iowa.

It was a time of turbulence. Hurricane Camille, the world's worst storm since 1915, lashed unmercifully at the gulf coast; the Reverend Jesse Jackson was arrested for demonstrating at the University of Illinois Circle Campus construction site; and in muddy farm fields near Woodstock, New York, more than four hundred thousand young people gathered to listen to rock music, smoke marijuana, and let it all hang out.

In Vietnam more than forty thousand American soldiers had already been killed and two hundred sixty-four thousand had been injured in combat. Another five hundred thousand remained on the battle lines while President Richard M. Nixon spoke of bringing them home.

Joe Namath had already won a Super Bowl and sold a saloon. Lew Alcindor joined the Milwaukee Bucks, Al Lopez retired from baseball, Bill Hartack won the Kentucky Derby aboard Majestic Prince, and Orville Moody was headed for a victory in the U.S. Open golf championship.

The Bleacher Bums were born at Wrigley Field.

And the Chicago Cubs had their greatest, and worst, season of baseball in four decades.

They had a pennant won and blew it.

It was a summer of ecstasy and trauma for the city of Chicago and a nation of Cubs fans.

This was the best Cubs team of a half-century, these Cubs of 1969, but something happened. Leading the New York Mets by 9½ games on August 14—the very day on which two decades of violence would break out in Londonderry, Northern Ireland—the Cubs collapsed to finish in second place, a humiliating 8 games behind.

The Mets' victory during baseball's 100th anniversary year was called a miracle. Winning 38 of their final 49 games, they swept onward to defeat Atlanta in baseball's first National League Championship Series and then humble the Baltimore Orioles in five World Series games.

But was it a miracle or only alliteration? Can defeat of such magnitude be rationalized away by divine intervention? Since the beginning of divisional play in the National League 20 years ago, only the 1969 Cubs have lost a lead of more than 2½ games after Labor Day. Only one other major league team, the 1978 Boston Red Sox, lost a larger post–Labor Day lead (5½). The Cubs, however, had led by 9½ in mid-August and led by 5, with only 25 remaining, at the beginning of play on September 5, 1969, only to lose their next 7 straight, 10 of 11, and 14 of 20 before being eliminated on September 24. During that same 20-day span the Mets went 19–5.

Those are numbers. But this is a book about humans— about the players, the manager, and the coaches who constituted the 1969 Cubs, what happened to them then and what has happened since, how they look back on that summer of '69, and how their lives have been affected by those unforgettable days.

It is also the story of a unique bond between men—call it a bond of combat, of compassion, of love—which has grown from within the heart of that team for more than 20 years.

Finally, and perhaps even more illuminating, is the witness of adoration and respect that the city of Chicago, and Cubs fans nationwide, still hold for their heroes in defeat. It has been said that love is not resentful—that it lets the past be past, moving people to new beginnings without settling the past. And it is indeed difficult to imagine the 1969 Cubs being more loved if they *had* won.

It was a mystique that began when Leo Durocher became manager in 1966 and was sustained, although somewhat shakily at the finish, until his dismissal during the 1972 season.

These were Leo's Cubs, a team that played together and stayed together longer than any in baseball since. Six position regulars, first baseman Ernie Banks, second baseman Glenn Beckert, shortstop Don Kessinger, third baseman Ron Santo, catcher Randy Hundley, and leftfielder Billy Williams, played together for five seasons—that's six men in the same spots in the lineup for five years. And when Banks retired after 1971, the other five remained together for yet another three seasons.

It all happened before free agency and, unless the rules of baseball are drastically changed, it will not happen again.

Banks batted in the heart of the Cubs lineup from the end of one war (Korea) to the conclusion of another (Vietnam); for 17 seasons he was either the regular shortstop or the first baseman. Banks, Santo, and Williams were the nucleus of the Cub batting order for 10 consecutive seasons, 1961–1970. Kessinger opened the season at shortstop for 10 consecutive years, 1966–1975. Beckert played second base for nine straight years, 1965–1973. Ferguson Jenkins pitched seven consecutive Opening Days, 1967–1973. Santo started 13 seasons at third base, 1961–1973, Williams 14 seasons in left field, 1961–1974.

Yet by the spring of 1969 the Cubs had not won a National League pennant since 1945 (and they still haven't). They hadn't won a World Series since 1908 (and they still haven't). Chicago cemeteries were (and still are) inhabited by people who had hoped to live long enough to see the Cubs win another pennant. The White Sox had won a pennant in 1959, the Black Hawks the Stanley Cup in 1961, the Bears a championship in 1963, the Bulls nothing at all—and all of those Chicago professional teams had also fallen on hard times in the mid-to-late 1960s.

Then surging came the Cubs, 41 in total, who careened aboard Durocher's ever-backing-up truck through that dramatic season of 1969.

The man who owned them, P. K. Wrigley, is now dead. So is general manager John Holland. So are coaches Pete Reiser and Rube Walker. So too is one player, Randy Bobb.

The others live with the memory.

It began with Willie Smith's home run.

Opening Day at Wrigley Field. Two-run shot, bottom of the 11th inning. Cubs win 7–6.

Rookie Barry Lersch of the Phillies threw the pitch, a 1–0 fastball that the 30-year-old Smith, an ex-boxer and substitute ballplayer, ax-handled into the right-field bleachers, scoring Randy Hundley ahead of him.

By the time Smith reached home plate, there was chaos. Hysterical fans poured onto the field to join Willie's 24 cheering teammates and form an uncontrollable committee of welcome.

Nobody could remember such an Opening Day. The largest modern Opening Day crowd in Wrigley Field history, 40,796, had begun congregating at 8 A.M. to vie for 5,000 bleacher and 22,000 general admission seats. First came the ceremonies. Capt. Ron Santo introduced Jimmy Durante and draped him in a Cubs jacket. Edgar Munzel of the *Sun-Times*, dean of Chicago baseball writers, threw out the first ball.

Then the ovations, first for 38-year-old Ernie Banks, beginning his 17th season with his 73-year-old father in the audience. Then for Banks again, and again, as he homered in his first two at-bats, driving in five runs.

But the Phils fought back on this day of balmy beginning and dramatic conclusion. Twice. Twenty-one-year-old Don Money homered two times, his second coming in the 11th off reliever Phil Regan, leaving the Cubs behind 6–5.

Lersch, meanwhile, had been magnificent, retiring 10 Cubs in a row until Hundley singled with one out in the 11th. Then manager Leo Durocher called upon left-handed hitter Smith to bat for Jim Hickman.

Leo began pleading: "Just a dying quail over third, that's all I want." Bill Hands, sitting nearby, said, "The hell with that, Skip. He'll hit it out."

"When the ball flew over my head," recalls Hundley, almost 20 years later, "it was like 'Hey, we're going to win. This is something special.' "

Afterward, there was bedlam in the clubhouse. Nobody considered taking a shower for at least 30 minutes.

"We knew right there," says Santo today, "that this was the season we were going to win."

One hundred and eight Smiths have played major league baseball—everyone from Riverboat Smith to Pop Boy Smith to Phenomenal Smith to Broadway Aleck, Germany, Klondike, and Skyrocket Smith, as well as four Red Smiths—but this day belonged to a Smith from Anniston, Alabama, called Wonderful Willie Smith.

Actually, it started *before* Willie Smith's home run.

The setting was serene. The swimming pool at the Ramada Inn, Scottsdale, Arizona, was cool and relaxing, as was spring training for the confident Cubs, eager to begin the '69 season.

"Leo Durocher has been a tonic for this ball club," said team captain Santo on March 27, 1969. "Leo is tough, he's real tough. He'll do anything to win, but he told us we were good, and we believe him. He's one in a million. You know, you don't have to love a man to respect him, but I know everybody on this club respects him. Other clubs respect him too."

Santo offered an example of what Durocher meant to the Cubs: "With five games to play last year [1968], we were in position to finish anywhere from third to sixth. Leo called a meeting. It was one of his great meetings. We got the message. Look it up. We won the last five games and finished third.

"It showed us what we can do under pressure."

A few days later Adolfo Phillips, his fractured hand in a cast, was seen shagging fly balls with his healthy hand. (Nevertheless, unable to please Leo, he would be traded on June 11 for infielder Paul Popovich.) Banks was tossing souvenir baseballs into the audience and singing ditties about "Sociable Scottsdale," and pitcher Regan was telling a reporter, "One thing you have to have is team spirit. Unselfishness. You can't have jealousies. You don't see or talk about it. But you can feel team spirit on a club and the Cubs have it."

It was a time for optimism. Even though the St. Louis Cardinals had captured consecutive pennants in 1967 and 1968 and were favored again, many were pointing toward the Cubs. And of the Mets? Dimitrius Synodinos, a.k.a. Jimmy (the Greek) Snyder, listed them at 100 to 1.

It was into an atmosphere of excitement and anticipation that this writer was to begin his first baseball season in Chicago, as sports editor of the *Chicago Today*. Fresh from nine years of apprenticeship in Rockford, Illinois, by way of San Francisco (UPI) and Carbondale (Southern Illinois University) and hometown Pinckneyville, a southern Illinois haven for coal miners, squirrel hunters, and jump shooters, I was a 34-year-old newsman prepared for anything.

The Cubs, on the other hand, coming east from Arizona were hardly prepared for what lay ahead.

Certainly, though, they didn't falter after that dramatic Willie Smith homer in game one. They swept the Phillies in the next two games at Wrigley Field, then won two of three over the Montreal Expos, an expansion team, and completed the 10-game home stand by sweeping both the Pirates and the Cardinals.

Wham, bam, and welcome to baseball, new commissioner Bowie Kuhn. The Cubs had won nine of their first ten and would remain atop the National League East for 155 consecutive days.

Meanwhile, George Archer was winning the Masters golf tournament, but the Cubs didn't notice. They were off to the frigid environs of Montreal, where they again won two of three from the Expos, then lost a doubleheader in Pittsburgh and, back in Wrigley Field, a single game to the Cardinals.

Having lost four in a row, they now faced the Mets for the first time in 1969, in a four-game series at Shea Stadium in late April. The Cubs won the opener as Fergie Jenkins outpitched Tom Seaver, and then they hammered the Mets behind Hands.

The schedule, backed up by cold April weather, had become an early adversary. The Cubs now faced the Mets in their third doubleheader within seven days, and, for the first time in 1969, manager Durocher faced some tough pitching decisions.

Rich Nye, then a 24-year-old left-hander, recalls the situation:

"We had just gotten Dick Selma from the San Diego Padres two days earlier [in a trade for Joe Niekro] and Leo named him for game one and me for game two. Selma got shelled but we won anyhow [Regan's fourth win in a row], then I pitched eight scoreless innings in the nightcap. But

Cleon Jones hit a three-run homer with one out in the ninth, and we lost 3–0.

"After that I figured since Selma got rocked and I had pitched so well that I'd be in the starting rotation. Instead Leo went with Selma and I went to the bullpen."

Jack Brickhouse, announcer for WGN-TV and later a bitter critic of Durocher, also recalls the Nye game vividly:

"I probably remember that home run by Cleon Jones more than any during the 1969 season. It was hot in New York, and you could see the kid was exhausted. Well, Ed Kranepool ripped the bejesus out of the ball, and it was caught. Now there's one out with a couple of guys on base, and Leo goes to the mound. But he leaves Nye in the game, and before Leo even sat back down in the dugout the ball was leaving the ballpark and the Cubs were beat. It was a judgment call by Leo, and it was no good.

"You know, when I first knew Durocher, he was one of the sharpest riverboat gamblers I ever saw in my life. You didn't have to tell Leo if a guy had thrown 87 pitches. He knew whether a guy was tired or not. In those early days, he was a son of a bitch, but he was a sharp son of a bitch. But by the time he was finished in Chicago, he was just an old son of a bitch."

Sharp, old, or whatever, Leo nevertheless had the Cubs on a roll. Having won three of four from the Mets, they won two of three in Philadelphia and finished April with a record of 16–7. The Mets had gone 9–11 and trailed by 5½, but nobody was noticing.

While the Cubs were traveling, a few things were happening elsewhere. The *Chicago's American* newspaper became the *Chicago Today*, a tabloid; the White Sox played before their smallest Comiskey Park audience ever, 619, on April 22; there was a foul claim in the Mississippi River steamboat race between the Delta Queen and Belle of Louisville; and the ABC television network had made a startling announcement. Get this: ABC was going to begin televising National Football League games on Monday nights in prime time during the autumn of 1970. Football in America's living rooms on Monday nights? A lot of people thought women would never stand for it.

The Cubs and Mets were back at it during the first week in May, this time in Chicago, where the Cubs won two but then lost a doubleheader, Seaver over Hands and Tug McGraw over Selma. The Cubs then won five of their next seven during the home stand versus the Dodgers, the Giants, and the expansion-team Padres, and the Mets were quickly forgotten. In the Padre series, in fact, the Cubs got three consecutive shutouts from Holtzman (now 5-1), Jenkins (now 5-2), and Selma (1-1), who pitched a 19-0 shutout.

It was that kind of month. The Cubs, winning 16 of 25 games in May, now stood at 32-16.

And while the Mets were struggling to finish the month with a 21-23 record, nine games behind the Cubs, a college student named Dan Quayle joined the Indiana National Guard and nobody noticed.

By June, of course, the Wrigley Field bandwagon was crowded with customers. The Cubs were ablaze and having fun, winning 17 of 28 during the month to go 22 games over .500 (49-27). Before June was finished, Jenkins would be 10-5, Ken Holtzman 9-2, Hands 8-6, Selma 6-1, and reliever Regan 8-5. The hitters were producing runs (during one six-game road stretch in mid-June, the Cubs scored 54 against the Braves, the Reds, and the Pirates), and there was even romance in the air.

Leo Durocher, at age 63, was getting married. For the fourth time.

The wedding to Lynne Walker Goldblatt was set for June 19, and the entire team was invited. Archie Reynolds, a 23-year-old rookie pitcher, was especially excited. For a kid from Tyler, Texas, this was big stuff.

"My wife and I both went, and she danced with P. K. Wrigley and I danced with Mrs. Wrigley," recalls Archie, "and I think that's when I became a favorite of Mr. Wrigley. He always did like me."

Wrigley's affection for Archie, however, did not keep the kid from Texas from being sent back to Tacoma soon after the wedding and being traded by Durocher ("I could never please him," said Archie) the following summer.

Leo's wedding did have other significance. It marked the beginning of his occasional disappearances. Even though the wedding was scheduled for a day off, Leo checked out of the team hotel in Pittsburgh early one day in order to attend a high-society bachelor party in Chicago on the eve of the wedding. The Cubs lost to the Pirates that night under coach Pete Reiser, 3-2 in 10 innings.

One other wedding item: Brickhouse was not invited, and Leo has always claimed that was the reason for his feud with the WGN announcer. Brickhouse's reply:

"Leo never invites me to his weddings."

At Wrigley Field, meanwhile, there was partying in the bleachers. This was the year the Bleacher Bums—the title emblazoned in red across their yellow helmets—appeared at Wrigley Field. Ron Grousl, a 24-year-old who worked a few hours each morning washing glasses at a saloon near the ballpark, was president of the not-so-tightly knit organization, and pitcher Dick Selma was its unofficial cheerleader.

Selma explains how his role evolved:

"Leo was very superstitious. He would chase the batboy out of the dugout if he moved the fungo bats from the end of the rack. So one day I'm on the bench, maybe in May or early June, and it's the second game of a doubleheader. I have to go to the bathroom, and in those days we had to walk down the left-field line to our door to the clubhouse. There was no entrance from the dugout. And Wrigley Field has a unique sound like no other ballpark—a sound all of its own, like a kids' sound, not an adult sound. Anyhow, I finish inside and walk back out, and you could hear a pin drop. Absolutely no noise. So I scream up to the bleachers, 'Start yellin'!' and I start waving my arms. Well, the next thing I know Ernie Banks hits a home run, and the place explodes.

"Now, the next day I'm back in the dugout, which is

where I like to sit because I can check information with the
hitters. But Leo makes me go down into the bullpen. 'Get
those Bums goin',' he yells, so I go down and start waving a
towel around. From then on, when I wasn't pitching that
was my job."

Selma's routine often concluded with a climactic cres-
cendo, as he'd leap into the air and point his finger at the
ground as the Bums chanted:

> Every time I go to town,
> The boys all kick my dog around.
> Makes no difference if he is a hound,
> You better stop kicking my dog around.

The Bums, meanwhile, were doing a good job of anger-
ing opponents. Pete Rose was a special target. So was Willie
Davis of the Dodgers, who got particularly angry one day
when the Bums kept mentioning the name of a Playboy
bunny he had known. Then there was the day Grousl
caught the 521st home run hit by Henry Aaron—the one
that put him ahead of Ted Williams. Grousl claims he
graciously offered Aaron the ball, but Aaron, unhappy with
the abuse he'd been taking, angrily threw the ball back.
The Bums retaliated by pouring beer over his head.

The original Bums even had their own pep song:

> Salvation Army, Salvation Army,
> Put a nickel in the drum
> To save another Bleacher Bum.

It was mania. Nothing like this had ever happened at
Wrigley Field, and management wasn't quite sure what to do
about the Bums. Cubs players loved them. But their opponents?

"Somebody's gonna get hurt out here," said Cardinal
Lou Brock in late June. "And it's too bad. The Cubs are
going great, but the fans may spoil it."

Brock, on that particular frenzied weekend when the

Cubs won three of four from the defending NL champions, was almost hit in the head by a dry-cell battery whizzing past his ear. Later, an orange bounced through his legs. And when he made a leaping, one-handed catch of Don Young's line drive in game one of a Cubs doubleheader sweep, a large apple went flying past his head. During the same series, Mudcat Grant was struck in the face by a hard rubber ball, and he retaliated by whipping baseballs into the bleachers as fans ran for cover.

The Bums, of course, claimed that none of their brethren had been responsible for anything being thrown. Indeed, they claimed to be watchdogs, pointing out those who misbehaved.

The situation got even worse in 1970, when on Opening Day hundreds of fans leaped the bleacher walls and ran onto the field. "A monster has been created," remarked one Andy Frain usher. And so, before the end of April 1970, the bleacher fence—a 30-inch diagonal basket, actually—was in place in Wrigley Field. So, too, were the Bums.

Longtime Cubs exec E. R. (Salty) Saltwell, who has been with the team since 1958, recalls the hoopla over the once-controversial basket. "The basket works," says Salty, "not only to keep fans from jumping out of the bleachers but to keep debris off the field.

"It was Opening Day 1970 when we had so many unruly fans, but we took a bad rap for that one. It turned out that a bunch of radical groups had been demonstrating downtown that day, and when they were finished they all decided to come to the ballpark. Those were not our regular fans."

But in June 1969 there was so much joy that nobody could assimilate anything negative. By the end of the month, 707,640 fans had already gone through Wrigley Field turnstiles. By season's end, that figure would reach an unprecedented 1,674,993, the greatest turnout in the history of Wrigley Field—a record that stood another 14 years until the division-winning 1984 Cubs surpassed two million and the 1985 team drew a record 2,161,534.

Those who couldn't make it to the ballpark tuned in

elsewhere, to Brickhouse on television and to Vince and Lou on radio. For 19 consecutive seasons, 1965 through 1983, it was Vince and Lou. Vince Lloyd, play by play, and Lou Boudreau, color. They were the WGN radio voices of the Chicago Cubs who traveled together, drank together, and flubbed together.

Vince, from the depth of those South Dakota tonsils, would say "at the end of 10 . . . it's still tied 2–1"; and when Lou described Jon Matlack pitching to Bill Madlock, it almost always came out Modlick and Malclack.

Listeners grew up with them and grew to love them, groaned at their imperfections but forgave them as easily as overlooking warts on Bob Ramazzotti and Bill Serena.

Remember, though, the climate of that time. The Cubs had failed for 15 straight years to attract even one million fans until Durocher's club of 1968 drew 1,043,409. Now it had increased half a million in only one year.

Durocher had begun his reclamation project with the 1966 Cubs, when he was credited with the infamous line that he really didn't utter at all:

"This is no eighth-place team."

In reality, that line came from the typewriter of Blake Cullen, who arrived in the Cubs' front office that year as assistant vice president in charge of road travel, statistics, and watching over Leo. Upon Cullen's arrival, he heard the voice of then-PR man Rip Collins (soon to be replaced by Chuck Shriver), say, "Kid, I'm going to let you write the press book."

So Cullen wrote the press book.

"Leo never said 'This is no eighth-place team,' " recalls Cullen. "I just made it up. I've always been sort of proud that I came up with Leo's second most famous line."

Actually Leo never uttered his most famous line ("Nice guys finish last") either. Not exactly. Durocher always claimed he was quoted out of context after saying to sportswriter Frank Graham about some of Mel Ott's New York Giants: "Take a look at them. All nice guys. They'll finish last. Nice guys. Finish last." Durocher said Graham quoted him correctly but that subsequent renditions made it sound as if he didn't think a decent person could succeed.

Durocher never denied the "eighth-place team" statement though, as his Cubs finished tenth (59–103) in 1966 and early critics giggled. Perhaps because he knew what was ahead, as the Cubs finished third in both 1967 (87–74) and 1968 (84–78).

Now, at last, in 1969 Chicago had a winner. It was heady stuff.

There was Ron Santo on the cover of *Sports Illustrated* ("They've got me running the bases," moaned Santo. "For nine years I've been trying to make that cover, and they've got me running the bases?") There was Kenny Holtzman joking about a rumor that he might be traded to the Phillies for Richie Allen. "We don't want Allen," said somebody in the clubhouse. "Sure we do. I'd trade Gene Oliver for Allen," joked Selma, looking directly into the eye of Oliver.

There was the doubleheader split with Montreal at Wrigley Field, when, two runs down in the ninth inning of game one, with two out and two men on base, Jim Hickman powered a homer to win it 7–6.

That was the first time Santo clicked his heels.

"I was so excited that I pounded Hick's head as he crossed home plate," recalled Santo. "Then I started running toward our clubhouse and just jumped into the air. It was a thing I did out of sheer joy. I don't think I'd ever been more excited because, for the first time, I felt we were going to win the pennant. So I hit Hickman on the head, ran down the field, and clicked my heels."

Heady stuff indeed.

So who was aware of Allied bases being blasted by the Cong, or 132 Yale students defying the draft, or a predawn raid on Black Panther headquarters? Actor Robert Taylor was dead at age 57, and Warren Earl Burger was succeeding Earl Warren as Chief Justice of the United States, and, would you believe it?, Mayor Richard J. Daley wanted to build an airport in the middle of Lake Michigan.

The Cubs were concerned only about the Cardinals coming into Chicago for that giant four-game series in late June. After losing the opening game, the Cubs swept the next three behind Hands, Jenkins, and Selma. By the completion of the last game of the Sunday doubleheader before 41,060, it was apparent the Cardinals would not win their third consecutive NL title. Already, on June 26, they trailed the Cubs by 14 games. The Mets trailed by 8, but who was keeping track of the Mets?

That weekend, too, belonged to Billy Williams on his "Day." Not only did he establish an NL record for consecutive games played (896), breaking Stan Musial's record, he also went five for nine in the doubleheader, including two doubles, two triples, and three standing ovations. He received, among other things, a new automobile, a boat, a trailer, and a weimaraner puppy that his four daughters adored.

Upstairs on the third-base mezzanine ramp, 69-year-old Andy Frain usher Malcolm Roland Reeser was leading the upper deck as they clapped along to the "Mexican Hat Dance" being played by organist Jack Kearney. And in the nearby press box somebody had discovered that on the Chinese calendar this was the Year of the Cock.

The last time the Cubs won a pennant, in 1945, it was also a Year of the Cock.

So was 1957, when the Cubs won 62 and lost 92. But this was 1969 with only one more day to play in June, and so far the Cubs had been on an untroubled joy ride.

Trouble came on that final June day. The site: Jarry Park, Montreal, on a cold, wet night. Play was delayed by rain, and the game didn't start until 9:51 P.M. Two minutes later Don Kessinger hit only his third homer in 77 games, over the right-field fence.

Then came the fireworks and the niftiest piece of fence kicking in Rusty Staub's career. The situation:

Ernie Banks homered in the second inning—a low line drive that soared through the darkness of the poorly illuminated Jarry Park outfield, cleared the wire-mesh fence, and rattled among the empty seats.

There was only one problem. Umpire Tony Venzon didn't see it that way. In fact, he didn't see it at all. He ruled it a ground-rule double.

"The ball went over the fence, no doubt about it. But it was obvious the umpire didn't see it," confirms Staub, who has since become a broadcaster for the Mets and a restaurateur in New York City, and was playing outfield for the Expos that confusing evening. "Anyhow, Joey Amalfitano was coaching that night, and he's out there in the outfield yelling for justice, and I stick my foot into a small hole in the bottom of the fence, kick it open a little larger, and say, 'Maybe it went through here, Joey.' Now, about that time here comes Venzon with Durocher after him, screaming bloody murder, and when Tony sees the hole in the fence he says to Leo, 'Look, it went under the fence through that hole.'

"Meanwhile, I'm having to turn away to keep from laughing out loud. I figure it's best to get out of there, so I retreated into right field. I mean, it's not like I misled the umpire. I didn't actually *say* the ball went through a hole."

Nevertheless Venzon's decision stood, and the Cubs not only didn't score; they eventually lost the game 5–2, near midnight.

"It was the worst umpiring I've seen in five years," said Durocher, who protested the game to no avail. And before the Cubs could escape the evening and month of June, there was yet another rhubarb, this time between Santo and Expos manager Gene Mauch. Somehow they got into a shouting match outside the Montreal dugout, near Santo's position at third base.

"I didn't say anything to Santo," said Mauch. "I did have a few words with my catcher. Maybe Ron has good ears."

For the record: Ernie Banks finished his major league career with 512 home runs. But take it from Rusty Staub, an honest man 20 years later: that number should be 513. Even Banks couldn't hit a baseball through a hole in the fence before the hole was there.

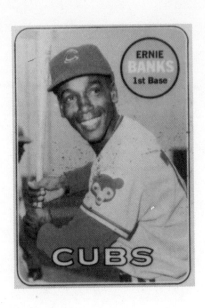

ERNEST BANKS
B. Jan, 31, 1931, Dallas, Tex.

YEAR	TEAM	G	AB	H	2B	3B	HR	HR%	R	RBI	BB	SO	SB	BA	SA
1953	CHI N	10	35	11	1	1	2	5.7	3	6	4	5	0	.314	.571
1954		154	593	163	19	7	19	3.2	70	79	40	50	6	.275	.427
1955		154	596	176	29	9	44	7.4	98	117	45	72	9	.295	.596
1956		139	538	160	25	8	28	5.2	82	85	52	62	6	.297	.530
1957		156	594	169	34	6	43	7.2	113	102	70	85	8	.285	.579
1958		154	617	193	23	11	47	7.6	119	129	52	87	4	.313	.614
1959		155	589	179	25	6	45	7.6	97	143	64	72	2	.304	.596
1960		156	597	162	32	7	41	6.9	94	117	71	69	1	.271	.554
1961		138	511	142	22	4	29	5.7	75	80	54	75	1	.278	.507
1962		154	610	164	20	6	37	6.1	87	104	30	71	5	.269	.503
1963		130	432	98	20	1	18	4.2	41	64	39	73	0	.227	.403
1964		157	591	156	29	6	23	3.9	67	95	36	84	1	.264	.450
1965		163	612	162	25	3	28	4.6	79	106	55	64	3	.265	.453
1966		141	511	139	23	7	15	2.9	52	75	29	59	0	.272	.432
1967		151	573	158	26	4	23	4.0	68	95	27	93	2	.276	.455
1968		150	552	136	27	0	32	5.8	71	83	27	67	2	.246	.469
1969		155	565	143	19	2	23	4.1	60	106	42	101	0	.253	.416
1970		72	222	56	6	2	12	5.4	25	44	20	33	0	.252	.459
1971		39	83	16	2	0	3	3.6	4	6	6	14	0	.193	.325
19 yrs.		2528	9421	2583	407	90	512	5.4	1305	1636	763	1236	50	.274	.500

2
Ernie Banks

"Start this book with me. I'm the senior citizen."
—Ernie Banks

Ernie Banks can fool you. He's been doing it for years. He bobs along in life, playing golf, signing autographs, attending Old-Timers Games, and making people feel good, and you think you've got a bead on what he's all about.

But then he says something like "I believe in the magic of change" or "Most of us fail—you must keep going," and you realize Ernie isn't just reciting a litany of armchair Pollyannaisms. There are thoughts behind those phrases, a depth of feeling behind that backslap and smile.

Banks's name first started to appear during the Korean War, alongside another simple five-letter name. Banks? Baker? The first blacks to play with the Chicago Cubs, you say? No kidding? Are they any good?

How quickly we learned. Gene Baker was very good, but

19

the skinny one, the kid from Texas with all that pop in his wrists—well, he was amazing.

How quickly, too, we learned to take him for granted. The Cubs were awful but there was always Ernie. The 1955 Cubs won 72 games, and Banks hit 44 home runs. The 1957 Cubs won 52 games, and Banks hit 43 home runs. Then he hit 47, and 45, and 41, and it didn't help, because the Cubs were on a treadmill to nowhere.

Banks, though, was above the torment.

Ernie's office is in the Dominguez Hills Industrial Park in Compton, California, part of the Los Angeles sprawl, where he has been employed as executive vice president, corporate sales, by the Chicago-based New World Van Lines, Inc., for the past five years.

Full-time job? Not exactly. Nothing has ever been full-time with Ernie Banks but baseball. But his boss loves him ("Mr. Banks opens a lot of doors for us," says Thomas Naegele. "It's a good partnership for both of us."), and certainly Ernie has had no problem fitting into the California lifestyle.

Chicago's own? Mr. Cub Man an Avocado Fan?

"I am three different people," says Banks, settling into a plain, hardbacked, plastic chair behind an empty desktop. No Cubs pictures on the wall. No Hall of Fame mementos. Just the telephone, which keeps him busy ("Hello, this is Einre Sknab! You don't know me? Sure you do, that's my name backwards!").

"Psychiatrists say I'm an open, giving, sharing person but that I can be very private, which is something I have been working toward. I can be with a group, and it's a blessing. Some people can't deal with strange people. I can. For 35 years all I did was deal with people I didn't know. But the facade was also me. I view people as if they have a sign on their chest which says 'Make me happy,' and I got happy by making them happy. I always view people as feeling worthless, not having self-esteem, and I try to focus attention off myself and onto them to make them feel important.

"The other side of me, though, is that I like to be alone. I never had that opportunity. I paid my dues being with people. I came from a large family of 12. I had my own family, twin boys and a daughter, and I always had a lot of people around.

"But never any privacy. My happiness is coming now because I have a chance for more solitude and privacy in my life. I like it, but I still like both sides, even as I get older."

Older is 58. When Ernie Banks became the first black man to represent the Cubs, Carl Furillo was hitting .344 in Brooklyn and guns along the 38th parallel were still smoking. The year was 1953, and on the day Banks came into the majors the Cubs lost 16–4 to the Phillies with a lineup of Bob Talbot, center field; Eddie Miksis, second base; Dee Fondy, first base; Ralph Kiner, left field; Hank Sauer, right field; Bill Serena, third base; Banks, shortstop; Clyde McCullough, catcher; and Don Elston, pitcher. It was 19 Septembers later that Banks walked away from Wrigley Field. Now a flag wearing number 14 hangs on that left-field pole, which stood sentinel while the majority of his 512 home runs sailed past.

But that was baseball, and now a third Ernie Banks is to be revealed.

"The third me is my strength in international business," says Ernie. "Now I understand it. I saw in the middle of my life, even back in 1969, that we would become a global society, and that people who can function must be international people or develop skills which will fit with the world. It's what we are coming to in a United States which is for sale. We don't own much of anything anymore. So I am becoming an international businessperson, and it's comforting. We started an international division last year. We're moving people internationally, and a big asset for me is that baseball is so popular in some countries. I like working with those people. If I have any regret, it's that I don't speak Japanese."

Since playing his final game at Wrigley Field on September 26, 1971—an awkward day because Cub management did not formally recognize his impending retirement ("I didn't want another year, but I didn't want a big deal either")—Banks has made several career changes.

"My long-range goal was to get a master's degree in sociology and eventually a doctorate," says Banks, "because people fascinated me so much."

He did indeed study sociology at Northwestern University after retiring from baseball, but he also embarked on what he calls a "career plan" that took him into marketing (two years with the Cubs), banking (ombudsman with the Bank of Ravenswood, Chicago), and insurance sales before he finally departed Chicago in 1983 to work for Associated Films Promotion, a Los Angeles–based company that gets products placed in movies. Now he's in the trucking business.

But Ernie, through all the uncertainties of career transitions, weren't there dark moments?

"Truthfully, I never had dark times. Before my father died in 1978, as I sat at the hospital with my mother—before I went into the Hall of Fame while he was on his deathbed—I decided then that I would not surrender to being 'down.' I'm alive, in good health, and living in a great country. Listen, I've seen 'down.' I can recognize it. I've been to the West Side of Chicago. I went to Vietnam to visit troops. I saw my sister's child, a catcher with the Texas Rangers named Bobby Johnson, drop out of baseball because of cocaine. But I refuse depression."

One of Banks's more troubling times came in February 1970, after a telephone rang in Scottsdale, and Cub pitching coach Joe Becker heard a voice say:

"I've got a rifle and I'm gunnin' for Ernie Banks."

"You can't do that," gasped Becker.

"Well, I'll get him . . . don't worry about that."

"But you can't . . . you can't do a thing like that."

"Oh, yes I can. I've got a rifle, and I'm going to use it."

The Cubs treated the call as a serious death threat, and so did the FBI. Banks remembers being called away from batting practice by coach Joey Amalfitano, then following general manager John Holland and Becker into the clubhouse.

"I thought I had been traded," Banks said a few months later. "Really. I don't know why, but I thought I had been traded, and I said to myself, 'If that's it, that's it.' I was really frozen up because I knew it was something big, and to a ballplayer the biggest thing was to be traded. Then I thought they were ready to put Roe Skidmore at first base and ask me to coach. And I thought, "Well, that's better than being traded.'

"At first, nobody said a word. There was Leo, not talking. So I kept quiet too. I wasn't going to say anything funny."

Then Banks got the word, was rushed into seclusion by a pair of Scottsdale plainclothes policemen, and left alone.

"I remember what had happened to people like Dr. Martin Luther King," said Ernie.

Shortly afterward a young man named Lawrence Bankhead was arrested by the FBI in Chicago (he had called from a YMCA telephone), and Banks was allowed to resume spring training. But he was deeply affected and began thinking more seriously about retirement from baseball.

Surely Banks encountered racial prejudice throughout his career, although he never showed his feelings about it. How did he handle racial injustices? What would he say to an angry young black man of today?

"I'd tell him that truthfully we learn little in a lifetime. Ralph Waldo Emerson wrote it: 'Success is going through failure after failure after failure without the loss of enthusiasm.' Most of us fail, but you must keep going, and my experiences in life have shown me that people all have the same kind of blood. I know that sounds naive, but if we could ever look past skin color as an excuse, how much better would we be?

"It's funny, too. When you get into higher business, it doesn't exist. If you and I were making a deal, the only important thing would be the deal. It's just unfortunate that when you're at a certain level of life there are injustices. But you just have to keep working against it.

"I've never been militant, but that doesn't mean I don't understand."

Because of that attitude, Banks has at times been viewed as an Uncle Tom, an accusation he chooses to ignore.

"At least they know I'm alive. You know, back when Leo Durocher was being criticized so heavily, I said that no one is above criticism, not even Jesus Christ. So I don't pay it any mind. It's just my style. There is nothing you can do to me to make me angry enough to do something or say something back to you. I've been criticized for that—by my wife, by my children. 'Why don't you stand up and fight?' they ask. 'Why don't you speak out? What's wrong with you?' But it isn't me.

"I couldn't be a Black Muslim, but I came through that era. I was an auto dealer in Chicago in 1976—first black Ford dealer in the U.S.—when the Blackstone Rangers dominated our neighborhood. They would drive past sometimes and break windows and cut tires in new cars, right there at 76th and Stoney Island, but it was their thing, not mine.

"Jesse [Jackson] was just starting then, back in 1969. I went back recently for an Operation PUSH anniversary. They're starting a new essay program for kids in school, to build their self-esteem. Jesse's success is no surprise to me. It's just the times, you know?

"It's like lights at Wrigley Field. It's just the times. It doesn't upset me. If you had to summarize what Ernie Banks is all about, it's that I believe in change . . . in the magic of change. So sometimes when it seems like 'Why does he care?,' you must understand you must flow with changes. Things are changing. It isn't as it used to be."

Ernie Banks, California. He works in Compton (population 78,611), which has a considerable black population, and lives in predominantly white Encino, the most affluent community in the San Fernando Valley, about 40 freeway minutes from his office. Ernie and his third wife, Marjorie, moved there in November 1987. She was director of human resources for the Chicago Transit Authority 15 years before marrying Ernie in 1983. He divorced his second wife, Eloyce, in 1980. Their twin sons, Jerry and Joey, soon to be 28, are also working in southern California—Joey, an actor and associate producer; Jerry, a banker. Ernie's daughter, Jan Elizabeth, 26, is active in a Jehovah's Witness church in Los Angeles, and his stepdaughter, Lindell, is a child psychologist.

"And I have a granddaughter named Tomorrow, just like the song in *Annie*," says Banks.

Joey gave baseball a serious try; he even accompanied Ernie on a goodwill barnstorming tour of Korea. "We roomed together, and it was like replaying my life," says Ernie. "Henry Aaron had his son along too, back in 1983 I think, and I was the designated hitter. So I told Hank, 'I'm gonna hit a home run off these guys,' and everybody just laughed. What was I, 52 years old? Well, we were playing in Taegu—you ever been to Taegu?—and I come up with the bases loaded and hit one over the fence on the first pitch. Here I come around the bases, and there was my son to meet me at home plate after a grand slam. I don't know who was thrilled the most, him or me."

Joey, however, was unable to duplicate his father's baseball prowess and turned to an acting career. Why? Why did Ernie Banks from a Texas family of 12 who picked cotton for $5 a day make it when the son of Ernie Banks could not? How many less-famous fathers have asked themselves the same question? Is it God-given talent and nothing more?

After a long pause, Ernie answers.

"I had discipline. I was very disciplined. I spent time hitting. I spent time alone. I mean hard practice and commitment. But you also have to have discipline of mind to do it without a whole lot of people around. I wish I could make young people today understand that. Their so-called friends don't help. It's so hard for a young man today to concentrate. They have so many things that we didn't have, but that can also be their enemy.

"The number-one nemesis of a young person today is drugs. My kids experienced it a little, but I got with Mitchell Ware, head of the Illinois Drug Abuse Program, and he had a lot of information on video. I showed them a lot of video and they got past it. One of my boys even got kicked out of high school once. But they were bright kids and they figured out their troubles. I'm very proud of my sons."

When considering the Cubs of 1969, there is one significant thing to remember about Ernie Banks: he was 38 years old with bad knees and had already hit 474 major league home runs before the first pitch of 1969 was thrown. Here's a man who won back-to-back league Most Valuable Player Awards in 1958 and 1959. His 129 RBI during 1958 were 47 more than runner-up teammate Bobby Thomson's; and one year later, when Ernie drove in 143, no other Cubs batter had 50.

But when help finally arrived, Ernie was in no condition to play two. The season of 1969 was to be his last full one at first base; Joe Pepitone arrived at midseason in 1970, and Banks retired after 1971. A dreaming Cubs fan can only fantasize about how powerful the 1969 team would have been with Banks in his prime. As it was, he hit .253 with 23 home runs and 106 RBI.

And there was the "situation" with his manager.

"Leo hated Ernie," recalls then–traveling secretary Blake Cullen.

"Leo had to be top dog," adds Brickhouse. "He just couldn't handle anybody else threatening that position in popularity. Ernie did."

It was September 1970, the Cubs team bus was parked in front of the Chase Park–Plaza Hotel in St. Louis, and Banks was a few minutes late. Said Durocher, "Where's Ernie?"

Somebody said Ernie wasn't on board.

"That figures," said Durocher. "He probably thinks he's too good to ride the bus with us."

There were at least two other occasions during Banks's final season on which Durocher, as he tried to justify dropping Banks from the lineup, deliberately sought to embarrass the future Hall of Famer. Once in New York he called on Ernie to play against flame-throwing Nolan Ryan, knowing well that Ernie couldn't get the bat around quickly enough. Banks struck out on three pitches. Yet after

Ryan was replaced by a soft-throwing left-hander, Ray Sadecki, Ernie was pulled for pinch hitter Jim Hickman.

Then there was the game against San Diego when the Cubs were leading 11–0 and Banks was on first base as a runner. Durocher called for a hit-and-run on the first pitch.

In those late days of Banks's career, Durocher seemed to have some justification. Ernie was slow. Ernie was making mistakes. But even as early as 1966 Durocher had been saying, "Banks has killed more rallies than anyone on the club. Just look it up."

"It was common knowledge that Ernie might miss the sign and couldn't run anyhow," says Cullen. "Leo simply felt he was saddled with a hero and couldn't take a full shot with him in the lineup.

"I'll never forget this scene in spring training. Ernie was playing first base during infield practice, and Leo shouts, 'Hey, old man, ever play shortstop?' 'Well,' Ernie says, 'I useta play a little . . . nine years at Wrigley Field,' and Leo says 'I believe you. Get over there. Ten balls for a Coke.'

"So Ernie goes to shortstop with his hat on backward, somebody throws him an infield glove, Leo grabs a bat, and they start. Leo hits one to his left four steps. Leo hits one to his right five steps. Then Ernie backhands one. Now he scoops a slow roller. Finally, he's damned near to third base and Leo is hitting him shots. There isn't a sound in the park. Everybody is watching. Ernie goes 10 for 10, throws the mitt into the air, and runs off laughing. Leo throws down the bat and says, 'You old fart, you're some kinda player. I'm taking my hat off to you.' "

Banks acknowledges there was a "situation" but says, "In Leo I saw a man in his 60s. Actually, it was joyful to see him so involved. How many men in their 60s can get that involved in something? And it couldn't have been easy for him, with all the travel. So when he got cantankerous, I figured that most of the time he just didn't feel so good. Just think about all that excitement of 1969. I saw him happy too. There was a lot of happiness there, him getting married and all. The sadness I don't remember much."

Which leads Ernie into his Ernie routine.

"Hey, let's go see Leo. What say you and me drive to Palm Springs and visit Leo? Call him up. Let's go now!"

When, indeed, was the last time they had visited?

"Old-Timers' Game in Houston last year. He was my manager, and I had all my family up from Dallas, maybe 15 people there," says Ernie, laughing, "and would you believe he wouldn't put me in the starting lineup? He started Mickey Vernon, who was 69 years old, and the first ball hit poor ol' Mickey in the knee. On the next one he slipped and fell down on a pop-up, and Leo looked down the bench at me and said, 'Why aren't you at first base?'

" 'I dunno, Skip,' I said. 'You're the manager.' "

Ernie's recollection of the '69 season:

"I'll always remember Willie Smith singing with that deep voice of his, 'I've got that lovely feeling . . . it's gone, gone, gone.' Every time we'd win he'd sing like that. I remember those things, the strong fellowship among players. Wasn't that home run by Willie Smith on Opening Day fun?

"It was the most happiness any of us had ever enjoyed in our lives. I feel more identified with the '69 team than any of the others, even though my career was almost ended. Winning constitutes love and togetherness that lasts forever. Everybody talks about money, the rings, and publicity, but fellowship you develop during that time is worth more than all of that. We stayed together a long time. That's unique.

"I remember more than anything about 1969 the difficult times in the United States. I remember the Chicago Seven trial, which started that fall. I remember Jesse with Operation PUSH, and people like Bill Singer and Chuck Percy. Me being elected to the CTA board.

"And I remember when we visited the White House at the All-Star Game, shaking hands with President Nixon, and him saying something about my last hurrah and how he hoped I would make it. Then he said, 'I can understand. I went for a lot of stuff I didn't make either.' I never mentioned that until now, but it was nice of him, wasn't it? Those are the kinds of things I remember. All of the sadness has gone away."

Why did there have to be sadness in 1969? Why did the Cubs lose?

"Well, a lot of people say we needed more rest, the bench, the black cat in New York, all of that stuff, but it wasn't pressure or outside activities or anything like that.

"It was fear. When you haven't won, it's scary, and that's life. Dealing with the uncertainties, the unknown. It's fearful when you get there, facing the unknown. And that's what I think happened to us in 1969.

"But the wonderful thing which makes the sadness go away is that the kids—I say kids, but all of us are grown now—those kids in their 40s have become so close. We have become each other's best friends, almost like brothers. Our kids and families know each other. We call each other. It's an interesting cross section, and that's why Randy Hundley's camps have been so wonderful. When we get together it's like a family reunion."

CECIL RANDOLPH HUNDLEY
B. June 1, 1942, Martinsville, Va.

YEAR	TEAM		G	AB	H	2B	3B	HR	HR%	R	RBI	BB	SO	SB	BA	SA
1964	SF	N	2	1	0	0	0	0	0.0	1	0	0	1	0	.000	.000
1965			6	15	1	0	0	0	0.0	0	0	0	4	0	.067	.067
1966	CHI	N	149	526	124	22	3	19	3.6	50	63	35	113	1	.236	.397
1967			152	539	144	25	3	14	2.6	68	60	44	75	2	.267	.403
1968			160	553	125	18	4	7	1.3	41	65	39	69	1	.226	.311
1969			151	522	133	15	1	18	3.4	67	64	61	90	2	.255	.391
1970			73	250	61	5	0	7	2.8	13	36	16	52	0	.244	.348
1971			9	21	7	1	0	0	0.0	1	2	0	2	0	.333	.381
1972			114	357	78	12	0	5	1.4	23	30	22	62	1	.218	.294
1973			124	368	83	11	1	10	2.7	35	43	30	51	5	.226	.342
1974	MIN	A	32	88	17	2	0	0	0.0	2	3	4	12	0	.193	.216
1975	SD	N	74	180	37	5	1	2	1.1	7	14	19	29	0	.206	.278
1976	CHI	N	13	18	3	2	0	0	0.0	3	1	1	4	0	.167	.278
1977			2	4	0	0	0	0	0.0	0	0	0	1	0	.000	.000
14 yrs.			1061	3442	813	118	13	82	2.4	311	381	271	565	12	.236	.350

3
Randy Hundley

"It was like a religious experience when we got together."
—Randy Hundley

The 69-year-old priest in double knits fed the ball into an automatic pitching machine as the attorney, face contorted, eyes locked on the ball, took uneasy practice swings.

Whang! The ball rocketed off the metal bat past the stumbling stab of a portly third baseman, then rolled toward the fence between a limping, white-haired leftfielder and bearded centerfielder with a $6 million portfolio.

As one runner rounded third, coach Gene (Beef) Oliver purred, "Go ahead and score . . . easy, easy, don't pull anything."

Back at second, there was a flurry. The ball rolled away, and the attorney, smiling broadly and rubbing his knee, stood to slap the dirt from his Cubs uniform. On a Little League scale of 1 to 10, the slide had been a 3.6.

"These guys don't slide," said Oliver, "they faint."

Randy Hundley, 46, showing reddish, permlike curls and tanned, crossed arms, grimaced, then turned his attention to field number two, just a few hundred feet away, where there was a dispute.

"That ball was fair!" shouted the lithe, angular ballplayer who appeared to be in his late 50s.

Before the umpire could argue, the nearby Glenn Beckert, wearing number 18 and a hand-cupped cigarette, said sardonically, "Listen, ump, Al has spent over $100,000 coming to these camps. He can call it fair if he wants to!"

It has been a phenomenon, these camps of fantasy. Hundley, the ex-Cubs catcher, fired and out of organized baseball and bitter about it, held the first one in 1983 and has conducted more than three dozen since. Adults over the age of 30 from all segments of society pay $2,895, plus air fare and spending money, to live their dream for eight days and seven nights: to play baseball, rub shoulders, and drink cocktails with former big leaguers, most of whom played with the Cubs.

And while the high-ticket, usually-held-in-Arizona camps—Randy Hundley's Official Big League Baseball Camps, to be precise—have provided Hundley with a more-than-comfortable income and brought joy and sore muscles to thousands of participants, many of whom repeat the experience, there has also been an unexpected and heart-warming residue: they have brought the 1969 Cubs back together.

"Some of us hadn't seen Hick [Jim Hickman] or Willie [Smith] for 10 years," says Hundley, recalling that first camp in Arizona. "And when we all saw each other, it was just as if we were getting ready for another season. The whole camp just got caught up in our love of one another. It was like a religious experience when we got together. I never dreamed it would happen that way."

The players return each year, sometimes to several of the half a dozen camps a year, for their reunion. Hundley pays them each $1,200 (the current rate), but most of them would probably come for continental breakfast. These guys didn't have agents when they played. They had each other.

There is also a delicious irony about the unprecedented success of the Hundley camps and reborn popularity of the 1969 Cubs.

Thanks should go to Dallas Green.

After Green, with his John Wayne walk and Philadelphia success, conned his way past the image-conscious Tribune Company executives into the Cubs' seat of power in 1981, he made a determined effort to eradicate the history of the franchise. Out with the old, in with the new. No more losers; there was a "new tradition" dawning in Wrigley Field. So, while flooding the Cubs' front-office and field positions with ex-Phillies employees (offering, along the way, a numbing display of how to rebuild a ball club with checkbook mercenaries), Green also began chopping off heads.

One of those fired was Hundley, who had been managing and scouting for the Cubs in the minor leagues.

"It really hurt me personally," remembers Hundley. "I was a Cub through and through. I kept remembering all those games I played when I was hurt. And I had been looking forward to working with Dallas because everybody kept telling me he was an up-front kind of guy. Well, he just came in and flat cleaned house. As soon as I met him in the clubhouse I said, 'Oh, crap, I am flat gone.'

"Everybody that was a Cub got caught up in it. Ollie [Gene Oliver] got it too; he'd been helping the Quad City club. Everything had to be changed. Dallas said to me, 'You've been a Cub for a long time,' and it was like '. . . and you haven't done anything.' It was like 'You've been a Cub player and a coach and in the minor league system, and you've never won a pennant!'

"It was his prerogative, of course, but I didn't understand it at the time. I thought Dallas was totally wrong, and I wanted to bad-mouth him, but I learned to respect him. He did what he thought was best for the situation. Maybe I would have done the same thing."

What Green didn't understand, of course, was that while

farm systems can be retooled, memories can't. Not in Chicago. And although Green's checkbook Cubs of 1984—the team managed by Jim Frey, who confronted the past by telling people "Fuck 1969"—won a divisional championship, the entire attempt to heighten the new by getting rid of the old backfired.

"I looked around in September of 1981," said Hundley of his firing, "and I said to myself, 'What am I going to do now?' " If Hundley hadn't been fired by Green, there probably wouldn't have been fantasy camps. Hundley's was the first. Others around the country have only copied him.

And as these camps have grown in public popularity for the past six years, so have the love and fellowship among the members of the 1969 team.

Dallas Green tried to make 1969 go away. Now he's gone, and those who played together 20 years ago have rediscovered the bond that made the team special.

Hundley stood before the spike-scraping assemblage in the Arizona locker room—businessmen and doctors and TV repairmen, now ballplayers all, snapping their jockstraps, bitching, laughing, checking to see if their sanitary socks were right-side out.

"All right, listen up!" he shouted. "There's a cocktail party tonight in Room 110 . . . and I know that's exactly what you guys need. Also, I need a count for the banquet Saturday night."

"Yeah," added Beckert, seated with the "instructors" in front of Hundley, "and extra for wheelchairs."

"Now, about the banquet," continued Hundley, "we will not be at Mesa Country Club. We have been barred from Mesa Country Club . . . yeah, you guys know why, because of three years ago when Hoyt Wilhelm drove his car down that cart path at 2 A.M. and ended up in the sand trap."

Hundley paused while the laughter subsided, and before he could continue instructor Fergie Jenkins said, "Any of you guys want chewing tobacco today, you can take it out of my locker."

"Yeah," needled Oliver, "and if you want anything stronger, he's got that too."

It was the usual prepractice clubhouse meeting at one of Hundley's camps. All part of the live-out-your-dream routine that's made the experience so successful.

"Today we do position work," continued Hundley. "Go to your number-one priority position and learn something about that position you can take home with you. These guys [the instructors] have an awful lot to offer. OK? Outfielders on field number one, infielders on field number two, pitchers and catchers in center field. Then we'll play some games. Remember . . . no bases on balls, no stealing, and you must strike out. Nobody gets called out. OK, let's go."

As the campers rushed for the exits, Oliver shouted, "And if you don't know everybody's name by the end of the week, I'll fine your ass. We drink together, we die together."

Then, spotting a couple of campers from his own team, Oliver added, "The way you guys keep kicking those ground balls, you should think about wearing those gloves on your shoes."

Hundley was a remarkable ironman performer with the Cubs from 1966 through 1969, catching 612 games; only severe damage to both knees, beginning in 1970, kept the boy from Martinsville, Virginia, from burning a deeper mark. As it was, Randy's career lasted through 14 seasons, finally ending after a comeback with the Cubs in 1976 and 1977. And while he takes good-natured kidding from ex-teammates about one citing of his name in the record book (one of the ten worst batting averages, .236, for players with at least 2,500 career at-bats), certainly Hundley was the heart of the Cubs defense.

He was fire and ice. Unafraid to think or speak (he drove umpires to distraction with nonprofane pleading), Randy was always ahead of the game, Durocher's manager on the field. In 1967, that year in which the Cubs began to believe they could become champions, Hundley set a major league record by committing only four errors. He also set the

National League mark that season with just four passed balls.

And by perfecting and advocating the one-handed style of receiving pitches, he literally changed the way the game is played. Nobody in the major leagues catches two-handed anymore.

It started with his father, Cecil, a contractor, earth mover, and semipro ballplayer. "The only thing my dad knew was that his hands were all broken up from foul balls," recalls Hundley. "He kept telling me, 'What good are you with busted-up hands? You can't play, you can't hit, you can't do anything.' So he taught me to catch one-handed. He'd make me sit there with my bare hand on my right leg and catch every ball with my glove hand, back-handing just like an infielder. I never missed a game because of a foul ball on my bare hand."

At first Randy played shortstop and pitched, but when his dad made him quit pitching ("He didn't want a sore arm ruining my career") and he found playing shortstop boring, he went behind home plate. That's when his dad told him, "If I ever see you catch a ball two-handed, I'm going to personally come onto the field and take you out of the game."

"He scared the daylights out of me," remembers Randy, "I guess I didn't realize how many umpteen times he'd had his own hand broken."

That it took so long for other major leaguers to realize the advantage of one-handed catching is amazing. Even Johnny Bench changed his style after observing Hundley's success.

"We were playing Cincinnati when Bench came up to the majors for the first time [the end of the 1967 season]," recalls Hundley, "and he catches a foul ball on his throwing hand and breaks a finger. That did it. Now he's in the dugout, blood dropping down his arm, watching me snap 'em one-handed, and that was it. He came back in 1968 as a one-handed catcher."

Hundley was paid a bonus of $110,000 when he signed out of high school in 1960 with the San Francisco Giants and immediately gave half of it to his father. He also wrote off the $55,000 on his tax return as a fee paid to Cecil Hundley for teaching him to catch one-handed.

Five years later the Internal Revenue Service screamed.

Instead of settling the issue by paying additional tax, however, Hundley took the IRS to court.

"It was a matter of principle," says Randy. "They were calling me a liar, and I was determined to fight. Dad wanted to settle, but I wouldn't do it. He had taught me. He lost jobs of his own to spend time with me."

So during the spring of 1965 Hundley left training camp to go into federal district court in Richmond, Virginia, and he took his catcher's mitt with him.

"There I was, wearing a catcher's mitt and squatting in front of a judge in the middle of the courtroom," recalls Hundley. "I must have spent 15 minutes down there demonstrating the unique advantages of catching one-handed. And, by golly, we won. It turned out to be a landmark case, and a couple of other guys, including Gaylord Perry, tried it later but lost. I guess I gave a good demonstration."

"You know," recalls Hundley, "you don't know where it comes from—why you love the game of baseball so much— but I really believe my bloomin' blood cells are made up with seams on them like a bloomin' baseball. I can't explain it. When I was two years old I was swinging a bat. I would go out at night in this little tobacco town and throw the ball into the air, just to see if I could catch it. I mean I couldn't even see the bloomin' ball, but it was a challenge to see if I could catch it. I got a lot of bloody noses doin' it, too. Shucks, I couldn't even sit still without wadding up a piece of paper and throwing it. It was just in my system."

What makes Cecil Randolph Hundley, Jr., mad? Call him a loser.

"Sure, we ended up on the losing side of the Mets in 1969," says Hundley, "but that doesn't make us bad people. It was just meant to be. The Mets won 100 games. What bothers me is that a lot of people think we're losers. They say things like 'You didn't know how to win,' and I say that's a bunch of crap. Don't tell me we didn't know how to win. You put a team out there that doesn't have the talent playing against a team that does. Don't give me that crap."

Excuse me? Is Randy saying that the 1969 Mets had more talent than the Cubs, who sent an entire infield into the All-Star Game *and* had a pair of 20-game winners?

"Pitching. The Mets had better pitching, and they used their players better. And I want to be perfectly clear about this: I am not criticizing Leo Durocher one iota. You know why? Because if I'd been manager I would have done the same bloomin' thing. Whether the guys were tired or not, I would have sent them out there. When it came to nut-cracking time, I would have my best players in the lineup.

"It's real easy to have hindsight, retrospect, and all of that stuff. But if Leo had taken me out of that lineup in those days, he would have heard from me. And do you think he was gonna get Santo or Banks or Kess or Billy out of there? No stinkin' way. You do what you have to do as a manager. You put your best guys on the field."

But weren't the Cubs tired?

"No question about it. It was a hard season. Not only physically but emotionally and mentally. And another thing. We just flat wore Phil Regan out. Leo started going to him all the time. What did he pitch, 112 innings in 71 games? That's a bunch for a short relief man. Now, if he pitches 80 or 90 innings in 71 games, he might survive. But Leo didn't feel he could count on the other guys out there, so he kept calling on Regan.

"Yet the fans want to put everything that happened on the position players. Hey, once Leo got through three starters and Regan, what was he going to do? The Mets had the arms and we didn't. We didn't have a stopper during the final six weeks. If you're going up against someone, I want some ammunition. I don't want to fight them with a bloomin' BB gun."

Frankly, when Hundley starts talking about 1969, he offers more than theories; he offers excuses. Three others:

1. "The umpires that summer were all over Regan about

throwing a spitter. They all but undressed him on the mound one day in Wrigley Field. Pete Rose flied out twice, and they let him come back and hit until he got a bloomin' base hit. It was the kind of stuff we put up with all summer. Umpires and the other teams. They couldn't stand the Cubs."

2. "We couldn't add players to strengthen the roster—not like they were able to do with the 1984 team in Chicago. In those days, without free agency, you just couldn't make those kinds of deals. You couldn't get a Rick Sutcliffe. Nobody wanted to help the Cubs."

3. "The heat. I'm sure it took a toll. It does every year come August. I lost so much weight I couldn't reach the warning track. But Leo wanted me out there every day handling the pitchers. That's basically all I concentrated on doing."

There remains a disbelief about what happened. "We all worried more about St. Louis than New York," recalls Hundley. "I remember I was at a banquet the night the Mets clinched the pennant. I still didn't believe it. It was just meant to be. But I'll tell you this: the Cub players did all they could do."

Hundley, batting seventh in the order, finished that season with 18 home runs and 64 RBI, hitting a respectable .255. Yet, as his weight dropped and the pressure built, he was able to drive in only four runs during the final month. It was his last healthy major league season.

As the campers filed slowly into the clubhouse, Beckert was deriding Holtzman about his appearance ("How many times have I told you to unpack those sweaters from your shaving kit?"), and Father John Pitzen from St. Patrick's Parish, Fairfax, Iowa, was telling someone how the Cubs saved his life.

"It was July 22, 1983," said the 69-year-old priest, "and I drove from my home in Jessup, Iowa, to see the Cubs play in Wrigley Field. Well, on that very afternoon a propane tank exploded across the street from the parish and demolished much of the town, including our school and rectory. Six million dollars in damage. When I returned the next day, there was this devastation, and my window in the rectory, facing the direction of the blast, had been shattered. Glass was everywhere. Had I been there working, as I normally would be, I would have been cut to ribbons or killed.

"So I've always felt," said the priest, pulling the baseball shirt over his head, "that the Cubs saved my life."

Greg Warner, camp photographer, was pinning examples of his work on the locker-room wall: color shots of campers standing in uniform with arms around Fergie or Beck or Billy, plus some of them leaping into the air to make a spectacular catch (simulated, of course, with the 350-foot marker in the background). Copies were for sale, as were the $65 silk jackets with RANDY HUNDLEY'S OFFICIAL BIG LEAGUE BASEBALL CAMPS emblazoned on the back.

"I was just a high school freshman in 1969," said Warner, who now runs his business out of Ft. Myers, Florida, "and I carried a Cub schedule in my pocket. Every day I lived and died with the Cubs. Every day I'd take out this tattered schedule and mark a 'W' or an 'L' on each date on the calendar. In September I quit marking."

Outside, Billy Williams spotted Vedie Himsl, a retired minor league executive who had wandered over to watch the camp games. "Don't step on the clipboard—you might be stepping on your name!" yelled Williams. Himsl laughed and Billy explained: "I remember him sayin' that 30 years ago. We were all just kids then, tryin' to make it, livin' in a barracks down the street here. Vedie and [scout] Buck O'Neil were gods to us."

Nearby, instructor Oliver, 53, just a shade (maybe 30 pounds) over his playing weight of 215, was exhorting a camper not to forget his "scully" (helmet) before going to the plate. Then he shouted, "Anybody who misses a sign, buys tonight!"

"I'm like Leo," said Oliver in an aside. "I'll do anything to win."

"Didn't do him any good," said instructor Lee Thomas, a

former Cub in 1967. "If he'd wanted to win, he'd have gotten rid of you."

Richard Lynn, a Chicago attorney who has represented athletes and paid full fare for this "major league experience," offered an observation: "This is a fantasy existence. I practice law, which is not a regimented routine. But this life, sleeping until 9 o'clock, drinking beer at night, now I see why athletes are like they are. I can see the transformation even in myself, and I've been here less than a week.

"I can see why these ex-players come back. They can't give up the life they once had. They can't handle the lack of joviality. Some of them can't handle responsibility either, in the outside world. They suffer terribly because they can't compete in an arena other than athletic, and it's tragic."

Beckert, now a successful commodities broker, is an obvious exception. Still, he admits that Hundley's camps serve as his escape from business. One night at the camp he had stumbled into the hotel lobby at 3 A.M. and telephoned Lee Thomas and roommate Joe Cunningham to report that he was in jail and needed help. Upon rushing to the lobby, Cunningham discovered Beckert, who wondered if he'd like to join him in a late drink.

Now, on a more serious note, Beckert pondered the phenomenal success of the camps.

"It's hard for me to imagine a millionaire wanting to come here and play baseball with me. But I ask myself: would I pay to go drink and eat and play golf all week with Arnold Palmer and Jack Nicklaus? I know I'd like to run one of these guys' conglomerates for a week, or operate this guy's movie studio or hotel. So I guess I do understand."

The ravage of Hundley's knees began in April 1970, when the left one was twisted in a collision at home plate. The knee was placed in a cast for three weeks, then Randy spent another three weeks of rehabilitation. Still, there was a "click" in there that puzzled doctors, who in those days did not have the benefit of arthroscopic diagnosis. So a decision was made and Hundley underwent surgery for cartilage damage.

"Actually, they could have waited until the end of the season," says Hundley, "because it turned out the cartilage damage wasn't that serious. They ended up just trimming it, but it kept me out of the lineup." He played in only 73 games that year.

Then, in spring training of 1971, Hundley tripped while trying to avoid Roger Repoz of the Angels in an exhibition-game rundown. Randy's spikes locked and his right knee popped.

"The pain was unreal . . . excruciating," recalls Hundley.

This time, though, doctors said it was just a sprain. So Hundley rehabilitated, played again, and went down again. Nothing definitive showed on x-rays, however, and he played again, and went down again, this time to surgery.

"The ligament was torn away from the bone," recalls Hundley, "but instead of making an incision on the medial side, they kept cutting down my leg, laid me open, and did a tendon transfer. Then they put me in a cast, even though the leg kept swelling and swelling. Finally they increased my blood-thinning medicine because I couldn't catch my breath and my heart was just pounding. Come to find out that a blood clot had broken loose and went through my heart and into my lung. I was one sick cookie for about eight weeks."

More specifically, Hundley endured everything from gallbladder attacks to high temperatures to stomach disorders, as his weight dropped from 185 to 155. The hospital denied he had been near death because of the blood clot, but certainly he was unable to return to the Cubs lineup. Doctors predicted his baseball career was finished.

"I just wish we'd had arthroscopic surgery," says Hundley, "because they said later that if they would have known it had torn the ligament away from the bone, they could have just gone in and wired it back and let it heal."

As it was, Hundley missed virtually all the 1970 and 1971 seasons, then came back to catch 113 games in 1972 and another 122 in 1973 before being traded to Minnesota—

where he reinjured the knees, which had never again been as strong.

"I got hurt in June, but [Twins owner] Calvin Griffith wouldn't let me go home for an operation because he'd have to put me on the disabled list. That meant he'd have to call up somebody and pay them big-league minimum pay, and he didn't want to do it. So I sat there on the bench for July and August while they played with 24 guys and I needed surgery. Finally, in September, I had the operation but got a staph infection from trying to rehabilitate too quickly. I came back to play in 1975 [with the Padres] and 1976 [with the Cubs], but I shouldn't have been playing. I wasn't anything near the player I once was. But, shucks, what else was I going to do? I think back to when I was a two-year-old tossing the ball in the air. It's what I wanted to do."

Hundley's frustrations, however, were not finished. From the collapse of 1969, he had gone to the surgical table only to return with pain as his companion. Now, finished as a player but back within the Cubs organization, he was to be frustrated once again.

He had actually hoped to play with the Cubs in 1977 but, because of neck surgery (he had slipped a disc after participating in a fight against the Giants in 1976), he found himself being offered a coaching job under manager Herman Franks. Hundley quickly accepted because already he was thinking he'd like to become a major league manager.

"I became Herman's right-hand man," recalls Hundley, "and I was doing everything for him—making out the lineup, everything you can imagine. I enjoyed it, too. Herman did about 75 percent of the things I suggested.

"But I really think Herman looked at me as a threat. I would go out and warm up pitchers, then come back into the dugout, and Herman would be standing in a corner and somebody would say, 'Why don't you just manage the ball club, Randy?' And I just wanted to crawl into a hole because I knew I wasn't ready. I felt that training under Herman was the best situation. Herman could have taken me from there and said to [Cubs general manager] Bob Kennedy,

'Bob, I've got a future manager for you.' "

Instead, the Cubs almost traded Hundley to Montreal, where Charlie Fox was general manager and manager Dick Williams was looking for a backup catcher to young Gary Carter. Hundley rebelled, however, knowing he could no longer play.

"I said to Herman, 'Give me a stinkin' break, will you? After all I've done for you? You know you could keep me here if you wanted to.' "

Herman Franks, retired in Salt Lake City, denies that he ever tried to inhibit Hundley's advancement.

"For some reason, Randy thought I didn't like him, but that wasn't true. Bob Kennedy wanted to send him into the minor league system to get managerial experience, that's all. I'm the one who called Randy and gave him a job scouting for the organization. Does that sound like someone who didn't like him? Look, Randy caught one-handed, and when I caught it was two-handed. But if you can do the job, I don't care if you catch the ball with your feet. If Randy didn't get the job advancement he thought he deserved, maybe he should take inventory of himself."

Hundley was given a choice: go to Montreal for a good salary as backup catcher or manage for the Cubs organization in the low minors.

"That's what got so frustrating," he recalls. "I was a Cub through and through. I couldn't stand the thought of going to Montreal. So, like a dummy, I did what the Cubs said because the Cubs were in my blood. Don't ask me why. I went down to the rookie league in 1978, and you can't get any lower than that unless you're a high school coach. Then I managed in Double A [at Midland, Texas], and by now Joey Amalfitano was managing the big-league club, and I wanted to go coach for him because I really wasn't getting along with C. V. Davis, our minor league farm director.

"C.V., you see, was one of those guys who thought all ex-big leaguers were prima donnas. He wanted us to wallow in the minors for the rest of our lives, but I had this desire to get back to Chicago. Sure, I wanted to manage, but I didn't have a cutthroat attitude about it. I just felt at some point I would eventually be a manager."

Would Hundley have been a successful major league manager?

"I was qualified. No question about it. I also felt then that I had the makeup for it, but looking back I'm not so sure. Umpires were my biggest problem, but I think that would have taken care of itself."

The Cubs didn't return Hundley to the big leagues as coach under Amalfitano. Instead they sent him to manage the Triple-A club, which was terrible in 1981. Once again, Hundley was frustrated.

"It's the last day of May and C.V. comes into town, and I think he's gonna make some player changes," recalls Hundley. "Boy, was I happy because my birthday was coming up and we really needed some new players. So what happens? He tells me he's going to change managers. I was fired.

"Well, I needed a job to survive, and all he offered me was another chance to work in the rookie league. But my wife, Betty, brought me back to my senses. She said, 'Why are you putting up with this? I'd rather have you dig a ditch than be treated like this,' and, you know, she was right. I was so stinking mad at C. V. Davis, I could have pinched his head off. So I told him he could take his rinky-dink job and shove it. I think the whole thing was premeditated anyhow. C.V. had tried to fire me four times, and I know Herman Franks had to give him the OK because Herman was now the general manager."

That situation was soon to change, however. Franks was to be replaced when the Tribune Company purchased the Cubs from Bill Wrigley for more than $20 million (one of America's great business heists). Before it happened, however, Franks offered Hundley a chance to become the Cubs' advance scout at both the major league and Triple-A levels. Once again Hundley saw career hope. He liked the scouting and learned about evaluating players. He was also expected to help run the instructional league following the season.

Then along came Dallas Green, and Randy was fired again.

But he hadn't quite run the baseball gauntlet. There was more. He went to the 1981 winter meetings in Miami, hoping to find a job with another organization.

Instead, he was embarrassed.

"I had reservations for three days but left after one," recalls Hundley. "Too much B.S. I was just not going to put up with all the B.S. from those people. I mean I was willing to start all over in somebody's rookie league—that's how badly I wanted to stay in baseball. But I just could not stand all the B.S., all those incompetent people in bloomin' high positions walking around like gods. It just made me nauseous, and I couldn't handle it. So I left. I'm sure pride had something to do with it. But I just had to leave.

"The problem, you see, is the structure of baseball. Everybody feels they have to hire their friends. Maybe I'd do the same thing, I don't know. Another problem is that there are so many guys out there willing to take almost no money at all just to be in uniform. They just want to stay in baseball."

Finally, though, Hundley was finished with organized baseball. (He had even tried to land a winter-league job in 1981 and failed.) Repulsed at every pass and fighting a great bitterness within himself at age 39, he had to consider the frightening future: a life away from The Game.

Camp instructor Gene Oliver's team had just scored five runs in the first inning and four of his players were wearing number 10 on the backs of their uniforms (each camper can choose his own number).

"If they knew Santo, they wouldn't be wearing that number," said Beckert, who without missing a beat then turned toward a cluster of wives in the nearby bleachers and said, "Look, groupies from Sun City."

Then the boss came out of the clubhouse—Randy Hundley, the Methodist who doesn't curse ("My mama wouldn't tolerate it") but *has* been known to complain.

"Elmer Gantry, we call him," said Beckert, laughing. "Hey, Ollie, did you tell me that that guy playing first base for you is a brain surgeon? That guy just dropped two in a row. With those hands he's a brain surgeon?"

Hundley has maintained his residence in suburban Chicago since first coming to the Cubs. He lives with his wife, Betty, and family in Palatine, just minutes from his office. His oldest daughter, Julie, 24, graduated from college as an interior design major and now designs and sells for a furniture business. Her sister, Rene, 21, is a junior at Wheaton College studying business. There are also two sons, Todd, 20, and Chad, 14. And, as his father did before him, Randy has prepared his sons for baseball.

Todd signed a professional contract with the Mets after high school graduation in 1987 and is currently a catcher in New York's minor league system. It is easy to calculate Todd's age: he was born in June 1969, only a few months before his father would be involved in emotional confrontations with the same Mets. ("In a selfish way, I've never had any fondness for the Mets because of what they did to us," says Randy, who serves as his son's agent, "but that was almost 20 years ago and my son is more important than the past. And what the heck, they had the money.")

How special, from the beginning, was Todd to Randy? Shortly after Todd's birth in 1969, Hundley said, "I've been waiting for a son for seven years. I felt like when I saw Todd for the first time that all my dreams had come true. When I went into that waiting room at the hospital when our first daughter was born, I was sure God didn't make anything but boys. Well, he fooled me twice, but this time I came out a winner. I love my daughters, but wait until you see Todd."

Because of Randy's influence, Todd became a switch hitter. There is a premium on switch-hitting catchers with great defensive ability. Randy says Todd has that ability: "I could tell when he was a little kid. I just wanted to eat him up. He was just incredible, throwing and hitting that ball. He just couldn't get enough of it. He was just like me."

Has it ever occurred to Randy that a father can expect too much from a son or push too hard?

"Sure, it entered my mind. But there are times when you have to push a kid to bring out whatever his talent may be. I felt that I would be cheating him if I didn't share my knowledge of baseball with him. I told him, 'Hey, if you want to be a player, pal, then you'd better work at it,' and I'll admit we had some tough times. He didn't want to work on balls in the dirt. So I'd throw them at him. Well, it paid off. I've never seen anybody block balls in the dirt better than Todd. I'm telling you, he can flat-out play. He wasn't hitting so well this summer [1988], but that'll come. And he can flat-out catch."

On Todd Hundley's chest there is a tattoo of a baseball and bat.

"He came home one day with that thing, and I told him he was nuts," says Randy. "But I guess it does tell you that his heart and mind are on baseball."

Father to son to son.

It hadn't been an easy week for Hundley. His father had been operated on for cancer and soon would be gone. But he had time to talk. He had time to gaze across the practice fields and wonder, even to himself, how this crazy thing had happened:

"If you'd have told me six years ago that I'd still be doing this, I'd have said you were crazy. I started first with kids' camps, and one day I asked Rich Melman [the Chicago restaurateur] to come talk with the kids about the importance of education. Well, Rich arrived early, and we let him go out and play with the 12- and 13-year-old kids, and he loved it. About three days later, we're having lunch and he says, 'A friend of mine, Barry Friedman, wonders why you don't do a camp for adults?'

"Well, I start thinking about it—take guys to Arizona, just like big leaguers to spring training, give them uniforms, the whole thing. That's how it started."

The publicity helped. Mike Royko wrote about the idea.

So did the *Wall Street Journal*. Hundley had to turn people away.

"My main concern was injuries," he says. "I was concerned about the expense of insurance. So I'm sweating it out and, so help me, the first day in Scottsdale, 1983, I look over and see a guy laying on the ground. I thought sure he'd taken a bad hop between the eyes. But he had caught his spikes in a clump of grass, and two days later he had a knee operation right here in Arizona. But that has been the worst injury we've had."

Hundley learned with each camp. He quickly learned to use metal bats ("Shucks, we broke 44 wooden bats in the first camp"), and he learned not to put his campers through aerobics so vigorous that they couldn't walk. He also learned that professional ballplayers aren't the only ones with a will to compete.

"One day we've got this guy, a really very successful businessman, and he slides into second and breaks his little finger. Oh, man, I can see a lawsuit. So what does he do? He gets a doctor to put a splint on it and comes back to play in our big game against the instructors on Saturday. I mean, this guy made the doctor mold the splint on his hand so he could hold the bat. It was absolutely incredible."

One of the frequent camp participants is 77-year-old George Goodall, who had undergone cancer surgery in early 1988 and was concerned Hundley wouldn't accept him for an 11th appearance. His comment to Hundley was, "Your only responsibility is that if something happens, just bury me at second base." And in Randy's camp advertisements and brochures, you can read Goodall's testimony: "Some people might think I'm nuts, but to be able to do this at my age is one of the most enjoyable experiences of my life."

"Every baseball person thought I was nuts to start these camps," says Hundley. "The big thing now is that wives and girlfriends use the camps as gifts. We probably get 80 percent of our business from women wanting to do something special for the men. And the guys, once they get here, make lifelong friends. They really do. My basic concept was to make them 'feel' like a big-league player—to go through the emotions, mental and physical. I mean we threaten to option them down to a lower team, the whole thing.

"A guy doesn't have to have played baseball. We had one guy who couldn't catch or hit. I was sure he would get hurt. But on Friday he finally made contact, and everybody was giving him high fives. He's been to eight camps since."

And from this extraordinary entrepreneurial success— from Hundley's gamble born of desperation and rejection— has come the rebirth of camaraderie among the 1969 Cubs.

Consider the scene in 1983, at the first banquet: Most of the 1969 Cubs were there, intermingling with the campers who were completing their first week of baseball fantasy. And at the podium was Durocher, then 78 and recuperating from recent open-heart surgery.

"Leo was at the microphone saying a lot of nice things about people," recalls Hundley, "and it was like he wanted to 'get things right' because he'd had a pretty good scare. Then, out of the blue, he says, 'And I want to apologize to Ron Santo.' Well, here was something that had happened 11 years ago [a brawl in the Cubs clubhouse after Leo insulted Santo in front of the team], and now here's Leo saying, 'I made a mistake, and I've been wanting to say so to Ronnie and his family for the longest time.'

"Well, I'm looking around the room, and it was incredible. Some of the players from the 1969 team had tears in their eyes. And the campers, well, they don't know what's going on. They really don't know what Leo is talking about.

"But you ask about what kind of bond our team has? I don't have the vocabulary to express how we all felt that night."

KEN HOLTZMAN   P
CUBS

KENNETH DALE HOLTZMAN
B. Nov. 3, 1945, St. Louis, Mo.

YEAR	TEAM	W	L	PCT	ERA	G	GS	CG	IP	H	BB	SO	ShO	Relief Pitching W	L	SV
1965	CHI N	0	0	—	2.25	3	0	0	4	2	3	3	0	0	0	0
1966		11	16	.407	3.79	34	33	9	220.2	194	68	171	0	0	0	0
1967		9	0	1.000	2.53	12	12	3	92.2	76	44	62	0	0	0	0
1968		11	14	.440	3.35	34	32	6	215	201	76	151	3	0	0	1
1969		17	13	.567	3.59	39	39	12	261	248	93	176	6	0	0	0
1970		17	11	.607	3.38	39	38	15	288	271	94	202	1	0	0	0
1971		9	15	.375	4.48	30	29	9	195	213	64	143	3	0	0	0
1972	OAK A	19	11	.633	2.51	39	37	16	265	232	52	134	4	1	0	0
1973		21	13	.618	2.97	40	40	16	297.1	275	66	157	4	0	0	0
1974		19	17	.528	3.07	39	38	9	255	273	51	117	3	0	1	0
1975		18	14	.563	3.14	39	38	13	266.1	217	108	122	2	1	0	0
1976	2 teams	BAL A (13G 5-4)			NY A (21G 9-7)											
1976	total	14	11	.560	3.65	34	34	16	246.2	265	70	66	3	0	0	0
1977	NY A	2	3	.400	5.75	18	11	0	72	105	24	14	0	0	0	0
1978	2 teams	NY A (5G 1-0)			CHI N (23G 0-3)											
1978	total	1	3	.250	5.60	28	9	0	70.2	82	44	39	0	0	0	2
1979	CHI N	6	9	.400	4.58	23	20	3	118	133	53	44	2	0	0	0
15 yrs.		174	150	.537	3.49	451	410	127	2867.1	2787	910	1601	31	2	1	3

4
Ken Holtzman

"I got my revenge. I beat the Mets in the seventh game of the 1973 World Series."
—Ken Holtzman

The rings make the difference. Five rings, one for each finger on Ken Holtzman's left hand. Five rings that represent baseball championships—four of the five coming in victorious World Series appearances, three with the Oakland A's and one with the New York Yankees.

Yet Ken Holtzman, 43-year-old businessman, is an ex-Cub, just like the rest of them. He can't shake it and doesn't even try. He makes his home in north suburban Chicago, does business in Chicago, and just as the rest of them do, remembers 1969.

But the rings *do* make a difference. He keeps them in a vault but wears the memories loudly and clearly.

"I find it strange that people still associate me with the

1969 Cubs when I was part of the best baseball team in the last 40 years, the Oakland A's," says Holtzman. "The A's were probably the most colorful bunch of men to ever play the game. It was a team Charlie Finley didn't deserve.

"But I understand the Chicago association. I do make my home here. I did go 17–13 with the team, so many people remember. But I can enjoy 1969 in a different way than the others. I feel fulfilled and they don't. The others—Ernie, Billy, Ronnie, Kess, Beck—none of them got to play in a World Series. I was in four. So when people look at 1969 and say, 'Geez, that was the best team that never won,' I don't have to feel badly. I can enjoy the memory for the fun we had.

"And I must admit that from start to finish that season had more excitement than did any of my seasons in Oakland or New York. Nothing compares with being in a World Series, but for a single season 1969 was something."

Holtzman was the first star of 1969 to walk away from the Cubs, and it was his choice.

"I was frustrated with the losing," says Holtzman, now in the insurance business. "I really didn't think I'd be part of a winner with the Cubs, so I asked to be traded. It was a tough decision, especially since I had come up through the Cub farm system and felt so close to all the guys. It was traumatic."

Teammate Santo recalls being distressed that Holtzman asked to be traded. "I asked him, 'Why do you want to leave?' and he just came right out and said, 'Well, I feel that if I stay, I won't help myself. It's going to get worse with Leo, and I've got to think of my future. I've got to go where I can pitch and be appreciated.' "

"I'll never forget the phone call from [general manager] John Holland," says Holtzman, "I was working that November [1971] in St. Louis as a stockbroker, and John called and said, 'I'm sorry you want to be traded, Kenny, but Mr. Wrigley said he would help any player who wanted to leave, so we made a trade with Oakland.'

" 'Where the hell is Oakland,' I asked. I knew it was out

West somewhere and that the A's had a good team. But the American League? It was such a short conversation, I didn't even ask John who the Cubs got in return."

It was Rick Monday who came to the Cubs, and Holtzman joined Vida Blue, Joe Rudi, Reggie Jackson, Rollie Fingers, Catfish Hunter, Blue Moon Odom, Dick Green, Sal Bando, Billy North, and the other characters of green and gold who swept to three consecutive World Championships in 1972, 1973, and 1974. He also pitched with Oakland's divisional championship team in 1975 and reached the World Series again in 1977 with the winning Yankees.

Bottom line: Holtzman's major league career spanned 15 seasons, and he won 174 games, 80 in a Cub uniform, while losing 150. Career ERA: 3.49. World Series record: 4-1. Career shutouts: 31. No-hit games: 2, both with the Cubs. He also holds a Series slugging percentage record (.6672 in 1973 for Oakland against the Mets) and was the last pitcher to hit a World Series home run (in 1974 for Oakland against the Dodgers).

And in the four seasons after leaving Chicago, Kenny posted records of 19-11, 21-13, 19-17, and 18-14. Then, at the end of his career, he came back to Wrigley Field in 1978 and 1979 and, while the disenchanted Yankees were paying most of his salary, won another six games.

All that, and people still ask him about the '69 Cubs.

"I think that team simply wasn't ready to win," says Holtzman, "I'm telling you, there is a feeling about winning. There's a certain amount of intimidation. It existed between the A's and the rest of the league. The others knew they couldn't beat us. It's hard to explain, but it's real. There's a certain time in most games when intimidation becomes a factor . . . when one team becomes a ball buster.

"The Cubs didn't have that. I'm not saying a great hitter like a Santo or a Banks or a Williams didn't have a certain aura about them. They did. Pitchers would look down at Billy and say, 'Oh, shit, I don't want to pitch to him.'

"But the overall intimidation never existed with the Cubs. I've told the other guys this: had we won in 1969, I would have bet my life savings we would have come back to win at least two more. You hear all that bullshit about 'it's hard to repeat' but it's just that—bullshit. In Oakland, when we took the field we knew things would happen. We would find a way to win. The Cubs never found that way.

"In 1969 I was just a kid. I was too young to understand how to handle the stress. I started the season weighing 185, and by September I was down to 162. What we went through was overwhelming. By the end of the year I was physically and psychologically drained, back and forth from the National Guard, the whole thing. I had just had it. I think my record in September was 1 and 5. At the end of August I was 16–8, and I finished 17–13.

"Our team started making tons of errors at the end, too. It's tough to measure what defense can do to a pitcher. Ask Fergie. As good as we were during the first five months, that's how bad we were in September.

"It wasn't managerial tactics that lost that pennant; nobody can blame Leo. But it is my contention that during that summer—even when we were ahead in July and August—that we had guys on the team waiting to get beat. I'll never forget one night in Pittsburgh. It was late after a game, and I was walking down the corridor, and Ernie Banks called me into his room. Ernie and I were very close. " 'Kenny,' he said, after we'd had a few drinks, 'we had a nine-game lead, and we're not going to win it.' Well, this hit me hard. This was Ernie Banks talking, and he was saying we weren't going to win. So I looked at him and said 'Why?'

" 'Because we've got a manager and three or four players who are out there waiting to get beat,' said Ernie. He told me right to my face. I'll never forget it. It was the most serious and sober statement I'd ever heard from Ernie Banks. And, you know what? He was right.

"I remember that era, too. I think it was Tom Seaver who was quoted as saying, 'If we can land a man on the moon, why can't we get out of Vietnam?' There was political discourse even among the ballplayers. Some of us were very aware of what was happening. I remember when the Houston Astros wanted to boycott a game after Dr. Martin Luther King got shot in April 1968. This was an era when politics finally crept into the game.

"Maybe that explains, too, why so many people identify with the Cubs of that era. We were the team they grew up with. A sense of history is involved. The baby-boomers that are now my age grew up with the Cubs. We were the team of the '60s, of the turbulent times."

There were, however, some laughs.

"How about the time Leo and I double-dated?" asked Holtzman.

Double-dated? A single 23-year-old pitcher with a 63-year-old manager who had gotten married 12 days earlier.

"True story. Our second trip into Montreal, first weekend of July 1969. I had already pitched in the second game of the series, so now the next night I'm hitting ground balls to Beckert and Kessinger in batting practice. And in old Jarry Park they had those French-Canadian usherettes standing at the bottom of the aisles really close to the field. Also, understand that I studied French for three years at the University of Illinois, so I could speak it pretty well.

"Anyway, I'm hitting ground balls and talking to this usherette on the side, asking her to meet me after the game. All in French.

"Well, all of a sudden I get a tap on the shoulder from Leo, and he says, 'You know that broad? You talking to her in French? You asking her out after the game?'

" 'That's what I'm doin', Skip,' and he says, 'Well, I've been watching, and that blonde right next to her is her good friend, so you ask her if she'll go out with me, OK?'

"Just like that. He wants me to fix him up. So, what the hell, the girls talked it over and my girl, Monique, said it was OK. The other usherette had agreed to meet Leo after the game.

"Now the game is over, and I'm walking out of the clubhouse to meet my girl, and here's Leo right beside me. So Leo and I go out. What else was I gonna do? But I'll say one thing for Leo: he picked up every check in every joint. Dinner, drinks, everything. We destroyed curfew.

"Finally, Monique drives us back to the Queen Elizabeth Hotel about 3:30 A.M., she gets into the elevator with me, and Leo takes the blonde to his room.

"There was only one problem. Apparently she was too much for him, and Leo didn't make the team bus the next day. He didn't make the game either. Monique said that, according to her girlfriend, Leo woke up at 9:30 A.M., threw up, then threw up again at 2 P.M., so he called Jake [Dr. Jacob Suker, the team doctor] and she finally went home.

"I think he missed the last two games of that series, holed up in his hotel room. Everyone thought he had the flu. The French flu maybe."

One of Holtzman's bachelor running mates during the early days of 1969 was another young pitcher of considerable promise, Joe Niekro.

"I didn't marry Michelle until 1971, and Joe and I are living out in Schiller Park, near O'Hare Field. There must have been 750 airline stewardesses living in our apartment building. It was paradise.

"But one day Leo calls a clubhouse meeting and says in front of everybody, 'We got a guy on this team living in a whorehouse.'

"Now we're all lookin' around—what is he talking about? But he's looking right at me and yelling, 'How in hell are you gonna get through the season living in that place with all those stewardesses? Can't you find a damned apartment in Evanston or somewhere?'

"Afterward half the guys came up and said, 'How come you never invite us up there?' "

Durocher took firmer action late in 1969 against another young Cub, Oscar Gamble.

"Oscar comes up in September, and he's living downtown and enjoying it. He's got a different girl each night, and some of them are white. Well, that's where he got into trouble. He either dated somebody's daughter or got a ride home from her after a game or made a move on her or one of her friends. Whatever he did, someone got hot.

"Leo calls a clubhouse meeting. Here we are in September trying to save our asses in a pennant race, and he's screaming at Oscar, 'If you ever do that again, I'm going to send you so far out of town . . . I'm going to send you to Outer Mongolia, where you're going to have to play games with bus trips without a piss break!' Those were exact words, and you know what happened to Oscar." For the record, Gamble and pitcher Dick Selma were traded soon after the 1969 season to Philadelphia for outfielder Johnny Callison.

But it wasn't the first time a Cub packed his bags after being flirtatious with the wrong woman. Holtzman was a firsthand witness to one of the most famous Cubs personnel moves of all (right up there with Lou Brock for Ernie Broglio):

"It's spring 1966," says Holtzman, "and we're warming up on the sidelines before a game at Wrigley Field. I'm probably 10 years younger than anybody on that team, guys like Billy Hoeft, Ed Bailey, Vic Roznovsky, Dick Ellsworth, Bob Buhl. Anyway, Bob Hendley and Cal Koonce are warming up with the two catchers, Roznovsky and Chris Krug, and Chris is crouched closest to the box seats. The next thing you know he's talking with this woman in the front row. Then he must have given her a phone number or said something wrong because the next day Leo calls a clubhouse meeting and gives one of his great speeches of all time.

" 'Boys,' he said, 'I've played this game a long time, and I've tried to get laid at the ballpark myself a few times. I've been laid at the hotel. I've been laid out of town. I've been laid as much as any of you sons of bitches.' And then he paused, looked right at Krug, and said, 'But *never once* did I ever try to fuck the owner's wife!'

"It turns out the lady in the front row was Allison Wrigley, then married to Bill Wrigley. Chris didn't get a chance to talk with her anymore. He was sent down."

Holtzman was a Jewish left-handed pitcher who threw high and hard and occasionally threw a hook curve, and that was enough to get him compared with Sandy Koufax, especially since Kenny was coming up as Sandy was leaving. That's the kind of pressure-generating comparison no ballplayer needs, but Holtzman didn't let it bother him.

"I pitched against Sandy in 1966, my first season and his last, and I beat him in the last game he ever lost," says Holtzman. "But I didn't feel any pressure to try to emulate him. I had nothing but respect for him, but I wasn't going to alter my style."

And what style was that?

"I went through two phases as a pitcher. When I first came up, I was a power pitcher—better-than-average fastball, better-than-average curveball, average control. Tee it up and let's go. Strikeouts were a big thing then.

"But after I got to be 26 or 27, pitching in Oakland, playing at night, I learned that by cutting down the number of pitches—and having a purpose for each pitch—you can be just as successful. That doesn't mean I lost anything; I didn't. I threw just as hard on the day I retired as the day I came up. I never had arm trouble because I never threw sliders or trick pitches. It's just that in those days a starting pitcher had an obligation to go nine innings if possible. We tried for complete games. Look at the statistics of Fergie, Hands, and myself in 1969. How many complete games between us, 53? That's not bad for three men. In those days you would get complete-game losses. You don't see much of that anymore.

"So I learned that you don't have to blow it past every hitter or throw a foot-and-a-half curveball every time. In Oakland during our championship years there were three main guys, Catfish, Vida, and me. Every fourth day you were expected to go nine. I had much better command of my pitches then: I was staying ahead of the hitters, and I didn't care if they grounded out instead of striking out. I became a complete pitcher."

Koufax and Holtzman actually had more in common

than their faith and their left arms. Both were also capable
of totally dominating an opposing lineup. Koufax threw
four no-hitters with the Dodgers, Holtzman two with the
Cubs. Kenny's first came during the 1969 season, and many
felt that the 3-0 victory over the Atlanta Braves at Wrigley
Field on August 19 was the last really good thing to happen
to the Cubs that summer.

"I know it gave us a 7½-game lead, and I know it was a
hot Tuesday afternoon with the place packed," recalls
Holtzman. "I didn't have good control, but I had an above-
average fastball, and the wind was blowing directly in
toward the hitters. That was the game Bill Heath caught
but broke his finger and Gene Oliver had to finish. I always
kid Randy Hundley because, of all the games he caught, he
didn't catch either of my no-hitters. The kid, Danny
Breeden, caught my other one in Cincinnati in 1971.

"But in the 1969 game, I had zero strikeouts and only two
walks, even though my control was off. Actually it was
almost a perfect game. I didn't throw many pitches.

"The big thing, of course, was the ball Henry Aaron hit
in the seventh inning. Should have been a home run. On
any other day it would have been over the houses across
Waveland Avenue. I remember the trajectory. It was one of
those high ones headed for distant places, and I remember
Billy backing up into that corner in left field, just standing
there with his right arm against the wall. He kept looking
up and looking up, and he knew it was going to land on the
sidewalk. The ball was suddenly suspended up there—it
seemed like 40 seconds between the time it left the bat and
the time it started coming down—and finally it just
dropped down into Billy's glove.

"I'll never forget the look Hammer [Aaron] gave me. Let's
face it, when Hammer hits it, you know it's gone. He had
those wrists and that top hand coming through, and when
he started into that trot, he *knew*. Well, he was almost to
second base when he saw Billy catch the ball. He made a U-
turn around second and ran about four feet from me as he
came past the mound. He just looked at me, puzzled, quizzi-

cal, and I just looked back at him. Nothing was said. Nothing needed to be said.

"Then Aaron comes up again with two out in the ninth, and Ollie runs to the mound and says, 'You want to walk him?' I say, 'If he gets a hit, he gets a hit.' So the count goes to 3-2, and he blasts a fastball to Beckert at second. Beck was so scared to death, he did a double pump before he finally threw Aaron out at first base. I still kid him today about being so scared."

Holtzman's second no-hitter was more dominating. He blanked the Reds 1-0 in Cincinnati on June 3, 1971, using 108 pitches (64 fastballs, 43 curves, one change-up) and striking out 6.

"It was 98 degrees then too," says Holtzman, "but it was one of those games where you go out and feel you can literally blow the ball past everyone. I had luck then too. You can't pitch a no-hitter without luck." Holtzman had lost one against the Giants in 1970 on Hal Lanier's single in the ninth. "Anyway, this time I got lucky in the seventh inning. Johnny Bench was up with one out and a man on base. So Santo, naturally, is playing Bench in shallow left field with a 1-0 lead and damned if Bench didn't bunt. If the ball stays fair, it's a double, for Chrissakes. Who expected Bench to bunt? But the ball rolled foul on that artificial turf just before it reached third base."

Bench then flied out to right and Holtzman finished strongly in that second no-hitter, throwing just 27 pitches over the final three innings. It was the first no-hitter in Riverfront Stadium history.

Because of his success after leaving Chicago, Holtzman earned more money than most of the 1969 Cubs. But it sure took a while.

"I played the entire 1966 year with the Cubs for $7,000. And then again in 1967, when I was in the military service for much of the season, I go 9-0 anyway and they gave me a $2,000 raise. If you go 9-0 today, what do you get, $1.5 million? I pitched in 1968 for $9,000, then got bumped to $16,000 at the end of my third full year in the majors.

"How about this? After the A's win the 1972 World Series and I'm coming off a season of 19–11, Charlie Finley sends me a contract for a $5,000 raise. I was making $37,500 at the time, and he wants to sign me again for $42,500. So I'm screaming on the phone at him and he says, 'Wait a minute, Kenny, how much money did you make for winning the World Series?' I told him about $21,000. And he says, 'Well, kid, that's what you're in the game for, isn't it? That's your raise.' "

Before Holtzman's career was finished, he had signed a million-dollar five-year contract with George Steinbrenner, making him one of baseball's highest-paid players. When he returned to the Cubs in 1978, in fact, the Yankees were paying $100,000 of Holtzman's $165,000-a-year salary, while the Cubs had to pay only the minimum $65,000. (He was also the first player to go through arbitration, in 1974.) Also, Holtzman somehow survived not only working for owners Finley and Steinbrenner but playing under managers Billy Martin, Dick Williams, Earl Weaver, and Leo Durocher.

"The only problem I ever had with Leo was that he would second-guess my pitches," says Holtzman. "He was notorious for it. He'd yell something like 'Why did you throw that guy a high fastball?' And I'd yell, 'Because I threw him a high fastball last time and struck him out. Are you tellin' me it was a great pitch last time and a shitty pitch this time?!'

"I remember the time Leo called Ferguson Jenkins a quitter in front of the whole team. *A quitter?* He had 23 complete games in 1969, and he was a quitter? I nearly fell over. That's when I thought Leo had lost it."

Any truth to the story that Leo once called Holtzman a "gutless Jew" in the same clubhouse?

Holtzman laughs.

"I don't remember, but he could have. He called everybody everything. But I had my day. Remember a couple of years later when Leo and Santo went at it in the clubhouse? That's the day Ronnie ran up into Leo's office and grabbed him by the throat. Leo's tongue was sticking out six inches before we pulled Santo off him. Big blowup. Anyway, that's when Leo came back into the clubhouse and announced he was quitting and John Holland came down to address the team. He's giving us that speech about how we can't let the manager quit and how it's not his fault, and different guys are defending Leo, and all of a sudden I shout:

" 'Let the son of a bitch go!'

"I think that's when Holland decided he would honor my request to be traded. But let me be clear about one thing: I still don't blame Leo for what happened to us. I never did and never will.

"It seems to me that the 1969 season was the ultimate Cub season. Baseball is always portrayed as a serene, pastoral game with hopes high in the spring, leading to eventual heartbreak in August and September, and what team better personifies that image over the history of baseball than the Chicago Cubs? It's the story of the Cubs franchise. The ultimate lovable losers.

"In '69 we just did it in spades, that's all."

JULY 31			
East	**W**	**L**	**GB**
Chicago	64	41	—
New York	55	44	6
St. Louis	55	49	8½
Pittsburgh	53	50	10
Philadelphia	42	60	20½
Montreal	33	70	30

5
July

"DUROCHER GOES AWOL"
—*Chicago Today headline*

It was during the month of July 1969 that the Cubs' universe subtly began its bizarre tumble.

The spinning began on day one in Montreal, when Durocher fired a verbal volley at Expo manager Gene Mauch.

"If the Expos stick with that little genius long enough," said Leo, "they'll continue to stay in last place."

Mauch's reply: "There is only one genius in this game, and his name is Leo, and he's in first place. But I remember a couple of years ago when he lost 103 games with Santo, Williams, Banks, Beckert, Kessinger, and Hundley in the lineup. Was he a genius then too? I'll say this about the Cubs this year: they have nobody to beat but themselves."

It was just a pithy little exchange between a couple of vain men, but it was indicative of the kind of opposition the

Cubs would encounter throughout the season. Their manager, their driving force, was not making any friends around the league. Atop the NL East standings with a record of 49–27, they had become the hunted.

From a four-game split in Montreal they traveled to St. Louis and lost three of four, including a doubleheader on July 6, the day Rod Laver defeated John Newcombe in the Wimbledon finals. Back in Chicago, meanwhile, representatives of the Bleacher Bums, unhappy over negative publicity they had been receiving (somebody had written they were "juvenile and disgraceful"), were threatening to take their act to Comiskey Park.

The silly threat was quickly forgotten. So was the first troop withdrawal from Vietnam, which began on July 8, because on that same afternoon something happened at Shea Stadium, New York.

The Don Young Incident.

The situation: The Cubs held a five-game lead over the Mets with Fergie Jenkins, 11–5, on the mound against Jerry Koosman. Jenkins was superb. He worked four hitless innings until Ed Kranepool homered over the right-field fence in the fifth, giving the Mets a 1–0 lead. But Banks homered in the sixth, and Beckert's RBI single gave the Cubs a 2–1 lead in the seventh. Hickman's homer over the left-field fence in the eighth gave Fergie insurance, 3–1. Three more outs and the Cubs would have a six-game lead.

What happened next came so quickly and unexpectedly that nobody could quite believe it.

Ken Boswell, pinch hitting for Koosman, looped a pop fly into right center. Young, the rookie centerfielder from Aurora, Colorado, and surprise starter in 1969 because Adolfo Phillips was injured and then traded, got a slow break on the catchable ball and managed only to play it into a double.

Tommie Agee then fouled out to Banks, but Donn Clendenon, pinch hitting for Bobby Pfeil, drove one toward the fence in left center. Young, racing backward and to his right, had the ball in his glove momentarily, then dropped it before he crashed into the wall. It could have been a brilliant, redeeming catch. Instead, Clendenon slid into second and Boswell stopped at third.

Jenkins, obviously shaken, then hung a slider that Cleon Jones drove against the left-field fence, scoring both Boswell and Clendenon to tie the game 3–3. Art Shamsky received an intentional walk and Wayne Garrett grounded out, moving the runners to second and third with two out and setting up a confrontation between Jenkins and Kranepool.

At first it looked as if Jenkins had won. He fooled Kranepool with a low outside pitch that the left-handed hitter just swiped at with his bat. He made contact, however, and looped a single to score the winning run 4–3.

The strange sequence of events sent shock waves through the Cubs clubhouse—waves that would haunt most of those involved for two decades.

It started with Durocher.

"It's tough to win when your centerfielder can't catch a fucking fly ball," he said after the game. "Jenkins pitched his heart out. But when one man can't catch a fly ball, it's a disgrace. He stands there watching one and then gives up on the other. It's a disgrace."

Then, with Young clearly within hearing distance, Durocher continued, "My son could have caught that ball. My three-year-old could have caught those balls!"

Santo, 20 years later, recalls his reactions:

"I felt sorry for the kid. But I was upset too. The other guys were also upset, but I was the captain. So people are taking their showers, and Jerry Holtzman of the *Sun-Times* comes over to me and asks, 'Did you hear what Leo said?' I said yes, and all I could think about was how Donnie had acted out there on the field. Jim Hickman had gone over to him in the outfield, but he had said to Hick, 'Go to hell.' Now, Hick's a very quiet guy, so he comes to me and says, 'Young is upset; you gotta calm him down.' So I did go to Don during the game to try to settle him down. But the next thing I know, he's throwing his bat and helmet in the dugout . . . really uptight, and I grab him before he runs back onto the field, and I say, 'Hey, do your job out there.' "

At that time, in the locker room with a reporter standing

over Santo saying, "What did you think of that?," Santo remained convinced that Young had carried his problems onto the field. And that's when Santo said:

"He was thinking of himself, not the team. He had a bad day at the plate, and he's got his head down. Don's a major leaguer because of his glove. When he hits, it's a dividend, but when he fails on defense, he's lost—and today he took us down with him. He put his head between his legs."

Another Chicago writer, Jimmy Enright, also heard Santo's remarks but refused to print them, saying, "One career has already been ruined tonight. I'm not going to ruin another."

And at 3 A.M. Santo got a phone call in his New York hotel room from a friend back in Chicago. The first edition of the *Sun-Times* had hit the streets. There it was: Santo criticizes teammate for losing game.

Young, meanwhile, had said nothing. He had rushed into the locker room, showered quickly, and departed Shea Stadium without waiting for the team bus. Later that evening, however, he was reached in his hotel room. Fighting back tears, he gave these answers:

"I didn't run into the wall on Clendenon's double until I had dropped it, and I didn't run into Billy Williams. I should have had that ball, but I dropped it. It hit my glove, and I dropped it."

Did he lose the first ball off Boswell's bat in the afternoon sun?

"I don't know . . . I don't know."

Did his performance at the plate (two strikeouts, two pop flies) affect his defensive play, as Santo had suggested?

"No . . . I just lost the game for us, that's all I did."

And the incident wasn't finished. Back in the Shea clubhouse, an obviously emotional Santo had said about the Mets, "I wouldn't put that infield in Tacoma. It's a shame losing to an infield [Kranepool, Garrett, Al Weis, and Pfeil] like that. Everybody thinks the Mets are so great. I'd almost forgotten them because we hadn't played them in so long. I was beginning to tell myself that maybe they were pretty good. But they looked like a bunch of rejects to me."

Santo had spoken himself into the center of a hurricane.

Suddenly the villain was the Cubs' third baseman, a captain who had publicly blasted his teammate. Young, who would be relegated to the bench and play little baseball for the rest of the season—or his life, for that matter—had overnight become the object of sympathy.

Santo reacted immediately and apologetically, calling Chicago writers to his hotel room the next day to explain. He had already given his personal apology to Young that morning.

"What I said, I did not mean," said Santo. "Don being upset, upset me. I am convinced that his not hitting caused him to put his head down between his knees and forget we had a 3–1 lead. I know this is true because it has happened to me. I have fought myself when I wasn't hitting and, as a result, messed up in the field. But I know I was wrong. Don has to be a great competitor to get as mad at himself as he did and to leave the clubhouse as quickly as he did. This was not good, and I said what I did because he had walked out.

"I want everyone to know my complete sincerity in this apology."

Jack Brickhouse remembers a related scene:

"I think Ronnie misunderstood Young leaving the clubhouse so soon. He thought it was because Young didn't give a damn. Ron wanted the guy to be sitting, grieving in front of his locker for an hour after the game. So Santo blasted the guy, then did a double take. His temperament got the best of him, and he regretted it.

"But the next day in front of the Cubs' hotel there was Santo with his arm around Don Young, talking to him for a good five minutes, trying to make it up to him. It was a touch of class by Ron, but you know, he never has gotten off the hook for that. At least he apologized. I'm still waiting for Leo to correct anything he ever said."

Billy Williams, who watched it all happen, also recalls the Incident:

"That first ball Donnie missed was in the sun. He didn't have his glasses on, and he broke back on it. Then I thought he was going to run through the fence trying to get that next one. So I run over and I say, 'Hey, you gotta take it easy, man. Relax a little out here.' So all that stuff happens in the clubhouse, and I'm back at the hotel and the phone rings. It's Fergie and he says, 'Can you come up here for a minute?'

"So I go to Fergie's room, and he's crying. 'That was a big game out there today, and I had to win it.' I said, 'It wasn't all your fault,' and he said, 'Don't matter. I had to win it.'

"Now, the next morning I see Santo talking with Randy, and he's saying, 'How can I make people believe something after they've already read something else and made up their minds?' I said, 'Ronnie, you may not be able to smooth it over in the papers, but you apologize to that kid.' "

The apology was made, but the Incident refused to be forgotten.

Somewhere, though, there was laughter. Johnny Carson had just signed with NBC for $75,000 a week, "The Beverly Hillbillies" and "High Chaparral" were popular on TV, you could buy a full-sized Ford for $2,305, and Big John, Chicago's Hancock building, was reaching for the sky.

And the image of another rookie centerfielder, just one day after the Don Young Incident, was indelibly imprinted on the memories of Cubs fans. His name was Jimmy Qualls.

Qualls got the call that July 9 because (a) Young was in the doghouse, and (b) Qualls was a left-handed hitter going against Tom Seaver. There were 59,083 spectators on hand that night, the largest crowd the Mets had ever had, and they *almost* witnessed history.

Qualls prevented it. In only his 43rd major league at-bat, the .243 hitter got a base hit off Seaver with one out in the ninth to break up Seaver's perfect no-hitter.

The scene: the banjo band behind home plate played another lively tune, umpire Chris Pelekoudas dusted off home plate, and Seaver took one long breath. Hundley had just opened the ninth by trying to bunt, but it hadn't worked. Now Seaver needed just two outs.

But two pitches and three minutes later, the perfect game

was gone—a victim of Qualls's sudden sharp drive into left field between Jones and Agee.

"I wanted the pitch to be low, but it was down the middle," said Seaver later. "I knew what might happen, but there was nothing I could do about it. Until then it was like a dream. Then the pressure just ran out of me, like someone opened a spout in my foot and let all the pressure run out."

Seaver threw only 99 pitches in that 4–0 victory over Ken Holtzman, and 71 were strikes. Never once did he have a three-ball count on a Cubs hitter. And on a night when thousands were turned away from Shea Stadium, the Cubs surely must have realized the Mets were for real.

Or did they? The Cubs salvaged game three of the series behind stopper Hands's 10th victory, and it would be another 48 days before the Mets would again inch up within reach.

"Were those the real Cubs we saw out there today?" somebody asked Durocher after the 6–2 victory.

"No," answered Leo, "but those were the real Mets."

July was just beginning.

There was a new Cub concern. Holtzman was in a slump, and pitching coach Joe Becker was convinced the left-hander was unconsciously tipping off his pitches. Despite his 10–1 start, Holtzman was now 10–5 and had completed only 6 of 23 starts. Even teammates noticed the tip-off: he was holding the fingers of his glove hand open before gripping the curveball, but closing the glove-hand fingers tightly before throwing the fastball. Despite thoughts of removing him from the rotation, it was decided Holtzman should remain. Durocher had no confidence in anyone else.

Meanwhile there was more fallout from the Mets' series. New York mayor John V. Lindsay, trying to make headlines on the political front, had telephoned congratulations to Mets manager Gil Hodges and said, "Tell Leo that Chicago is still the Second City."

Durocher's response: "You can take your mayor, I'll take mine."

Richard Daley versus John Lindsay, best two out of three?

"Mayor Daley is number one," said Leo. "At least the people of Chicago aren't up to their fannies in garbage."

And the Cubs were still rulers of the NL East. Ballots were being counted for the upcoming All-Star Game in Washington, D.C., a gala event to celebrate baseball's 100th anniversary. After their 90th game on July 12, the Cubs could savor these statistics:

Record: 56–34. Lead over the Mets: 4½ games. The team was 32–10 at home, 9–2 in extra-inning games, and 16–15 in one-run games. The pitchers had 16 shutouts, and Jenkins led the staff with a record of 12–6, followed by Holtzman at 11–5, Hands at 10–7, Selma at 7–1, and Regan at 9–5 with 8 saves. Santo lead the league in RBI with 79, and Banks had 74. Beckert was hitting .305, Willie Smith .305, Williams .303, Kessinger .299, and Santo .295. Santo led the team in homers with 18, Banks had 14, Hundley 13, Williams 9, and Willie Smith 8.

And when the All-Star teams were announced, Santo and Kessinger were top vote-getters, with Beckert, Banks, and Hundley named as reserves. As usual, the quiet Williams was ignored by voters. And Cub pitchers Jenkins, Hands, and Holtzman were bypassed by Red Schoendienst, manager of the NL All-Stars. "I must be losing it as a pitching coach," said Becker, and in retrospect it is difficult to imagine how Jenkins, who would finish the season at 21–15 with 23 complete games, could not have been an All-Star in 1969. The same might be said for Hands, who was 20–14, and Williams, who hit .293 with 21 home runs and 95 RBI and played in 163 games. Schoendienst's dilemma was that the Cubs were already so well represented.

As Don Kessinger would reminisce 20 years later, "One of my big thrills in baseball was looking around the infield during the 1969 All-Star Game and seeing every position filled by a member of the Chicago Cubs."

For the record, Hundley started that game at catcher— even though he had finished second in voting to Johnny Bench, who faced an untimely military obligation. And with Santo starting at third, Kessinger at shortstop, Banks substituting for Willie McCovey, and Beckert for Felix Millan, the Cubs did indeed have a complete infield of All-Stars. There was nobody out there named Kranepool, Garrett, Weis, or Pfeil.

Before the All-Star Game would arrive, however, there was another series to be played against the Mets, this time at Wrigley Field.

The Cubs had spent the previous weekend at home against Philadelphia, winning three of four, and when the Mets arrived on July 14, they still trailed by 4½. That lead soon became 5½ games when Hands outdueled Seaver 1–0.

Santo was seen leaping into the air and clicking his heels that day as he ran for the left-field locker-room entrance. It was not the first time: he had been doing similar heel-clicking leaps since late June.

The Mets, however, took it personally.

"Who saw Santo's victory dance today?" asked Tom Seaver in the clubhouse.

"Bush," said the Mets.

"I'm just jumping for joy," said Santo.

But the Mets won the next two games, thanks in part to Al Weis, a journeyman infielder who only 18 months before had been employed by the White Sox. Now filling in at shortstop for Bud Harrelson, who was serving a military hitch, Weis homered off Selma in the fourth inning with two men on base. Yes, the wind was blowing out, and yes, it was a two-strike pitch. He had hit only one home run in 1968 and none the two years before that. And what was he thinking as the ball soared over the Bleacher Bums onto Waveland Avenue?

"To touch every base."

The Mets then won the series finale, giving them four of six over the Cubs in July by pounding Jenkins for four runs in the first inning. And, yes, Weis homered in that game too.

"My ambition," said Met Ed Kranepool, "is to come into Wrigley Field for the last two games of the season with a three-game lead. Then I'm going to go over and stand on the Cubs dugout and wait for that smiling Ernie Banks to come out. Then I'll start singing, 'What a beautiful day to play baseball.' "

In the meantime, the world was waiting for Apollo 11, the first manned voyager to the moon, to reach its destination. Astronauts Neil Armstrong, Edwin (Buzz) Aldrin, Jr., and Michael Collins had been launched successfully on July 16 (about the time Weis was launching his second home run of the series) and were expected to land on the 20th.

So great was the Apollo 11 anticipation that in retrospect it is no wonder that another story that broke on July 18 took some time to build momentum. Sen. Edward Kennedy of Massachusetts had driven his car off a bridge on Chappaquiddick Island, Massachusetts, and a passenger, Mary Jo Kopechne, was dead. It was several days before details of the accident would be made somewhat clearer. A confused nation waited for answers while Apollo 11's lunar module headed for touchdown.

The Cubs were now in Philadelphia, and for the first time, were showing signs of physical exhaustion. Bone-tired, having played 30 games in the last 27 days, there was a psychological weariness too. Santo, following those last two losses to the Mets in Chicago, looked like a man who had just bellied his way through an army infiltration course and had been told he would have to do it over again. Unquestionably, the Don Young Incident was preying on his mind.

Others were showing signs of stress too. The team had not been out of first place since Opening Day, and the daily fight-for-your-life schedule had been wearing.

"It's time to regroup," relief pitcher Hank Aguirre said. "We've been after it every day, and the pressure has been extreme. We just haven't had much rest. Now it's time to go out and have a few cold drinks, take a deep breath, and regroup."

Ironman catcher Hundley, who had been swinging a tired bat for weeks, added, "You ask if the All-Star break is welcome? Are you kidding? I said a month ago that if we survived to the All-Star break we'd be OK. It looks like we'll make it, but it's been murder."

And it was only mid-July.

The spacecraft *Eagle* had landed, and on the night of July 20, Neil A. Armstrong of Wapakoneta, Ohio, and Col. Edwin E. Aldrin, Jr., of Montclair, New Jersey, walked on the moon as Armstrong said, "That's one small step for man, one giant leap for mankind."

On the late afternoon of July 20, Dick Selma of Fresno, California, looked from his place on the bench in Philadelphia's old Shibe Park and said to teammate Beckert, "Hey, with those guys on the moon tonight and me pitching, no way we can lose."

Selma and the Cubs did win, completing a doubleheader sweep of the Phillies and maintaining their lead of 4½ games over the Mets. And from that day until he was traded the following spring, Selma would be known to teammates as "Moonie" or "Moonman."

Now, though, it was time for a break, unless you were one of five Cubs headed for the All-Star Game and the Nixon residence, Washington, D.C.

"He gave me three years," said Banks, flashing a grin as big as the White House porch while heavy rain soaked the outside lawn. "The president thought I was only 35. Then the commissioner said, 'No, Mr. President, I think Ernie is 38,' and Mr. Nixon said, 'Well, he looks 35, and don't tell any of those other fellows, but this man deserves a pennant.' "

More than 400 other baseball All-Stars, celebrities, and reporters joined in the informal two-hour reception at the White House, with Nixon admittedly showing off his knowledge of the sport. He praised Santo about the entire Cubs infield reaching the All-Star Game, he told WGN radio announcer Lou Boudreau that he recalled the famous second-base pickoff play of the 1948 World Series, and he even found something nice to say about sportswriters.

"I like the job I have," said the president, "but if I had to start over again I'd like to have been a sportswriter."

Tired or not, the Cubs apparently enjoyed themselves, as Beckert said, "I'm glad I came. Now I know how part of our tax money is spent."

Unfortunately the president's enthusiasm had no impact on the weather, which postponed the game until the next day. Nixon had to miss the National League's 9–3 victory in order to depart for the splashdown area of the Pacific Ocean to greet the returning moon men.

It marked the first time an All-Star Game had been rained out before even beginning. Actually, there had been a lot of firsts that week, and visitors weren't sure which was more astounding—men on the moon or sportswriters drinking booze in the East Room.

All-Star postscript: The two young men sitting in the first-class section of the jet out of Washington, D.C., studied their sports pages closely, analyzing a list of the best "All-Time" team ever. Finally, Reginald Martinez Jackson, age 23, discarded the newspaper and said:

"What did Ty Cobb ever do?"

"And what did Pie Traynor ever do?" asked Jackson's teammate, Sal Bando. "Could he charge a slow roller better than Ron Santo? It isn't possible."

Camp Ojibwa, located in Eagle River, Wisconsin, at the intersection of state highways 32, 70, and 45 in Vilas County, became part of Chicago Cubs lore soon after the Cubs returned from All-Star break.

Camp Ojibwa—a pleasant place to visit, and that's exactly what manager Leo Durocher of the Cubs did on the weekend of July 26–27, 1969. No problem, except that his team was playing the Dodgers at Wrigley Field that weekend while Leo was AWOL.

President Nixon was also traveling that weekend, visiting a fellow named Ferdinand Marcos in the Philippines—but he hardly drew the attention that Leo did. Why? Because Durocher almost lost his job.

The situation: Leo left Saturday's nationally televised game during the third inning, and it was reported to the press box that he had a "stomach disorder." In truth, he was grabbing a taxi for Meigs Field. There he met his new bride, Lynne, and flew to Camp Ojibwa, where her son, 10-year-old Joel, was waiting for them on Parents' Weekend. Leo stayed through the weekend, missing the game on Sunday (his 64th birthday) as well.

But instead of his visit being kept secret, it became news when the *Chicago Today*'s baseball writer, the late James Enright, received a tip from another Camp Ojibwa parent. Enright, no favorite of Durocher's, then phoned Cubs owner Wrigley at his home in Lake Geneva, Wisconsin, for a reaction. Wrigley responded by angrily wondering what Leo was doing in Wisconsin and suggesting—strongly— that he owed his players an apology.

"Mr. Wrigley almost fired Leo that weekend," says Jack Brickhouse. "I don't think it's wrong to tell this now, inasmuch as P.K. and his wife, Helen, are both gone. But for about two hours, Leo *was* fired. Wrigley was really upset, but Helen calmed him down and warned him to cool off before making a decision. He did cool down, thought it over, and gave Leo a chance to explain. That's when Leo came back, met with John Holland and P.K., and almost got down on his hands and knees to kiss their shoes."

Lynne Durocher, who divorced Leo in 1981 and now works in public relations in Chicago, offers this insight on what really happened that weekend:

"In a way, it was all my fault, strictly out of ignorance. I didn't know the ways of baseball, and I figured the head man of any corporation ought to be able to take off whenever he wanted. Joel and Leo liked each other, and I just thought it would be nice if Leo could fly up for Parents' Weekend. But baseball? I didn't know anything about baseball. That was Leo's business."

So the whole thing was Lynne's idea?

"Oh, sure. You know, I said something like, 'Gee, it sure would be nice if you could go with me to see Joel,' and at first he said, 'No way!' So I said, 'Well, after all, you are the boss of the Cubs, aren't you? How serious could it be to miss one or two little old games?'

"Well, this appealed to Leo's crazy sense of humor, and he started thinking about it, I could tell.

" 'Nahhhh,' he said, 'no way.' But then he got that smile on his face and said, 'I'll call you if I can meet you at the plane.' So I went to Meigs with my two daughters, and had Leo's ticket with me just in case. And, sure enough, he called me from the dugout during the game and said, 'I think I can make it. We can't lose this one!' "

Actually, the Cubs could—and did—lose that one to the Dodgers in 10 innings with coach Reiser managing. However, they came back on Sunday, still without Durocher, to win.

"Well, anyhow," says Lynne, "he made the plane, and we got to Wisconsin, but after we rented a car and drove to camp, I knew this would be no secret. There were banners saying 'Welcome, Leo.' But we had a great time. He really enjoyed himself, meeting the counselors and everything. He was just like any of the other fathers. It was no big deal.

"He did it to please me. I'm sure he didn't think of the consequences. Leo was like that, very impetuous. It would drive me crazy because I usually do think of the consequences. In this case I just didn't understand them, and he was just trying to play the big man. That was part of his charm."

Was Leo surprised at the reaction and the aftermath?

"He was stunned."

Leo, always the survivor, escaped Camp Ojibwa with a scolding and wrist slap from Wrigley and Holland. None of the players can recall whether he ever apologized or not. It didn't matter much to them anyway. Pitcher Jenkins, who pitched and won the July 27 game during Leo's absence (the same day the Cubs went over one million in attendance), recalls, "There was a lot of hype and publicity about the whole thing, but we were playing good ball, so we weren't really bothered."

Recalls Hundley, "It didn't bother me that he left. I didn't think anything about it. Certainly I didn't think we had been deserted."

"I don't think anybody was upset," remembers Santo. "He told me he was going to camp. I can't believe he told the press he was sick, but he told us in the clubhouse he was heading out in the afternoon. I said, 'Go ahead, have a good time.' "

"The whole thing was a joke," says relief pitcher Hank Aguirre. "We all knew what kind of guy Leo was. I think the only guys upset were the writers."

Joey Amalfitano, at age 35 the youngest member of the 1969 coaching staff and now a coach with the Los Angeles Dodgers, adds, "Perhaps there were a few players who looked at it like a child thinking their father had abandoned them, but if players have to lean on something like that, they are weak players. Frankly, I don't think our players knew what was going on, or cared."

"I thought the whole thing was terribly overplayed," says Lynne Durocher.

Leo, however, was personally embarrassed, especially when Chicago baseball writers gave him the "Camper of the Year" award at their midwinter awards dinner, and *Tribune* columnist David Condon showed up wearing a Boy Scout uniform. Durocher's feud with reporter Enright also intensified. Result: Soon after the incident, when the club's chartered plane stopped for fuel in Las Vegas and Enright departed to make some phone calls in the terminal, Durocher ordered the pilot to take off. Enright, having left his coat and wallet on board, was stranded without money or credit cards.

Durocher loved to hold grudges. It was part of his persona. Example:

It was 10 A.M. August 14, 1969—just 18 days after the Camp Ojibwa flap—when the telephone rang at my home in Crystal Lake, Illinois.

"Hello, Rick? This is Leo Durocher."

It was a surprise. Even though I was sports editor of one of Chicago's four daily newspapers, Leo had never called my home. And, since the Cubs were playing that night in San Diego, it was 8 A.M., coast time, for Leo.

He didn't waste a minute. "When I took some time off [to visit Camp Ojibwa], your man Enright called my boss and talked to him about it, didn't he?"

"Yes, he called Mr. Wrigley."

"And he got me into trouble over it, didn't he?"

"Well, yes, there was some criticism about you leaving the team, Leo."

" 'Durocher Goes AWOL' . . . isn't that what the headlines said?"

"Yes . . . but what's this all about?"

"Well, right is right, don't you agree?"

"Yes, I agree."

"Well, do you know where your man Enright is today?"

I knew. Jimmy had been assigned to leave the Cubs in San Diego and travel to nearby Camp Pendleton to interview White Sox star Carlos May, who was hospitalized after blowing off his thumb with a mortar during a U.S. Marines training exercise.

But I didn't tell Leo I knew.

"He's with the Cubs, isn't he?"

"No," answered Durocher triumphantly. "We're going to go into Tacoma for an exhibition game tonight, and he isn't going along. You'll probably find him at Del Mar racetrack, then he'll skip Tacoma and go into San Francisco to pick us up."

"So why are you telling me this?"

"When I took a day off, he called my boss, right? I just wanted *his* boss to know what *he* was doing."

"So what am I supposed to do, Leo? Run a headline that says, 'Enright Goes AWOL?' "

"If *I* were to miss the Tacoma game, you'd run the headline, wouldn't you?"

"Yeah, probably."

"Well, I just thought you should know. Fair is fair, and right is right. If he can call my boss and get me into trouble, I think this is only fair."

That was Leo. There was no way to ever predict what he

might do or say, but there was one man in the Cubs organization whose main job was to do just that. It was traveling secretary Blake Cullen's job to caddy for Leo Durocher. He did other things too, like make travel arrangements—book hotels, charter planes, leave tickets, represent the team on the road, handle ticket requests, etc.—but with the Cubs being Leo's "bo-bo," i.e., one who served and protected him, was a consuming task.

"When I first joined the Cubs after the 1965 season right out of the Sheraton Hotel chain, no baseball background, the first thing John Holland told me was, 'You're Leo's personal manager. Open his mail and take it to him. Whatever it takes. Watch over Leo.' Well, sometimes it took some watching but we hit it off, we really did.

"Leo wasn't much of a drinker, but there were many times I had to cover for his actions on the road. Remember that Indian-looking woman who always sat behind third base, the one with the good-looking daughter? Well, they came to Cincinnati, and Leo promised them tickets. They got their tickets OK, but then Leo called their room and said, 'Hello, honey, I want you to come down to my suite in your nightgown.' The only problem was that he was talking to the mother and he thought it was the daughter. Needless to say, shit hit the fan. The mother filed a lawsuit against the club, but we kept it quiet.

"Leo took care of himself. He went to the Mayo Clinic every year. He dressed like a million bucks. He's the only guy I ever knew who carried spare teeth. He had these two false front teeth and he always carried two spares in this little jeweled cuff-link box, just in case somebody took a swing at him and knocked out his teeth."

Cullen, who left the Cubs after the 1975 season because he was passed over for the available general manager's job, reveals that Durocher had a master plan for running the Cubs.

"Leo wanted to run the team. He had it all figured out. He would be under Mr. Wrigley and be my boss. I would be general manager, and Joey Amalfitano would become the manager. But it didn't work."

After leaving the Cubs, Cullen joined the National League and worked under President Chub Feeney for 11 years serving in various capacities—director of public relations, administrator of umpires, schedule maker, in charge of publications, etc. But when A. Bartlett Giamatti (now commissioner of baseball) came into power as NL president, Cullen once again was frustrated.

"I went into Bart's office and said, 'Could we talk in private about your plans for me?' And he said, 'I have no plans for you. I want you out by the first of the year.' So I took a nice settlement and left."

Cullen, 52, currently lives in New York City and serves as a management consultant to the sports industry and has ownership in several minor league franchises. Financially, he has done well. But, as so many did, he left a piece of himself with the Cubs.

"It's funny how a team can get into your heart. I'm a Chicago guy, born there, and when my dad had to move to Akron, Ohio, I remember rebelling and refusing to go because I was so sure the Cubs were going to win the 1945 pennant. My parents had to promise they'd bring me back for the World Series before I'd go, and they did.

"Then 24 years later I could see that pennant getting away in August. Suddenly the Mets were everybody's darlings, and we were the bad guys."

What about Camp Ojibwa? Did Cullen play a role?

"You can't blame me for that one. Leo just left. First I heard about it was when somebody called me in the press box. I said, 'Excuse me? He did what?' "

What about the Durocher-Brickhouse feud?

"It was programmed by Leo from day one. Leo wanted feuds. It allowed him to release his frustrations. But he put us in a real awkward spot with Brickhouse. I remember once, back when Leo and Brick were still speaking, we were sitting in a saloon in Philadelphia, and you know how Leo liked to play silly games. Well, we were playing one of those 'do as I do' drinking games, and Brickhouse could never get it right. Every time he'd screw up Leo would yell, 'Wrong!' and Brick would have to take a drink. Finally, after about 19 drinks, he turns over his scotch glass and his hand is bleeding. Somehow he had cut his hand. Well, everybody is laughing, and somebody is wrapping his hand, and he's yelling to Leo, 'I did it right . . . I did it right.' And Leo yells, 'Wrong, I didn't bleed!' "

Cullen wasn't the only Cubs employee keeping a watchful eye on Durocher. Chuck Shriver joined the club in 1967 as the "Information and Services Manager" and was ushered into a room and shown a large paper box filled with unopened fan mail.

"I guess you could start there," Shriver was told, and that's how he began as the Cubs PR man.

Shriver's biggest PR nightmare involved—guess who—Durocher.

"We were in Los Angeles to play the Dodgers, and it was time for Leo to tape his pregame radio show with Lou Boudreau on WGN. Well, Leo and Lou weren't too fond of each other, but the show was part of Leo's contract and he was getting paid good money, so he had to do it. But he hated it and always tried to embarrass Boudreau. He was always swearing on the show, which was usually taped, so they'd have to do it again.

"So now they're down on the field at Dodger Stadium, and they've already taped the show once, but something had gone wrong technically and Lou rushes back onto the field to get Leo. They would have to do the show 'live.' Well, he finds Durocher in front of the dugout talking with Milton Berle, the comedian, and explains the situation. Leo, though, thinks Lou is putting him on—at least that's what he said later—so when the interview begins, Durocher hands the microphone to Berle, who asks, 'Leo, you've got your club in the first division: can they stay there?', and Leo responds, 'Fuck the first division!'

"Boudreau jerks the mike away, there is a long, pregnant pause on WGN, and finally Lou says, 'And that was . . . Durocher in the dugout.' "

Shriver also had to deal with Leo's "no comment" penchant during the 1969 pennant race.

"He thought the press was after his scalp even then. He

didn't like Ernie Banks because he was so popular, and he didn't like Don Kessinger because he was too nice. He didn't think either one of them had enough killer instinct. He didn't like Jimmy Enright either. I remember the time he gave Enright the names of some players to be involved in a trade, then took Ray Sons of the *Daily News* aside and gave him a different set of names. Well, he had deliberately given Enright wrong names, and Jimmy printed them in the *Chicago Today*. That's when their war began."

That's the way Leo played the game. And he had tried to instill into the Cubs that same us-against-the-world attitude as they headed into their final series of July, one against the Giants at Wrigley Field.

The Cubs won the opener with Rich Nye getting the victory, then lost game two with Ted Abernathy taking the loss in rookie Jim Colborn's second (and final) start of the season. They also lost game three, as Holtzman departed for military duty, and Nye took the loss. Finally, they completed the four-game series, and the month, by hammering the Giants 12–2.

Elsewhere, the Bears were wondering what to do with their number-one draft choice, Mike Hull; Sox fans were still savoring a 10-year reunion of the 1959 pennant winners (Al Lopez, Luis Aparicio, Jim Rivera, et al.); and in Hempstead, New York, training camp of the New York Jets, quarterback Joe Namath had reported for duty, having decided that maybe he wouldn't retire from football after all.

And the Cubs, having struggled through July with a record of 15–14, still led the Mets by six games.

At least one newspaper had begun to publish the magic number, which, heading into the month of August, was 59.

DONALD WAYNE YOUNG
B. Oct. 18, 1945, Houston, Tex.

YEAR	TEAM		G	AB	H	2B	3B	HR	HR%	R	RBI	BB	SO	SB	BA	SA
1965	CHI	N	11	35	2	0	0	1	2.9	1	2	0	11	0	.057	.143
1969			101	272	65	12	3	6	2.2	36	27	38	74	1	.239	.371
2 yrs.			112	307	67	12	3	7	2.3	37	29	38	85	1	.218	.345

6
Don Young

"Don Young? Nobody knows."
—Jim Colborn

He has cleaned golf clubs and fixed model airplane motors and worked as a janitor, and nobody can find him.

At least I can't. God and Pacific Bell know I've tried.

Donald Wayne Young, age 43, social security number 523-56-7717, born October 18, 1945, in Houston, Texas, raised in Aurora, Colorado, 6'2", 185 pounds, brown hair, glasses, lacking in self-esteem, has been known to wear disguises.

Last known addresses: Scottsdale, Arizona, and Pagosa Springs, Colorado.

The trail is cold, but he's out there somewhere.

Much has happened to Don Young following that fateful afternoon in Shea Stadium, July 8, 1969—that bright but hazy day when Young misplayed two fly balls and the Mets beat the Cubs 4–3, and Ron Santo's resulting criticism was blown out of proportion.

Young completed the season a forgotten man, batting only 69 times in August and September yet finishing with a respectable-for-his-role average of .239 with 6 home runs and 27 RBI. Young had been hired to catch fly balls and hit eighth. He was the team's second-best defensive outfielder (.975), handling 191 putouts, 4 assists, and 5 errors.

But in 1970, on a rainy April morning in Tulsa, Oklahoma, as the Cubs were boarding a bus headed north from spring training, pitching coach Joe Becker called Young aside and told him he had been sold outright to Tacoma. Young had hit .357 in spring training.

"I never saw Leo Durocher," said Young, a few months later, after he was back in the minors. "He never said a word to me about being cut. By then, too, most of the players were on the bus, so I just went back into the clubhouse, packed my bags, and headed for the airport. At one time I was ready to say some things about the way I was treated, but I've thought about it and I don't want to be a complainer. I got a letter from Chicago just the other day, in fact, from a man who said he was an alcoholic. He said the thing he admired about me was that I didn't complain when they sent me down."

After his 1969 season Young never played again in the major leagues. He had, however, played before 1969, and how he landed with the Cubs is an extraordinary story.

His first major league game, at age 19, was September 9, 1965, the day Sandy Koufax of the Dodgers threw a perfect game against the Cubs. Young played only 11 games for those '65 Cubs, hit .057, and spent the next three seasons back in the minors. By 1968 he had reached bottom, playing outfield in Lodi (Class A) under manager Jim Marshall and hitting .242.

Young seemed almost finished. Then the strange circumstances began. Former Lodi teammate and friend Jim Armstrong explains.

"Don was dating a girl in Denver during the off-season, but she was also dating some guy with hoodlum connections. One night this guy stuck a gun in Don's face and told him to leave the girl alone. So he headed off for Los Angeles. From there he wrote a letter to John Holland, asking if he could come into spring training early as a nonroster player."

Holland said OK. After all, a strike was being threatened, and the Cubs needed bodies in Arizona. Then Durocher became disenchanted with youngsters Jim Dunegan and Oscar Gamble in the outfield, and when veteran Adolfo Phillips fractured his hand, Leo turned to Young as his starting centerfielder.

At age 23, Young had gone from Lodi to a team of All-Stars in one season, and even though he carried his load and made some spectacular catches in center field, Young was an uneasy rookie.

"He told me about the time Leo called for him to pinch hit," says Armstrong, "and Don was so nervous that when he reached for the bat, Leo looked down and saw goose pimples on his arm, and Leo just said, 'Aw, forget it.' "

After Durocher forgot Young in 1970 (Leo was infatuated with outfielder Boots Day, who never did much), Don played one full season and part of another in the minor leagues. Then, in midsummer 1971, while playing for Oakland's Triple A team in Des Moines, Iowa, Young laid down his glove and quit baseball.

"He walked away from a $2,000-a-month salary to clean golf clubs at Camelback Country Club in Scottsdale, Arizona, for $2 an hour," says Armstrong. "Don walked to the beat of a different drummer.

"One day the following spring, Don was busy loading golf clubs on the backs of carts, and here came Ernie Banks and some other players. Don tried to hide because he was embarrassed, but Ernie saw him. Don put the clubs on their cart."

Armstrong and Young kept in touch during those early years away from baseball but one night got into a knockdown fight in a Phoenix restaurant ("tables and chairs went flying, the damage was $400, and that was our parting of the ways").

Armstrong says he last heard that Young was working as a janitor at a college in Scottsdale.

Young did show up for Randy Hundley's first adult camp the winter of 1983, but it was not a comfortable experience.

"We were all in the clubhouse getting dressed, and Don was just standing outside," recalls Billy Williams. "Some of us had to go outside and talk him into coming inside."

"He thought he felt animosity from some of the other players," says ex-roommate Rich Nye.

"All the publicity from the Santo thing just shoved him right into his shell," comments Bill Hands.

"I could never find him again after that first year," says Hundley.

Nye tried. In 1984 he searched for Young when he returned to Arizona but only reached him at work by telephone.

"He was working as a machinist, fixing model airplane motors, and living in a trailer," says Nye. "He told me he was making about $400 a month, so I figured he didn't have enough money for a phone of his own. I tried to talk him into joining us at Randy's camp, but he wouldn't do it."

"Don became sort of a hermit," says Armstrong. "He wasn't mad at Santo or the Cubs. It was more like he hated himself for what had happened. He became hot-tempered, almost self-destructive."

Nye, who has always been a defender of Young, recalls what happened after that Incident in Shea Stadium in 1969:

"When I got back to the hotel, Don already had his bags packed. He was going home. After a couple of drinks, I finally talked him out of it. People said he had left the clubhouse before any of that criticism from Leo or Santo, but that wasn't true. He heard it from the shower. That's why he got dressed so fast and left.

"People should understand this about Don. He has always been a loner. When he lived in an apartment in Chicago, over near Lake Shore Drive and Irving Park, he would go out at night alone wearing dark glasses and a wig. He would go down to Division Street wearing that wig and sit in the corner of a bar so nobody would recognize him. I remember once he brought the wig on the road—one of those long-haired things—and I shook up the hotel lobby by wearing it to breakfast.

"So what if he screwed up one game for the Cubs? So what? So who cares? How many games did other guys blow that season?"

Yet it would be almost five years after he had quit baseball and was tending bar at Dirty Dingus McGee's, a saloon in Mesa, Arizona, that Young would say anything to absolve Santo. It was spring 1974, and a Chicago writer had run across Young by accident.

"It wasn't Santo's fault," said Young. "It never was. I should have spoken out and said that years ago."

Did Young, at that time, feel haunted by that eventful 1969 afternoon in New York?

"I remember it," he said, "but it doesn't haunt me. I didn't miss those balls because I was pouting over striking out, as some people [such as Santo] said. In fact, I can remember running toward the outfield in the ninth inning, clapping my hands and saying, 'Let's go.'

"But do me a favor, will you? Make my life complete. Explain that the incident didn't end my career . . . explain that if it hadn't been for Santo taking a liking to me in the spring of 1969 that I probably wouldn't have stuck with the club in the first place. He was always the first to speak up for me."

Why then had Young remained silent during that 1969 pennant race while Santo took the backlash?

"I thought it best to just keep quiet," he said. "I was wrong. I was listening to my friends rap Santo, and I was feeling sorry for myself. It's always easier, I guess, to rationalize and listen to people tell you something wasn't your fault.

"But I wasn't being a major league ballplayer in 1969. I couldn't throw a lick because I'd injured my arm, and I never was much better than a .235 hitter. And in that big

Mets game, I dropped two fly balls, and Ron Santo took the blame.

"Hell, that incident didn't end my career. I just wasn't good enough. Now I'm at peace. When I first quit baseball, it was really a tough decision. But I'd spent nine years playing baseball. Then six months after I quit I was saying to myself, 'How could I stay in baseball so long?'

"Now I sleep at night. No hassle. No internal disruption over whether I hit the ball or didn't hit the ball. I have no regrets about playing baseball. I made some money and I got to travel. But I'm a happier man now."

In 1988 I became obsessed with trying to find Young.

I talked to ex-Cubs Ken Rudolph, Pat Bourque, Jim Dunegan, and Jim Marshall, all who still live in the Phoenix area and knew Young. All had lost track of him.

I called Joe Gilmartin, sports editor of the *Phoenix Gazette*, who said, "No problem, we'll find him for you by next Monday if he's in Arizona."

The *Phoenix Gazette* never found him.

I called Charley Briley, owner of the popular Pink Pony restaurant in Scottsdale.

"I'll find him and get back to you," said Briley, but I never heard from him again.

"I'll ask around," said Don Carson, owner of Don and Charley's rib restaurant, as did Chuck the bartender at El Chorro, and Nancy the bartender from the Caddy Shack, but I never heard from those prominent Arizonans, either.

Then I called a friend of mine from *Sports Illustrated* who had a strong connection within the attorney general's office in Arizona. "If your man is in Arizona," said my friend, "we'll find him."

They didn't find him. Nor could the Major League Baseball Players' Association, which had no address for Don Young. He didn't qualify for a pension. The Association of Professional Ballplayers of America said they hadn't corresponded with Young since 1970.

Ex-Cubs manager Jim Marshall said he thought somebody told him Young was tending bar in Hawaii. It's a rumor I wish he hadn't heard.

There are five Don Youngs listed in the Oahu directory. Three are Oriental, another said he once played infield in Little League, and the fifth asked if my Don Young was a surfer.

One Sunday evening in September, while serving as an analyst on a cable television pro football show, I got so desperate that I said into the camera, "The Phoenix Cardinals play their first home game on Monday night. If anybody headed for the game knows Don Young, will you please give me a call?" The director was not thrilled.

I continued to inquire about Young. The answer was always the same.

"Nobody knows," said Jim Colborn. "Don always had a self-image problem. He has now fulfilled his prophecy by dropping out."

The search turned northward into Colorado, where Young had been a high school baseball star. John McGrath, columnist for *The Denver Post* but also a Chicago native and lifelong Cubs fan, provided me with names of men who had coached Young as a youth.

"We've lost track of him," said Mert Letofsky, who coached Young with the American Legion Post 106 state championship team in 1961 and 1962. "Everybody here has wondered about Don, but nobody has seen him for four or five years. The last time I saw him he was bitter. I'm afraid he'll be bitter toward Leo Durocher for the rest of his life."

Herb Buchkowski, retired, coached Aurora High School to the 4-A state championship when Young pitched and played outfield. He also coached Cincinnati pitcher Danny Jackson. "Don stayed at my house about a year and a half ago," said Buchkowski. "I've got an old Christmas card here with a telephone number, but I didn't get one last year."

The number was for Slimline Manufacturing Company, Scottsdale, Arizona. Yes, said the owner, Peggy Leonard, Don Young had worked for her late husband, Jim, running a milling machine to repair model airplane motors.

But after Jim Leonard died in December 1984, Don stayed only another six to eight months, then one day left a note and the key on Peggy's desk and walked away.

"I still owed him some money," said Peggy Leonard, "but Don was like that. He was unsatisfied with life in general. He never talked much about baseball. Didn't he run into a fence or something? I liked him a lot, and he was an excellent worker, but he was always changing cars and apartments. One day he would be on a health kick taking vitamins, and the next night he'd get rip-roaring drunk. Not that he was a steady drinker, not at all. People really liked Don. I liked him. But he didn't say good-bye."

Did she know his whereabouts since leaving the key?

"Oh, no. I wouldn't have a clue. I don't even know anybody who would know. He did, for a while, live up in Pagosa Springs, Colorado. He would go back and forth between here and there. Maybe he went back again."

Pagosa Springs is a town of 3,000 located about 45 minutes northwest of Durango in the San Juan range of the Rocky Mountains near Wolf Creek Pass, elevation 7,000 feet. It is perhaps one of the most beautiful pieces of real estate in North America. Anyone living there, doing anything, is luckier than most of us.

I made a few phone calls, expecting nothing and finding nothing. By now, though, it didn't matter. The compulsion had run its course. Already I knew as much as I needed to know about Young. There was no answer he could give that would tell more than his own lifestyle had already revealed.

But, still, it would be nice to know that Don Young has either learned to live with the past, or learned to block it out.

One would like just to be able to tell him that it was only one game, so long ago.

RONALD EDWARD SANTO
B. Feb. 25, 1940, Seattle, Wash.

YEAR	TEAM		G	AB	H	2B	3B	HR	HR%	R	RBI	BB	SO	SB	BA	SA
1960	CHI	N	95	347	87	24	2	9	2.6	44	44	31	44	0	.251	.409
1961			154	578	164	32	6	23	4.0	84	83	73	77	2	.284	.479
1962			162	604	137	20	4	17	2.8	44	83	65	94	4	.227	.358
1963			162	630	187	29	6	25	4.0	79	99	42	92	6	.297	.481
1964			161	592	185	33	13	30	5.1	94	114	86	96	3	.313	.564
1965			164	608	173	30	4	33	5.4	88	101	88	109	3	.285	.510
1966			155	561	175	21	8	30	5.3	93	94	95	78	4	.312	.538
1967			161	586	176	23	4	31	5.3	107	98	96	103	1	.300	.512
1968			162	577	142	17	3	26	4.5	86	98	96	106	3	.246	.421
1969			160	575	166	18	4	29	5.0	97	123	96	97	1	.289	.485
1970			154	555	148	30	4	26	4.7	83	114	92	108	2	.267	.476
1971			154	555	148	22	1	21	3.8	77	88	79	95	4	.267	.423
1972			133	464	140	25	5	17	3.7	68	74	69	75	1	.302	.487
1973			149	536	143	29	2	20	3.7	65	77	63	97	1	.267	.440
1974	CHI	A	117	375	83	12	1	5	1.3	29	41	37	72	0	.221	.299
15 yrs.			2243	8143	2254	365	67	342	4.2	1138	1331	1108	1343	35	.277	.464

7
Ron Santo

---

*"No doctor will look me in the eye and tell me
I'm not going blind."*
—*Ron Santo*

Ron Santo was always the team hypochondriac. If somebody discovered a new African virus, Santo would blow his nose. Cancer? Santo fought the fear of cancer as often as a drunk fights a hangover. Name a terminal illness, and Santo not only knew the symptoms but recognized them in himself.

That doesn't mean he had a low pain threshold. To the contrary, it was difficult to get Santo out of the lineup. He played 2,243 games during 15 major league seasons; and during a span of 11 years, 1961 through 1971, he averaged 159 games per season at third base for the Chicago Cubs. (During 7 of those 11 years, he appeared in more than 160 games.) Billy Williams was establishing a new National

League record for endurance, but the man who batted behind him, cleanup man Santo, traced Billy's steps almost daily.

Now there is the fear of blindness, and it is real.

Santo, 49, a diabetic since age 18, was diagnosed more than seven years ago as having proliferative retinopathy—a disorder caused by the diabetes, which damages the retina, that instrument of vision in the human eye connected to the brain by the optic nerve. He undergoes laser treatments every three to six months; so far more than 4,500 laser burns in each eye. The laser treatments don't cure, but they stop the bleeding behind the retina.

He still sees well enough to carry a three-handicap at North Shore Country Club in suburban Chicago and to score consistently in the low 70s during frequent visits to the Desert Highlands Golf Course in Carefree, Arizona, where he is a member. And certainly he sees well enough to operate his business, Unipoint Corporation, which owns and operates Union 76 truck stops throughout the United States. Santo is one of three equal partners in the company, which employs more than 900 people, and he also owns four Kentucky Fried Chicken franchises in the Chicagoland area.

Santo is, obviously, a successful businessman. Unipoint facility islands on interstate highways are currently located in North Carolina, Georgia, Texas, Oklahoma, California, Arizona, and Oregon. But the golf scores and business success can't stop the degeneration of the retina. Only the laser treatments can help.

"Ten years ago, if I had been diagnosed for retinopathy I'd have been legally blind within three years and totally blind within five," says Santo matter-of-factly. "But because of laser treatments, because of the monies spent for research in recent years, I can fight it. I just don't see as far, that's all. But I don't wear glasses because they wouldn't do any good. This is all a matter of the blood vessels."

Santo is all too aware that one of baseball's great players, Jackie Robinson, was nearly blind from diabetes before his

death. Yet, because of technological breakthroughs, specifically the miracle of lasers, Santo also realizes his odds for a
normal lifestyle have increased dramatically.

"There are some side effects," he shrugs. "You sign a piece
of paper each time you go in for treatment. It's a chance you
take. I'll admit I was scared to death the first time. The
procedure is so perfected . . . but no doctor will look me in
the eye and tell me I'm not going blind."

Diabetes, a disease that has stricken more than 12 million
Americans, is the number-one cause of blindness in the
United States and the number-two cause of kidney failure.
Santo knows all of this because he's a prominent member of
the board of directors for the Juvenile Diabetes Foundation,
an organization that raises money to combat the disease.
Santo has spoken in front of House and Senate appropria-
tions committees in Washington, D.C., and personally
helps raise thousands of dollars each year via his Ron Santo
Walk and Bike-a-Thon and other charity events.

"It's amazing," says Santo, who learned he was a diabetic
back in 1958, "that no money went into diabetes research
until 1974. Now more than $200 million a year comes from
the federal government, plus what JDF raises. Finally people realized how serious this disease can be: it's our third-
largest killer."

Because of the lack of information about diabetes, Santo
kept his own affliction secret for much of his career. Team
doctors knew it, and some of his teammates learned, one by
one, in the mid-1960s. But Santo didn't admit it publicly
until Ron Santo Day at Wrigley Field, August 11, 1971.

"In those days nobody talked about it," recalls Santo. "I
wanted to prove to myself that I could stay in the major
leagues with diabetes. I didn't want anyone knowing. It was
a subconscious thing. The last thing I wanted was any
sympathy or special treatment. And believe it or not, *major
league clubs never took blood tests.* You just had your heart
and blood pressure checked. So I was always careful not to
give myself a shot of insulin in the locker room in front of
anybody. I always did it in private."

And he has done it daily for 31 years. He usually told his road-trip roommates, though—first Jimmie Schaffer, then Dick Ellsworth and Cuno Barragan, and finally Glenn Beckert. Therein lies one of the better Santo-Beckert stories, of which there are many.

"I forgot to tell Beckert," says Santo, savoring the story. "So we're in Cincinnati in June at the Netherland-Hilton Hotel, one of those older places with full-length mirrors on the inside of the bathroom door. Well, each morning after a night game, I would do my routine, go into the bathroom, come back, drink orange juice, then go back to sleep. So on this morning Beck just happens to look into the bathroom-door mirror and see me giving myself a shot. But he doesn't say a thing. Just goes back to sleep.

"Now, I go three for four in the game that night, and I'm hitting about .320. Beck went 0 for four, and he's hitting about .230. So after the game we go out for drinks and dinner, and after a while he looks across the table and says, 'OK, roomie, I don't care what it is, I want it.'

"What are you talking about?

" 'I saw you this morning. I saw that needle go into your leg. I don't know what it is, and I don't care. I want it.'

"I'm a diabetic. That was insulin.

" 'What's a diabetic? Never mind, I don't care. I want some of it anyway.' "

Pick any controversy of the 1969 baseball season, and Ron Santo was close to its vortex. The Don Young Incident. The clicking of heels. The fastball deliberately thrown into his arm by Mets pitcher Jerry Koosman, Dick Selma's costly overthrow of third base in Philly in September. Arguments, tears, and ecstasy. Santo wore it all in the open, creating an often-volatile love-hate relationship between himself and others.

And, along the way, he hit .289 with 29 home runs and 123 RBI and fielded his position brilliantly.

Perhaps no player took the loss of the 1969 pennant harder than Santo.

"It affected my life a lot," he says candidly. "For one

thing, it was the first time I was booed [during the days and weeks following the Don Young Incident]. And there was the pressure which kept building into the years that followed. We thought we had a good enough team to win the next year, then the year after, but we didn't win. It was traumatic. Losing became a habit.

"For much of that 1969 season, we knew we couldn't lose. Then things started to happen, and I'll have to admit there came a time after the losing started that we were *waiting* for something to happen.

"But we did not wear out. People say we should have been rested, but I don't see why anybody should have been out of the lineup. I'll fight that argument to my dying day. How could we wear out when we'd never been there before? Now finally we were number one, and all year we were thinking, 'Oh, God, here's my opportunity,' and we were just *up* for everything. How could anybody be tired in that kind of atmosphere? I agreed with Leo: we had to keep our best team on the field to win.

"Remember too that nobody in those days had guaranteed contracts. Who wanted to come out of the lineup under those conditions? Now, in Kessinger's case that's different. He was a slightly built person to begin with. I remember when he came up, Leo took one look and said, 'Plug up the drains, or he'll slip through and we'll lose him.' Physically, Kess just wasn't very strong, and I can understand how he might think now that he should have been rested."

Does Santo believe that his own physical condition—the highs and lows of diabetes, the constant checking of his blood sugar, the shooting of insulin into his body—affected his play and, eventually, his career longevity?

"No, but that's one reason I played so hard. I kept thinking my career could end any day. I never really wanted out of the lineup. The diabetes thing was hanging over my head all the time.

"But it didn't make me quit. What affected my longevity was the losing!"

What happened?

"The Mets won, that's what happened. That's the only way I can look at it. Every time we looked up at the scoreboard, the Mets won. What'd they win, 38 of the last 49? It was their year."

Does Santo feel guilty about the Cubs not winning that pennant?

"No, not at all. We had the best team on paper. And, looking back, maybe we should have had one more relief pitcher. But just think about what the Mets did. When you lose by eight games, as we did, that's a big swing. The Mets just came out of nowhere, and of course it always galled me the way the New York writers and some of the players rubbed it into our faces."

When the 1969 season was finished, Santo and Beckert decided to get away by taking their wives to Las Vegas. Even then they couldn't escape the Mets.

"We're at the Flamingo Hotel playing blackjack," recalls Santo, "and all of a sudden they open this big curtain in the casino, and there's this huge screen with the Mets playing Baltimore in the World Series. Believe me, nobody in that entire city was rooting for the Orioles except me and Beck. So the game starts, and Baltimore beats the Mets in the opener. Now I'm fretting to myself saying, 'Geez, those guys aren't good enough . . . that should be us in the World Series,' that kind of thing. Then I look at the TV screen, and there's Tony Kubek interviewing [Oriole] Frank Robinson, and Robby says something like, 'How did the Mets get here?' I say to myself, 'Frank, you never should have said that.' Sure enough, the Mets win the next four games. It was just their year."

Despite the rationale, Santo has not been able to shake his feelings about the Mets (as many Cubs fans have been unable to do). He was the only prominent member of the Cubs to bypass the so-called Dream Game promotion in 1984 in Arizona, the 15-years-later rematch between the '69 Cubs and '69 Mets—which was once again won by the Mets.

"I wouldn't go to *anything* that had to do with the Mets at all," says Santo. "Nothing against individual players. Just

the Mets, period. I've never forgotten how they rubbed it
in."

The Mets, of course, said the same thing about Santo
earlier in the season, when he began the heel clicking. Still,
he has no regrets about his method of victory celebration.

"I even did it last winter to Gene Oliver after my team
beat his team at Randy's camp. Listen, a lot of people
remember the joy they felt when I clicked my heels. The
only thing that surprised me is that I've talked to a lot of
ballplayers since who resented it. I knew opposing pitchers
didn't like it, but that didn't bother me. I just didn't know it
bothered other players."

So contagious was Santo's heel clicking in 1969 that fans
were also doing it—with varying degrees of success. One
couple sent him a picture of them both with legs in casts.
"But when the casts come off," they wrote, "we'll be clicking again." Santo had created a new way for victory-starved
fans of Chicago to celebrate. People wouldn't leave Wrigley
Field until he had given them at least one click. He even had
a double click planned for the Cubs' pennant victory.

"I remember Kessinger taking me aside and asking me to
please be careful," says Santo. "He was afraid I'd fall, twist
a knee, and blow the pennant."

But then came another kind of fall, and the clicking
stopped.

"That's when some fans got vicious," recalls Santo. "It
started going sour after the thing with Don Young."

Perhaps the thing that bothered Santo most about the
Young affair was that, of all the Cub veterans, he had spent
more time trying to build the rookie's confidence than
anyone. And Santo, realizing the ramifications of his words
in that Shea Stadium locker room, had quickly and openly
apologized to Young and the public. But it hadn't mattered.
By then, nothing mattered.

Santo lives with his second wife of almost seven years,
Vicki, in Chicago's northern surburb of Bannockburn. His
oldest son, Ronnie, 28, works with his father at Unipoint.

Jeff, 25, who graduated from Miami University of Ohio, works at the Mercantile Exchange in downtown Chicago. Santo's daughter, Linda, 18, attends Texas Christian University.

Both of his sons were good ballplayers, but, like a high percentage of other baseball-loving kids in America, not good enough to play professionally.

"They were both around the clubhouse a lot as kids," recalls Santo, "and I think because Ronnie grew up with it, all the ups and downs, he had enough of it. Both kids played in high school though, and Jeff played in college. But I definitely left them alone. I would never push them. Jeff, even in college, would ask me, 'Dad, do you think I have a chance?' And I would say, 'You're the only one who knows that, son, not me.' "

The Santo kids who once played catch on the Wrigley Field sideline are now young men making their own way. And the father, although still carrying faint scars from the summer of '69, nevertheless savors the good memories.

"I would not trade it," says Santo. "If you had to take my whole career—and everybody says, 'Oh, God, you probably don't want to talk about 1969'—I wouldn't trade it. The excitement was incredible. The Bleacher Bums, all of it. I know we lost, and that hurts. But we had so many great moments. It was incomparable to anything that has ever happened to me."

By comparison, Santo recalls the team atmosphere when he joined the Cubs for spring training as a rookie in 1960:

"The only guy to even say hello was Ernie Banks. Nobody else in the clubhouse even said boo. All a bunch of veterans, and nobody even wanted to talk to a kid.

"In high school I had been one of those holler guys, always yelling 'C'mon, babe' from the dugout, and one day I'm yelling and Dale Long is batting, and he steps out of the batter's box, turns, and yells 'Will you shut your fucking mouth?'

"Long was tough. One day at batting practice, I'm not sure when it's my turn, so I jump in and the first ball is a bad pitch, so I don't swing. Next ball is away, and I let it go too, and I hear Dale say, 'Get the hell out of here, you make me sick.'

"I went out for breakfast one morning, and I'm early so I sit at one of those big, round tables for six people at our hotel dining room. Then the guys start coming in and filling up the other tables, and nobody will sit with me. The whole place is filled, and I'm the only guy eating at this table. It was like I had a disease.

"But in those days, that's just the way it was for a rookie.

"But the closeness from the '69 team is something special. We were close when we played together. We really were. Billy and Ernie and I were together 14 years. Think about that. We had nine guys together eight or nine years. You can't find that anymore. Now, with Randy's camps, we find ourselves drawing even closer together as we get older. It's like I never left these guys. It's a wonderful thing. Sure, we have our different personalities, but these are compassionate men I played with. We love each other.

"When I left baseball I had already made up my mind that was it. I was going to stay out of the game. Then along came Hundley with his camps, and it has given me an outlet I really appreciate. It gives us a chance to get together. We really do care about each other. We compare careers. We talk about families.

"Maybe some of the guys aren't as happy as they would like to be, but who is? Some guys got into big money, some guys don't have much money. So what?"

Did the losing have anything to do with this special bond?

"I don't know. We talk about it sometimes. Everybody calls us 'the team that never won,' yet everyone seems to relate to us. I can't explain it. Maybe it's because our teams of the late 1960s and early 1970s seemed to relate so much to the fans. God, I remember trying to drive home after a game and those kids running alongside the car along Berteau Avenue. And we did have some talent."

Some talent? Banks and Williams have already been

inducted into the Hall of Fame. Jenkins became an eligible contender for Cooperstown balloting in 1989. Durocher too, with a colorful career as player, coach, and manager spanning 48 years, perhaps will one day gain enough support from the Special Veterans Committee (as his bitter enemies fade away). Holtzman, Kessinger, and Hundley will probably not reach Cooperstown, yet they all enjoyed All-Star status. Hands and Hickman also certainly had their seasons of glory.

And what of Santo? Certainly a strong Hall of Fame case can be made. There have been only four full-time third basemen installed at Cooperstown—Pie Traynor, Fred Lindstrom, Eddie Mathews, and Brooks Robinson—and, statistically, Santo compares favorably. Another third sacker, Judy Johnson, has been honored for his tenure in the Negro Leagues, and there are two part-time third basemen who have been enshrined: Harmon Killebrew, who also spent considerable time at first base; and Jackie Robinson, who played approximately 30 percent of his major league career at third base.

Santo unquestionably was the dominant National League third baseman of his era, while Brooks Robinson was equally dominant in the American League. Brooks played 22 seasons, Santo only 15. But even with that seven-year difference in tenure, Santo hit more home runs (342 to 268) and drove in almost as many runs (1,331 to 1,357) as Robinson. Also, Santo's career batting average was 10 points higher (.277 to .267). His numbers also far surpass those posted by Traynor (except for batting average, .320) and Lindstrom (except for batting average, .311).

	Yrs	Games	AB	H	HR	RBI	BA
Santo	15	2,243	8,143	2,254	342	1,331	.277
Lindstrom	13	1,438	5,611	1,747	103	779	.311
Mathews	17	2,388	8,537	2,315	512	1,453	.271
Robinson	23	2,896	10,654	2,848	268	1,357	.267
Traynor	17	1,941	7,559	2,416	58	1,273	.320

Careers of all of the Hall of Fame third basemen, however, share one ingredient: all played in the World Series—Brooks Robinson in 21 games, Mathews in 16, Traynor and Lindstrom in 11 apiece, Killebrew in 7, and Jackie Robinson in 38.

All but Judy Johnson, who had no opportunity, and Santo, who played with the Cubs.

About the significance of the World Series, Billy Williams, who reached Cooperstown in 1987, says, "Great players make big plays in big games, and it always ate on me that I didn't have that opportunity. I always wondered, 'How would I have played?' You always wonder how Ernie Banks would have performed, how Fergie would have pitched, how many spectacular plays Ronnie would have made at third base.

"Can you tell me that those great fielding plays by Brooks Robinson in the Series didn't help him reach the Hall of Fame? Don't get me wrong; he deserves it. But was he a better fielder than Ron Santo? I played left field behind Santo all those years, and I'm telling you that sucker was quick. I saw him make plays nobody else could have made. He was out there every day, hurt or not, he had marvelous instincts, and he could hit. As each year passes, Ron Santo's numbers are going to look better and better."

Santo, however, was virtually ignored by Hall of Fame voters when his name was first placed on the ballot in 1979. He drew such scant support, in fact—less than the 5 percent to remain on the ballot—that his name had to be reinstated. Since then he has received more support, yet Santo, finishing 12th in balloting, getting 75 out of 447 ballots (17%), still has not received Hall of Fame recognition. Is he being punished for lack of postseason exposure? Will he continue to be plagued by such nonstatistical memories as the collapse of the 1969 Cubs, the Don Young Incident, or the protrusion of his rear end? Santo's thoughts:

"I'm the wrong person to ask. Obviously, I don't like to compare myself to Billy Williams. I prefer instead to compare myself to Brooks Robinson and Eddie Mathews, and certainly both of them are deserving. But I do think I lack recognition because we never won. Billy, for that matter, should have been voted into Cooperstown before he was.

"I guess the only way I can explain the voting situation is this: A writer called me. I think he said he was 33 years old. Said he was doing an article on Billy Williams, so I gave him everything I knew about why Billy was deserving. Well, two days later he called me back. He said, 'Geez, I want to apologize to you. I just looked up your statistics, too.'

"I hate to say it, because maybe it'll hurt me in the future, but the whole Hall of Fame process is terribly political. And it's sad."

When Santo, barely 20, broke in with the Cubs in 1960, he was still struggling with the recent diagnosis of his diabetes. At first, in fact, he refused to take insulin, believing he could control the disease with a strict diet (no alcohol, no sweets, no carbohydrates, etc.). But during the winter following his promising rookie season, Santo started losing weight, dropping from 185 to 165 pounds in just three weeks.

"It started with bad pain in my right leg and went out of control, like a cancer," he recalls. "That's when I went to a diabetic specialist in Chicago, and he told me quite bluntly, 'You're walking out of here on insulin, or you'll lose that leg.' It was that simple."

So Santo set out to learn his own symptoms, something every diabetic eventually realizes is crucial to survival.

"I took a buddy of mine to a gym," recalls Santo. "And I took along some sugar, like the doctor told me. Sugar and orange juice. Then I said, 'OK, start the clock,' and I began running up and down the basketball court, having fun, while he watched the clock. Then I started getting tired, so I sat down to rest. He looked at me and said, 'Ron, you're as white as a sheet.' Then I began to slur my words and my vision was blurry. I was like a drunk. So I finally said, 'Give me something,' and he gave me straight sugar.

"It took me about 10 minutes to come back, but now I knew my symptoms. Now I knew when I would have to take something, whether it was a day game, night game, double-header, or whatever. I knew with my traveling schedule a strict diet would be impossible, so insulin became part of my life. I took it every morning, but with my body burning up sugar I had to learn to regulate it. I had to fluctuate according to my playing schedule . . . one day 15 units, another day 30. I learned about myself. It was too important not to. I had to to play baseball."

Santo had been a star athlete as a youth in Seattle, always one or two years ahead of his class, always in the spotlight. He did it all—basketball, baseball, quarterbacking football, and turning down college grid scholarships because baseball was always his goal. His father had abandoned Ron, his mother, and his sister, Natalie, when Ron was six, and it wasn't until he was 11 that his new stepfather, John Constantino, became a force in his life.

"I called him Dad, and I meant it," says Ron. "God, did he come along at the right time. I had been on my own, and I was one of those kids who could have gone either way. But he shaped me up. I didn't like it at first, but that's because I had been getting away with murder with my mother."

The family moved into an ethnic part of Seattle known as Garlic Gulch, and Ron turned all of his energy toward sports, particularly baseball, and became a catcher–third baseman. The Cubs, in fact, signed Santo as a catcher after he was drafted by all 16 major league teams and turned down considerably higher money offers. The Cleveland Indians offered Ron a bonus of $80,000, but, anxious to get to the majors and knowing the Cubs needed a third baseman, he signed with the Cubs for $20,000 and went into Double-A ball for $600 a month. The man who signed Santo told him he would never make it in the big leagues as a third baseman.

When 20-year-old Santo showed up for spring training in 1960, he was impatient to be recognized. Third baseman Alvin Dark had retired and the Cubs needed a new one;

Santo, promised a full shot by manager Charlie Grimm, was impressive in spring training and appeared to have won the job.

But on April 8, 1960, the Cubs sent pitcher Ron Perranoski, infielder John Goryl, minor leaguer Lee Handley, and $25,000 to the Dodgers for a third baseman named Don Zimmer. Santo went back to the minors while Zimmer went to third base at Wrigley Field.

But Santo was back in Chicago by midseason, playing third base, while Zimmer was shifted to second.

"That's when Zim sort of took me under his wing," recalls Santo, "and one night he put me under the table.

"Remember, I was just a kid and had never drunk hard liquor, only beer. So when we went into Milwaukee to play the Braves, Zimmer took me to this restaurant and started feeding me gin and tonics. Well, they tasted great to me. So we sat there for a couple of hours and I had 10 gin and tonics. Then I tried to stand and couldn't. I went right to my knees."

Indirectly it was because of Santo that Zimmer was released by the Cubs after the 1961 season. By that time the Cubs were being run by committee, the infamous College of Coaches, and young Santo was confused.

"Every two weeks I had a new boss telling me to change my stance or play third base differently," recalls Santo, "and Zimmer noticed I was having trouble. So he went on the radio with Lou Boudreau and said something like 'The Cubs are ruining their best young prospect and they should get rid of the rotating coaches.'

"Instead, they got rid of Zim."

Yet Santo is now considered the greatest third baseman in Cubs history. He did play one final season (1974) with the White Sox, but it was not a memory he savors. With Bill Melton at third base, Santo not wanting to be the designated hitter, and manager Chuck Tanner bowing to Richie Allen, Santo soon determined the situation untenable.

"The only reason I went to the Sox was because I wanted to remain in Chicago after the Cubs decided to break up our team," says Santo. "I really had no problem with Melton. We're good friends. But I didn't get along with Tanner and all of his bullshit. I saw Richie Allen getting away with murder—showing up five minutes before a game and Tanner asking him, 'Do you want to play?'—and I knew I had to get out."

Despite having a contract guaranteeing him more than $120,000 for another season, Santo let the Chisox keep their money. He retired from baseball, his business future ahead.

"Everything I've done certainly hasn't been a success," says Santo, businessman. "But I've had more success than failure. I lost money in the pizza business when I was a player. I made some money in the crude-oil business and land investment. But real success came when we [Santo and partners] sank $1.5 million [much of it borrowed on Santo's collateral] into this company in 1981."

How much business success can be traced to baseball?

"I know what you're saying, but in fact when I would make calls on steel mills and large industry, even back when I was in the crude-oil business, I would never walk into an office as Ron Santo, ex-Cub. It's amazing, especially around the country, the number of people who don't know who that is anyhow. Sometimes it comes up later down the line but never up front. That's not how I do business.

"But that doesn't mean I don't enjoy walking into a restaurant and having somebody say, 'Hey, Ron Santo.' "

For 24 years, since they started playing together at Wrigley Field in 1965, Santo has been walking into restaurants with one of his best friends, Glenn Beckert. They roomed together on the road, vacationed together with their wives, and, for a while after baseball, even worked together. Since the beginning of the friendship, they have never lived more than 20 miles apart.

"But I could never stay with Beckert's one-liners," admits Santo. "He's got them all. But because he was always joking, people didn't realize how keyed up he was as a player. You couldn't get him to stand still. He was always pacing up and down in the dugout, stepping on people. Then after the games on the road we would go out, always looking for music and a couple of beers. He loves wine too.

"If you go out with Beckert, he does the pouring. Can't keep his hands still. And those aren't the greatest hands in the world either. That's why we call him Bruno. When you go out with Beck, you just automatically figure he'll spill something before the evening is finished. When he and his wife, Mary, would come to our house for parties back during our playing days, she kept threatening to set up a chair in our garage where Glenn could sit. That way he wouldn't spill anything on the rug.

"So we're out one night with friends at a black-tie affair, five or six couples seated at a round table, and Beck is sitting with his back to the dance floor. On his right is a bottle of red wine, and sitting next to him is a woman wearing a white mink stole.

"Well, the music starts and every time Beck hears music, his hands start moving. So he turns and knocks the red wine all over our friend's mink stole. He doesn't even realize he's nailed her. He just turns to me and says, 'Hey, Dag, not bad music, huh?' Then he turns toward the lady, sees this wine all over the white mink, and says, 'What happened?'

"That's Beck. I love him."

GLENN ALFRED BECKERT
B. Oct. 12, 1940, Pittsburgh, Pa.

YEAR	TEAM		G	AB	H	2B	3B	HR	HR%	R	RBI	BB	SO	SB	BA	SA
1965	CHI	N	154	614	147	21	3	3	0.5	73	30	28	52	6	.239	.298
1966			153	656	188	23	7	1	0.2	73	59	26	36	10	.287	.348
1967			146	597	167	32	3	5	0.8	91	40	30	25	10	.280	.369
1968			155	643	189	28	4	4	0.6	98	37	31	20	8	.294	.369
1969			131	543	158	22	1	1	0.2	69	37	24	24	6	.291	.341
1970			143	591	170	15	6	3	0.5	99	36	32	22	4	.288	.349
1971			131	530	181	18	5	2	0.4	80	42	24	24	3	.342	.406
1972			120	474	128	22	2	3	0.6	51	43	23	17	2	.270	.344
1973			114	372	95	13	0	0	0.0	38	29	30	15	0	.255	.290
1974	SD	N	64	172	44	1	0	0	0.0	11	7	11	8	0	.256	.262
1975			9	16	6	1	0	0	0.0	2	0	1	0	0	.375	.438
11 yrs.			1320	5208	1473	196	31	22	0.4	685	360	260	243	49	.283	.345

8

Glenn Beckert

---

*"Emotional scars . . . we all have them. We all went
down together."*
—Glenn Beckert

He is at home in the octagonal pit, eyes and hands in
synchronization with the frenzied movement, ears in har-
mony with the babble of those about him. This is the
Chicago Board of Trade, Glenn Beckert's arena.

He came here 13 years ago, having borrowed heavily to
pay $130,000 for a "seat" that is now worth more than three
times that amount. Wearing the pale-green jacket and identification badge of the Shatkin Trading Company, Glenn
trades primarily in wheat futures (contracts sold in lots of
five thousand bushels), calling upon the discipline he
learned in baseball to survive in the jungle of commodities
and finance.

"I know it looks scary," says the 48-year-old Beckert to a

morning visitor, "and it can be. But my secret is simple: Get out of losses as quickly as possible. Don't wait for a comeback. Cut and run."

Beckert is a success, but, as he also learned in baseball, there is a price to pay for success. He can't quit smoking, and his joints occasionally swell with the pain of rheumatoid arthritis.

"Sometimes my wife has to tie my shoes," admits Beckert. "Maybe the attacks are stress related. When it happens, I just take a lot of aspirin and back off. I'll take a few days off until I start feeling myself again."

There are no guarantees on the trading floor, one of those unique marketplaces where you can sell before you buy. When Beckert first arrived in 1976, one year after retiring from a nine-year career with the Cubs (and enduring one year–plus of pain with the Padres), he sat and observed for four months. He learned the hand signals for buying and selling, quantity and price, and learned to read the price boards and tickers.

Then he began. He spent most of his first three years on the floor trading soybeans, before deciding to concentrate on wheat. Beckert usually leaves his suburban home by 6:30 A.M., has breakfast downtown, studies trading sheets, then reaches the floor before 9 A.M. And when the bell rings at 9:30 A.M. to signal the beginning of trading, organized confusion prevails, and Beckert is in the middle of it.

"All my seat really gives me is a ticket to ride the train," says Beckert, acknowledging the uncertainty of his chosen profession. "You have to be here to make a living. But I like the freedom of working when I want. I'll probably always trade."

On this day Beckert is apologetic. "Usually it's more frantic," he says, grinning. "This is a slow day. The real action is in the bonds pit."

As he watches the traders, mostly young men, elbow and push and exchange scribbled bits of paper worth staggering amounts of money, Beckert laughs and says, "I put some time in that pit, but you have to watch yourself. Once I waved my hand and it cost me $2,700 before I blinked. The action here is a bit too fast for me. I'm too old for it."

When Beckert began, smoking was allowed on the trading floor.

"Not anymore," he says, "and it's just as well. I've still got burn marks on my hand. It was pretty hectic down here during the years 1977 through 1981. I would go home limp."

From 1965 through 1973, as the starting second baseman for the Cubs, Beckert compiled a lifetime batting average of .283 and a reputation for being one of the more adroit bat handlers in baseball. Batting second behind Kessinger in the lineup, Beck was a master at the hit-and-run, seldom struck out (only 20 whiffs in 643 at-bats in 1968), and was always a team player, always scratching for more. Durocher loved him. If they ever exchanged a harsh word, nobody can remember it.

"I think maybe I reminded Leo of some player he admired from the old days," reflects Beckert. "All I know is that we always got along. The last time I saw him was an Old-Timers Game, and he looked absolutely terrible. Then I heard he started looking good again. That doesn't surprise me. Leo has a way of surviving. He always did."

Beckert, in many ways, was a "throwback" ballplayer, a blue-collar kid from the sandlots of Pittsburgh. A 1962 graduate of Allegheny College, he was originally signed as a shortstop by the Boston Red Sox and was snared by the Cubs in the first-year draft of 1962. It was a selection of guess and hope for the Cubs, who had lost their fine 22-year-old second baseman, Ken Hubbs, in a private plane crash near Provo, Utah, in February 1964.

By 1965 the second-base job belonged to the rookie, Beckert. He has been a Chicagoan ever since, building a home in 1971 in north suburban Palatine, where he and his wife of 21 years, Mary, and his daughters, Tracy and Dana, still live. Tracy, 20, works with her father at the Chicago Board of Trade. Dana is a senior in high school.

Beckert carries no emotional scars from the 1969 season,

only a few physical ones. On April 16 in St. Louis, he was broadsided at second base by baserunner Mike Shannon, knocked unconscious, and hospitalized. On May 12 at Wrigley Field against the Padres, he was hit in the face by a pitched ball, and his chin required 15 stitches. On June 6 at Wrigley Field, he broke a thumb while tagging Cincinnati's Tony Cloninger in a rundown at second base. Because of these injuries, Beckert played only 131 games yet accumulated 158 hits and a batting average of .291 nevertheless.

Beckert, however, was one of those players who figured that bumps, bruises, stitches, and scars came with the territory. He's also one who doesn't mind reminiscing about what happened in 1969.

"I enjoy talking about it," he says. "The memory has slipped on a lot of things—I guess that's a sign of getting older—but I consider myself fortunate to have played during a season of such intensity. I think what happened still bothers the big guys more than me. Kess and I were just the little guys. But I know it still bothers Ronnie and Billy, and I think Fergie is concerned now that he's eligible for the Hall of Fame. Not winning makes a big difference. But when you ask about emotional scars . . . sure, we all have them. We all went down together."

Why?

"I don't know. Tired? I don't know, we just came up short. More than anything I think we were emotionally drained. None of us were accustomed to the crowds and the intensity. An awful lot of what happened was mental. The whole thing was such a sobering experience, but we were young. It bothered me more later when I started wondering what it would have been like to play in the Series. It's something that's always in the mind of any athlete—to reach the top. And I still believe that if we had won in 1969 we would have won again and again.

"But, you know, maybe we lost the pennant, maybe we crashed and blew the big one and all that stuff, but maybe we're winning the game of life together. I don't think there has ever been a baseball team that has stayed closer together. We get together at least once a year now at Randy's camps. It's crazy too about the Chicago fans. To this day if you ask most fans about the '69 Cubs, they'll say, 'Oh, you guys were great.' Well, we weren't *real* great because for some reason we didn't win it."

Beckert's version of the post-1969 trip to Las Vegas with Santo and their wives:

"I remember sitting there playing blackjack and hearing Ronnie say, 'At least we don't have to watch that damned World Series,' and just then this giant curtain opens, and there's the game on a big screen. I wished I had a camera to record the expression on Santo's face.

"I'm trying to remember if that was the same trip to Las Vegas where I got so smoked—just a couple of extra drinks, actually—that I was standing at a crap table with a hamburger in my hand, and the burger slipped out of the bun and flopped right onto the table.

"I'll never forget it. I'm standing there with a stupid look on my face and the croupier just looks at me, real cool, and says, 'Do you want that on Pass or Don't Pass?' "

None of it came easily for Beckert. His father, Al, who died in 1980, was a florist, and Glenn and his sister, Carol, grew up in a family of German heritage, a family of work. His mother still lives in Pittsburgh.

"I must give my parents credit," says Glenn, "they gave me the opportunity to play ball. Sure, we worked all the time. Got out of school and worked. But they also let me play. I knew a lot of kids with ability from that area, and their parents just wouldn't let them play ball because they thought it was a silly game. When I finally reached the major leagues [in 1965], it was like a dream world. For years I had gone out to Forbes Field to sit in the Knot Hole Club and watch Ernie Banks play. Then all of a sudden I was beside him. For a kid who grew up loving sports, it was the American dream."

Nine years later, however, after being traded to the San Diego Padres for Jerry Morales, Glenn's dream became a nightmare of pain.

"It started with fluid on the knees and ankles. They diagnosed it as rheumatoid arthritis, and I went through all the doses of aspirin and analgesic medications and draining of the joints. Then came the 'gold shots,' a series of 21 shots. Also a lot of cortisone shots, but it wasn't helping. I couldn't run, and my left ankle was totally swollen. I knew then the end was in sight. Maybe in a way the health problems eased the pain of getting out of baseball. I just wanted to walk. I wanted to feel better.

"Don't misunderstand. I was never looking for sympathy, but I was in real pain. I really hurt. Finally I just got out. Then they started flushing out my knees, a total cleanup job on the ankles too. I guess I had four or five operations, and I was still hurting. After I was away from the game I started feeling better. That's when I asked the doctors if any of it had been stress related, and I guess maybe it was."

Beck's evaluation of himself as a ballplayer:

"I was a guy with average ability who got the most out of it. I think maybe my upbringing in Pennsylvania had a lot to do with how I played. You played as hard as you could, and if you couldn't do it, you played harder.

"I was average on defense. They kidded me a lot about my hands, but I really was a decent fielder, especially when I first came up. Near the end I had some problems, especially going to my right. I think when I tore out the tendons in my thumb (caught in the seam of Houston's Astroturf in 1971) it just wrecked my throwing. I just couldn't get the velocity, and I lost confidence. And when that happens to a ballplayer, it's tough."

Beckert never lost it with the bat. He was the best "choke-up" hitter of his time, and nobody executed the hit-and-run play better. He became so proficient, in fact, that opposing defenses began to pay him the ultimate compliment: when the runner broke for second with Beckert at the plate, they wouldn't even try to cover. Both the shortstop and second baseman would hold their positions, so certain were they that Beckert's bat would strike the ball.

How did Beckert learn to spot the hole and drill a ground ball into it as the defender was evacuating?

"At first I watched and listened. Alvin Dark was great at it. So was Dick Groat. Then I really worked on it. I'm not boasting, but I became really good too. I could take a quick glance, even as the pitch was being delivered, and tell who was breaking. Just any movement and I could go there with the bat. Of course, I didn't always succeed. Jack Hamilton hit me in the face with a three-and-two pitch once, and it was my fault. I was trying to pick up movement and didn't get out of the way."

The key with Beckert was that he seldom missed the pitch. In 5,208 official major league at-bats, he struck out only 243 times, once every 21.4 at-bats.

"I had an inside-out swing," says Beckert, "and it helped me stay on the pitch longer. Also, for some reason I could hit through the shortstop hole easier than to the right side of second base. The key was movement. When the fielder moved, even after the ball left the pitcher's hand, I adjusted. Sometimes Leo called for it, but a lot of times Kessinger and I just did it on our own.

"I wish I saw more hit-and-run in baseball today, but I don't. I keep watching on TV, but I don't see it. It's too bad because they're taking a great thing out of baseball. I think it's because everybody is down on the bat going for distance, not worried anymore about contact. Hey, when I came up I was down on the bat too. Then I moved up about an inch to an inch and a half. My goal was to stay in the major leagues, and I wasn't going to do it down on the bat. I didn't have the power.

"Consider the pitchers at that time too. I'm not trying to say ballplayers from one era are greater than those from another, but think of those pitchers: Sandy Koufax, Juan Marichal, Bob Gibson, Don Drysdale. And they were expected to go nine innings. Nowadays what do they want from a pitcher? Five innings? Six? There are different theories now. The game has changed."

Speaking of change, what about lights at Wrigley Field? Would they have saved the 1969 Cubs?

"No, I don't think so. The only problem I felt was the adjustment on the road after a long home stand. It was the jet lag and change of bodily functions, the going from day ball to night ball, eating at different times, and learning to sleep different hours."

Many of those Beckert hours over nine seasons were spent with Santo, his road roommate.

"We've been friends ever since. He's a super guy. Emotional, sure. He hates to lose, whether it be at putting on shoes or flipping pennies. But he's a caring person who just wears his feelings out in the open. You have to understand Ron Santo. Maybe the diabetes had a lot to do with it. Unfortunately I think his emotions hurt him with how the public perceived him. All you had to do was read the newspaper. People either loved Ronnie or hated him. And in some ways he invited it. He was a team captain and top gun. But the Don Young thing was blown out of proportion. So was the heel clicking. But if we'd won that pennant in 1969, it would have been the greatest thing in the world."

Unlike Santo, Beckert was never involved in controversy and was always a favorite with the fans. When one Chicago newspaper ran a contest in 1973 to find the most popular Cub, Beckert even got votes for "looking like Paul Newman."

His biggest difference with management came when owner P. K. Wrigley, frustrated in 1971 by dissension within the team, purchased a full-page newspaper advertisement backing Durocher. That didn't bother Beckert, but the postscript to the "open letter" certainly did: Wrigley had written, "We need more team players like Ernie Banks."

Beckert, the quintessential team player, was crushed, feeling that all those days of hitting behind the runner and absorbing body blocks at second base had gone unnoticed by management.

But for Beckert, as for most of his ex-teammates, memories of those "bad times" have faded, leaving only the comfortable glow of fellowship.

"I think we understand each other as to what happened," says Beckert. "It's a good feeling, the bond. We get together and laugh about things that would be meaningless to the rest of the world. Take Ernie, for instance. You know Ernie. We all know Ernie and we love him. So he calls me one day and says, 'Let's all go to Cooperstown to see Billy go into the Hall of Fame.' And I say, 'Look, Ernie, it sounds great, but I've got a brother-in-law who's very ill, so get back to me with the details so I can work it out.'

"The next time I see Ernie is on television from the Hall of Fame ceremonies. He never did call back."

Unlike Santo, Beckert participated in the Dream Game against the Mets—and loved it. He walked around introducing himself to Mets he'd never met ("Hey, they're good guys too") and particularly enjoyed the company of Koosman, the pitcher who had drilled his buddy Santo with that memorable fastball in September of 1969.

And reflecting on the Dream Game defeat, Beckert says:

"I think maybe in another 20 years we can get them. We'll play the game at Sun City."

BILLY LEO WILLIAMS
B. June 15, 1938, Whistler, Ala.

YEAR	TEAM		G	AB	H	2B	3B	HR	HR%	R	RBI	BB	SO	SB	BA	SA
1959	CHI	N	18	33	5	0	1	0	0.0	0	2	1	7	0	.152	.212
1960			12	47	13	0	2	2	4.3	4	7	5	12	0	.277	.489
1961			146	529	147	20	7	25	4.7	75	86	45	70	6	.278	.484
1962			159	618	184	22	8	22	3.6	94	91	70	72	9	.298	.466
1963			161	612	175	36	9	25	4.1	87	95	68	78	7	.286	.497
1964			162	645	201	39	2	33	5.1	100	98	59	84	10	.312	.532
1965			164	645	203	39	6	34	5.3	115	108	65	76	10	.315	.552
1966			162	648	179	23	5	29	4.5	100	91	69	61	6	.276	.461
1967			162	634	176	21	12	28	4.4	92	84	68	67	6	.278	.481
1968			163	642	185	30	8	30	4.7	91	98	48	53	4	.288	.500
1969			163	642	188	33	10	21	3.3	103	95	59	70	3	.293	.474
1970			161	636	205	34	4	42	6.6	137	129	72	65	7	.322	.586
1971			157	594	179	27	5	28	4.7	86	93	77	44	7	.301	.505
1972			150	574	191	34	6	37	6.4	95	122	62	59	3	.333	.606
1973			156	576	166	22	2	20	3.5	72	86	76	72	4	.288	.438
1974			117	404	113	22	0	16	4.0	55	68	67	44	4	.280	.453
1975	OAK	A	155	520	127	20	1	23	4.4	68	81	76	68	0	.244	.419
1976			120	351	74	12	0	11	3.1	36	41	58	44	4	.211	.339
18 yrs.			2488	9350	2711	434	88	426	4.6	1410	1475	1045	1046	90	.290	.492

9
Billy Williams

"Racial barriers in baseball? Of course they still exist."
—Billy Williams

The Chicago Cubs marketing department cannot be found without personal guidance or a map and compass. It has somehow been wedged between girders and ancient concrete deep in the left-field corner of Wrigley Field, just a dalmatian's trot across Waveland Avenue from the fire station. Admittance is gained through an unmarked green door. There may be no exit. Billy Williams wasn't sure.

His office was within, a single-windowed cubicle with a door that sticks, a framed poster of the 1969 Cubs, and a ceiling affixed with hooks—the same hooks from which once hung a 16-millimeter movie screen used by Williams to study flickering images of his inimitable batting swing.

Only a few hundred yards away, past the brick wall, old

clubhouse entrance, and white chalked line, is the green and ivy freshness of left field, where Billy Leo Williams paced.

Symbolic, perhaps.

Symbolic, perhaps, of being stuck in a corner.

Williams, 50, is black, and wanted to manage the Cubs in 1988. Instead Don Zimmer got the job when Jim Frey became director of baseball operations, and it wouldn't have mattered anyway. Williams wasn't going to get it. The Cubs and WGN hired a black radio announcer, Dave Nelson, instead.

Williams, fresh from his Hall of Fame induction and a Cooperstown speech that made the old guardsmen squirm in their folding chairs, was then given a new assignment with the Cubs: special player consultant, whatever that meant, reporting to Frey.

But Billy didn't like the travel ("I would have gotten lost out there scouting in minor league parks. I didn't grow up no fool"), and that's how he landed back in the left-field corner, a black man behind a green door.

In midsummer 1988, just a few days before that first night game that so angered Mother Nature, Billy was in charge of the Cubs speakers' bureau and seemingly happy in his work. Seemingly.

"But I will be back," said Williams, "if not on the field, in some baseball capacity."

There have been only three black managers in the history of baseball: Frank Robinson with the Indians (1975–1977), Giants (1981–1984), and now Orioles (1988–); Larry Doby with the White Sox (1978); and Maury Wills with Seattle (1980–1981). There are more than a few who are qualified and hopeful—specifically, Williams, Willie Stargell, Dusty Baker, Tony Taylor, Fergie Jenkins, Hal McRae, Joe Morgan, Bill Robinson, and Elrod Hendricks.

Williams, for example, has coached on the major league level for 10 seasons, seven with the Cubs and three in Oakland, as well as managed in the instructional league.

"He always has himself under control, and when you

have yourself under control, you can control other people,"
said Henry Aaron when once asked about Williams's capa-
bilities. "He's going to be a big-league manager. I'm sure of
that."

Billy sent out his own message in the summer of 1987,
when he gave his Hall of Fame acceptance speech, a surprising challenge to the baseball hierarchy from an even more
surprising challenger.

Billy Williams, the Quiet Man, rocking the boat?

"I like to think about that quiet image, about the time I
spent as a player, as a person observing and grasping
information," says Williams. "I guess over the years you
can't be both a talker and a listener. I listened. And on the
40th anniversary of Jackie Robinson breaking into baseball, I decided it was time to do some talking."

Williams still chuckles about the speech, which raised
the issue of racism within baseball.

"While I was waiting to speak," recalls Williams, "people would ask, 'How long is your speech?' And when I'd say
'Oh, about 10 minutes,' they'd say, 'Really? That long?' "

The speech, actually considerably longer, bored nobody.
And when Williams talked about being a minor league
player and unable to eat with the rest of his team at a lunch
counter in Corpus Christi, Texas, as late as 1959, he looked
down into the audience and saw Yankees owner George
Steinbrenner shaking his head as if in disbelief.

"And I thought to myself, 'These people at the top still
don't even know.' The only people who really know are the
peons who run around in the minor leagues, and they're
people who either can't or don't want to make noise.'

"We minorities," said Williams at Cooperstown, before a
live national (ESPN) audience, "for the past four decades
have demonstrated our talents as players. Now we deserve
the chance and consideration to demonstrate similar talents
as third-base coaches and managers on the field, as general
managers and executives in the front office, and, yes, as
owners of the teams themselves. . . . We ask for nothing less,
and we seek only what is just."

The speech was Billy's idea. Nobody got to him. No activist group influenced his thinking.

"Racial barriers do exist in baseball," says Williams, "and that's why I said those things. I knew a lot of people would be listening. I felt strongly then, and still feel strongly about which direction baseball should go. I think my speech made a few people open their eyes."

Williams was criticized for having a professional writer help prepare the speech and for choosing that particular forum to air his views. He is unfazed.

"Those were my thoughts, my feelings. I knew what I wanted to say. I'd seen too many things happen in baseball not to say them. I just had a writer help with the words. I didn't tell anybody what I was going to do, and I didn't ask anybody. I didn't want to hurt anybody either. I just wanted to tell the facts about the game.

"My four daughters loved the speech. That's because kids today don't take anything. I've always told them to be nice to people but don't take any bullshit, and they don't."

Williams had been on the Hall of Fame ballot for six years before attracting the necessary 75 percent of votes. During that time he saw several of his contemporaries enshrined—Hank Aaron, Frank Robinson, Luis Aparicio, Harmon Killebrew, Lou Brock, Juan Marichal, Brooks Robinson, and in 1986, when Williams missed by just four votes, his close friend Willie McCovey.

Now he can be driving on the highway, or standing on a golf tee, or waiting for a phone call, and he will think about it, the Hall of Fame.

"I was blessed," says Williams. "Here was this kid from Whistler, Alabama [population 1,500], in the right place at the right time. My brother, Franklin, two years older than me, was always the best athlete in our family. I wasn't recognized as a ballplayer until I was in 10th grade [one year before he met his wife-to-be, Shirley]. Then all of a sudden I'm in the big leagues, and people back home are saying, 'The Williams boy made it into the big leagues,' and everybody would say, 'You mean Franklin?' And they'd say, 'No, Billy.'

"Franklin was a great athlete. He scored 16 touchdowns one season for Mobile County Training School. Held the record until Cleon Jones broke it. A lot of us came from that area. Henry Aaron and his brother, Tommy. Me and Cleon, Tommie Agee, Amos Otis, Jimmy Mason, Frank and John Bolling, Willie McCovey, a whole bunch. We all played a lot as kids, just gathered up sides. There were a lot of good ones too, who just didn't want to leave home.

"I knew Henry [Aaron] as a kid. He was four years older than me and played with my brother, Clyde, who pitched for the Mobile Black Bears semipro team. Henry played second base and batted cross-handed. Nothing special about Henry then. He didn't stand out any more than anybody else. I first met Willie Mac when my brother, Franklin, who had signed with Pittsburgh, got as far as the Georgia State League. But he just didn't think he was movin' fast enough. Then I got him a tryout with the Cubs, but that didn't work, and he just went out to California and forgot about baseball. He's been driving a bus in Sacramento for 20 years now, but he came to Cooperstown. All of my brothers played ball. Clyde, Franklin, Adolph, and then me, the baby. I used to go watch them play."

Eventually Billy also played with those Mobile Black Bears. They toured throughout the South—Hattiesburg to Birmingham to Montgomery to Maysville.

"They'd call and say, 'We want a game,' and we'd go," recalls Billy. "Most I ever got was $5 or $6 a game, but they'd feed us too. I barnstormed with Satchel Paige through Florida one year too. He's from Mobile, and he was amazing even when I knew him. We'd go start the game, but people had come to see Satchel. Finally he'd show up about the seventh inning, maybe dress in the hotel or out of the trunk of a car, and he'd go down to the bullpen to warm up. We're out there playin' our asses off, and everybody is 'oooin' and 'ahhin' over Satch in the bullpen.

"Then ol' Satch would take out a stick of gum, throw down the wrapper, and say, 'Hey, Catch, stand behind that. Lemme go back and see how many I can throw over that.' And he was right there with every pitch. He could swing the bat too. He took a liking to me . . . always giving me $5 on the side. Then he'd say, 'C'mon, Blood, I'll show you how to swing the bat.' "

There is the popular theory, of course, that nobody showed Billy Williams how to swing the bat, that he was a "natural" with a swing so sweet that honey would drip from the end.

This offends Williams.

"Somebody once wrote that you could wind me up like a doll and just let me go . . . that the swing would always be the same. I know it was meant as a compliment, but I got kind of mad about it.

"Sure, I had some natural traits. I always had quickness as a kid. Arms and wrists. Ernie was quick, too. But I also worked hard. I became a good hitter by *staying behind the ball*, not pulling it but hitting sharply, driving the ball to all fields. There's a difference between driving a ball and miscuing it. Aaron, Stargell, Roberto Clemente, McCovey . . . we all did it. Stand back, see the pitch, then be quick. That's where the natural ability was."

At first Billy was a free swinger. He never saw a pitch he didn't think he could hit. He hardly ever walked.

"Then Rogers Hornsby taught me the strike zone," said Williams, "that you get only one good pitch to hit, to be patient, and the quick hands helped me be patient, to get that bat into the hitting area.

"Good hitters don't have bad swings. My stance and my swing were always the same. So was my bat [34½ inches, 32 ounces], and it helped me against power pitchers." Billy had 10 lifetime home runs off Bob Gibson and also hit well against Sandy Koufax.

What, then, was the "book" on pitching to Williams?

"Junk."

That's it?

"Anything to get me out front," says Williams, "fastballs up and in, then change-ups. Ray Sadecki owned me. If other guys had watched Sadecki pitch to me, I'd have never made it to Cooperstown.

"I also had technical flaws, but the key is knowing yourself. Ernie and I would watch those films taken by Barney Sterling, the team photographer. Keep the hands in a certain spot. Keep your balance. Don't overstride and swing too hard. That's how I kept in the groove longer than some other hitters. I knew myself, and I watched myself on film back when a lot of guys weren't doing it. If I remember right, Ernie and I bought Barney's camera for him."

What about all those years Williams played alongside Banks?

"He was so special. Just think of all those years when he was the only hitter in the Cub lineup, the only guy who could really hurt other clubs. Nobody around him, no pitches for him to hit. It was amazing the way he would still get his home runs. He's an amazing person too. He's absolutely the same man now as when I first came up. I honestly believe he did want to play doubleheaders every day. Somebody once said to me, 'Sure, you and Ernie want to play two because you know you're gonna get two or three hits. No wonder you guys are so jolly.' And I said, 'Maybe that attitude is why we're getting the hits.' "

Billy sits, chair tilted back, gazing at the colored framed poster of the '69 Cubs on the wall, at the sketched faces of Santo, Banks, Kessinger, Durocher, Beckert, and all the others. He knows where the conversation eventually will go. It always does.

"I think of those guys up there," he says without prompting, "and I know they lost out on some things because we never got into a World Series. We could have been recognized as one of the great teams of the half-century. That's how close we were. But we never got over the hump."

He holds up his thumb and index finger just a half-inch apart and says:

"This close. We were in position to win. We saw ourselves going into the World Series. Then we got right there [his thumb and finger almost touching] but didn't know how to get past it. We just couldn't cope, and if we had I know we would have won two or three more times. We were that good.

"And the damned Mets," he continues, still gazing at the

poster. "Koosman, Ryan, Gentry . . . they came at us at the right time. We felt the pressure, Randy and Kess lost a lot of weight, but I don't look at the grind and the sun. I look at it as the Mets winning, not the Cubs losing. They just kept coming.

"None of us had been there. Most of the time there is somebody on a club who can tell you how to feel. We had nobody. Just a bunch of guys who made it so far and couldn't get over the hurdle. I remember wondering to myself, 'How are we going to regain our momentum?' and going into the clubhouse with a bar of soap and writing on the mirrors '$17,000,' because that was the money from the World Series. I was just looking for any way to motivate the team. Meetings just weren't getting it done. Everybody was calling meetings.

"And don't let anybody tell you ballplayers don't look at the scoreboard. Every time we looked up the Mets were winning. They just didn't give us a chance to breathe. They just kept winning."

Williams hit .304 during the month of September 1969, while the rest of the Cubs hit .219, although the team's batting average for the season was .253.

Williams always hit.

He hit 20 or more home runs in 13 straight seasons.

He was an All-Star six times.

He played in 2,488 games, including a then–league record of 1,117 straight, from September 22, 1962, to September 3, 1970.

He averaged more than a hit per game, 2,711 in all.

He finished with 426 home runs, 1,475 RBI (31st on the all-time list), and a career batting average of .290.

He also finished second twice in MVP balloting in 1970 and 1972, and the fact that he didn't win it in 1972 remains a mystery.

Actually, there is no mystery. The panel of baseball writers chose Johnny Bench of Cincinnati over Williams because: (a) the Reds won their division and pennant, while the Cubs finished second in the NL East to Pittsburgh; (b)

Bench was considered for his defensive contribution; and (c) Bench had more charisma. But that didn't make it right. Williams blew away Bench in many offensive categories.

Williams indeed almost captured the rarest of baseball hitting jewels, the Triple Crown (batting average, home runs, and runs batted in), last achieved by Carl Yastrzemski of the Boston Red Sox in 1967 and still unclaimed in the National League since Joe Medwick in 1937.

In 1972, amid all the strife at Wrigley Field (which included an open revolt within the clubhouse and Durocher being fired at midseason), Williams at age 33 hit .333 with 37 home runs and 122 RBI. His batting average led the NL, but Bench, who hit 63 points lower, finished with three more home runs and three more RBI.

Bench also received 11 first-place votes from MVP voters, while Williams got only five. Bench won the total point balloting 263–211, and one panelist didn't even list Williams among his top 10 choices. Interestingly, another Chicago player, Richie Allen of the White Sox, was a landslide MVP winner that season in the American League although his team also finished second. For those who consider numbers, compare these:

	AB	R	H	2B	3B	HR	RBI	TB	PCT
Williams	574	95	191	34	6	37	122	348	.333
Bench	538	87	145	22	2	40	125	291	.270
Allen	506	90	156	28	5	37	113	305	.308

Chuck Tanner, who coddle-managed Allen on the south side of Chicago, would later remark that his star's 1972 season was the "greatest individual year" he had ever witnessed. And indeed it was something special considering Allen's supporting cast. Yet, just a few miles north via the elevated transit, Williams was surpassing Allen in every category in a league with tougher pitching.

Williams's reaction at the time, to the MVP voting:

"I think I was done an injustice by the Baseball Writers of

America . . . I was bitter about it for a while. I think the only way I could have won was to win the Triple Crown or the Cubs win the pennant."

Williams was the first Cub to earn $100,000. He got it in 1971, leaving general manager John Holland kicking and screaming in the wake of negotiations. Holland simply didn't want to open the door on a club loaded with super-stars. Others, including Jenkins and Santo, followed the unprecedented advancement into the six-figure bracket. Jenkins, in fact, one year later signed a two-year pact (1972–1973) for $125,000 a season.

That prompted Williams, at age 34, to ponder the amount and duration of his next contract. It also prompted Holland to say to Billy, "We didn't announce that Jenkins figure. You know you can't believe everything you read in the newspapers."

"No," countered the Quiet Man, who eventually got $150,000, "but I can believe Fergie."

Billy and Fergie had a close friendship, not just because they were black but because of shared interests. They hunted and fished together and counseled each other. And although there had never been any hint of racial tension within the Cubs clubhouse—Durocher was certainly color-blind—that wasn't the situation in the Cubs front office.

Charles (Chuck) Shriver, manager of information and services ("Mr. Wrigley didn't like the term public relations") for the 1969 club, looks back:

"Holland was very prejudiced. That's why he got rid of Oscar Gamble after the 1969 season, because he'd been dating white girls. He didn't like Italian players either. John was just a product of his era, born and raised in Oklahoma, and he was very prejudiced."

But Billy kept getting his money from Holland, and it's a good thing. He never made any elsewhere. While others were speaking before groups, signing autographs at auto agencies, or endorsing products, Williams was heading out the side door.

"It just wasn't me, getting close to people for business," reflects Williams. "After a three-hour game I was on my way home."

At home were Shirley and the four daughters. Billy and Shirley, who currently live in suburban Glen Ellyn, have now been married for 29 years. Their daughters are Valerie, 28, married and working for a bank in Atlanta; Nina, 26, Julia, 24, and Sandra, 20, all working for banks in the Chicago area. About the daughters Billy says simply, "They've been a joy." Family has always been important to Billy. His own father, Frank (Susie) Williams, worked the railroads and boatyards in Mobile, Alabama, unloading goods, playing baseball ("Dad was a switch hitter"), and raising four sons and a daughter, all of whom attended all-black schools. Billy's mother, Jessie Mae, did day work for white families and raised her own in the Methodist church.

"Satchel Paige gave my dad his nickname, Susie," recalls Billy, "because he always said my dad, who played first base on the Whistler Stars with Satch, was as graceful as a girl."

And if those who attended Williams's induction into the Hall of Fame in 1987 had known anything about his background, particularly about his grandfather, Louis, surely they wouldn't have been surprised by Billy's comments. Louis Williams, you see, was born with an exceptionally light skin color. He could, and did, pass for white whenever it suited him, particularly when working as a foreman at the wharf and supervising both white and black. In Williams's autobiography, *Billy* (with Irv Haag, published in 1974 by Rand McNally), he recounted this particularly incisive anecdote about his grandfather:

> One day coming back from fishing, he had me wait outside while he went into a restaurant to get us something to eat. They had the usual signs, "White" and "Colored." Of course, the best food was near the "White" sign. That's where grandpa went. When he came out with some sandwiches, he was sort of laughing to himself.
> "What's so funny, Grandpa?" I asked.
> "People, Billy, people! When I went inside, they didn't

know whether I was white or black. It's the outside of a man they care about. But, the inside is what's important. Never judge a person by the color of his skin."

Williams was serious about wanting to manage the Cubs. He didn't see why he couldn't.

"I first talked with Dallas Green about it in 1987, and he sent me to manage in the instructional league after the season," says Billy, "I did a good job, and it didn't surprise me. After all those years as a hitting coach on the major league level, managing was no different. It's all relating to people, knowing personalities, and knowing the game.

"I could see there would be changes in Chicago. I knew Russ Nixon and some others had talked with Dallas, so I thought, 'Why don't I just let him know I want to manage the Cubs?' "

Green's response was that he had several other coaches, specifically John Oates and John Vukovich, who were also qualified but that he didn't want to subject any of them, including Billy, to the "pressures" of 1988. Therefore, he was going outside the organization to seek a manager.

"That's when he offered me the Triple-A managing job," says Billy, "but I just couldn't make up my mind. I really had misgivings about going back into the minor leagues at this stage of my life. I had plenty of major league experience, and I'm not just talking about coming off the field as a player like Pete Rose did. I'm talking about coaching and instructional league managing. I'd seen it all, so why manage Triple A?

"Then I found out that Dallas was going to sit Vukovich on the bench and give him the apprenticeship, and that sort of pissed me off. I didn't quit the Cubs, but I did say I wasn't going to Triple A. I told [Cubs exec] Don Grenesko and [Tribune Company exec] John Madigan how I felt, that I wanted to stay in Chicago, and for a while there it got a little sticky."

Then came changes and compromise. Green resigned, Frey became general manager, Zimmer became manager, and Williams eventually ended up behind the green door. But he refuses to let it slam behind him.

This wasn't the first time the greatest left-handed hitter in the history of the Cubs found himself unwanted by the Cubs. It had also happened back in 1974 when the breakup of the Class of '69 was almost complete. Only Williams, Jenkins, and Kessinger remained, and it was only a matter of time for them. Heads and checkbooks had turned toward Bill Madlock, Andre Thornton, Jose Cardenal, and a 26-year-old pitcher named Steve Stone, who had just arrived from the White Sox in the trade for Ron Santo and, according to reports, hadn't thrown a low strike in three major league seasons. It would be another seven years before Stone, after posting ERAs of 4.13, 3.95, and 4.08 in Wrigley Field, would enjoy his magical Cy Young Award season in Baltimore (25–7, 3.23).

Billy Williams could be found that spring standing alone in the outfield, hands stuffed into the warmup jacket, a pensive superstar who had refused to be traded over the winter.

"I'm here," said Williams, then almost 36. "That's all I can say. If I said anything else, I'd be lying. It would just be a bunch of crap. It hurts, you know? It hurts when you've been with a club for 14 years. I wanted a two-year contract, but they were stubborn. So I signed for one. Maybe I was wrong. But I have my pride, and now I'll play the best baseball I can."

It didn't work for Billy that last year in Chicago. The manager, Whitey Lockman, kept benching him at first base in favor of Thornton. Billy was getting the insult treatment. He got only 404 at-bats (16 homers, 68 RBI, .280) that season and afterward accepted a trade to Oakland, where he performed as a designated hitter with Charlie Finley's A's for two more seasons before retirement.

"Actually, Holland wanted to trade me to Baltimore because he could make a better deal," recalls Williams, "but I had already given Mr. Finley my word. The A's were winners, and I was still hoping to get into a World Series."

It was not meant to be for Williams, however, as it had not been meant for Banks, Santo, Jenkins, Kessinger, Beckert, Hundley, Hands, or others. Williams contributed 23 home runs and 81 RBI in 1975, but the A's were beaten by the Boston Red Sox in the American League Championship Series. Billy retired after the 1976 season and coached another three seasons in Oakland.

Each year as the World Series approaches and the Cubs remain absent, Billy Williams, the son of a man named Sue, finds himself reaching again toward those comrades of the past, his teammates of 1969. Another Hundley camp is always just around the corner. Another visit with Fergie, Ernie, Ronnie, and Beck.

"We have a lot of fun together," says Billy. "There isn't two weeks goes past that Beck doesn't call. He can hardly walk from the last camp he went to. Now he's ready to go again. I wonder if he'll bring his own cigarettes this time. Most of us stay in touch; I called Kess the other day. Lasting friendships are important. I'm not saying we didn't have some arguments. Man, I remember one day walking out of the clubhouse and there was Santo and Beckert wrestling on the ground. But they were OK the next day.

"I'd like to see Leo again too. I really would. I had only good things with Leo. He sent me a telegram in Cooperstown that said, 'Whistler: You were a manager's dream to have on a ballclub.' It got rough with Leo and some of the other guys toward the end, but we only had harsh words once. Curt Flood had a sore arm out in center field for St. Louis, but instead of me going from first to third, I stopped at second. I just wasn't sure. And when I got back into the dugout Leo's yelling, 'Dammit, don't you know he can't throw?' I think I yelled something back, but that was the only time I ever had bad words with Leo. We embrace every time I see him."

Billy stops talking but keeps staring at the poster on the wall, one that will surely go with him when he departs through the green door.

"There are a lot of memories there," he says. "We just kept trying so hard, you know? I guess it helped keep us together."

WILLIAM ALFRED HANDS
B. May 6, 1940, Rutherford, N. J.

YEAR	TEAM		W	L	PCT	ERA	G	GS	CG	IP	H	BB	SO	ShO	Relief Pitching W	L	SV
1965	SF	N	0	2	.000	16.50	4	2	0	6	13	6	5	0	0	0	0
1966	CHI	N	8	13	.381	4.58	41	26	0	159	168	59	93	0	4	0	2
1967			7	8	.467	2.46	49	11	3	150	134	48	84	1	3	6	6
1968			16	10	.615	2.89	38	34	11	258.2	221	36	148	4	0	1	0
1969			20	14	.588	2.49	41	41	18	300	268	73	181	3	0	0	0
1970			18	15	.545	3.70	39	38	12	265	278	76	170	2	0	0	1
1971			12	18	.400	3.42	36	35	14	242	248	50	128	1	0	0	0
1972			11	8	.579	2.99	32	28	6	189.1	168	47	96	3	0	1	0
1973	MIN	A	7	10	.412	3.49	39	15	3	142	138	41	78	1	2	3	2
1974	2 teams		MIN A (35G 4-5)				TEX A (2G 2-0)										
1974	total		6	5	.545	4.19	37	12	1	129	141	28	78	1	2	0	3
1975	TEX	A	6	7	.462	4.02	18	18	4	109.2	118	28	67	1	0	0	0
11 yrs.			111	110	.502	3.35	374	260	72	1950.2	1895	492	1128	17	11	11	14

10
Bill Hands

"We folded. I don't want to hear all the bullshit about day games and the guys being tired. I don't buy that."
—Bill Hands

If you drive 103 miles due east from Manhattan past Shea Stadium to Exit 73 at the very end of the Long Island Expressway, then take Routes 58 and 43 to Sound Road before traveling another 23 miles past vineyards and truck farms, then slow down in time to keep from driving into the Atlantic Ocean, you might find Bill Hands.

Unless he's fishing.

Hands did it. He did what many of us have only fantasized about doing. He walked away from all the bullshit, bought the only gas station in Orient, New York (population 900), and pointed his 28-foot boat, *Froggy III*, toward Gardiners Bay. Farewell, concrete and traffic. Hello, seagulls.

"Welcome to the end of the earth," says Hands, smiling. "Three more miles and you would have run out of road."

Hands, 48, still lanky and trim, his hair gray and his face tanned, stands outside the Orient Service Center (formerly Joe's Garage), wiping one hand clean while pumping gas into somebody's Jaguar with the other. There is no pretension about Bill Hands. There wasn't when he won 20 games for the 1969 Cubs either. If he didn't like the way a hitter stood at the plate, he'd knock him down just to be doing it.

But that was baseball. Hands is a fisherman now, and he likes to spend his time on the ocean, where there aren't any telephones ringing. It's only a half-mile or so from the garage to the Orient marina, and he drives there in the Hands Fuel Company truck ("Our Fuel Makes Warm Friends"), then heads out into Gardiners Bay aboard *Froggy III*, the 28-foot Flybridge Sleeper.

Flybridge?

"Yeah, I love the word," laughs Hands, steering past fishing boats toward the calm open sea, "it's got a flying bridge on it. Sleeps four crowded, two very nicely. I use it mostly for fishing, but we take it on a 45-minute trip over to Montauk, 15 miles straight across, and I've been all the way out to Block Island with it. It's too bad it's not clear today because this is really a beautiful area. See, there's the state park over there . . . and if you went around that point, the Sound would be on the other side. Great shellfish out there . . . soft clams, hard clams, scallops, blue-claw crab, and for eating fish you've got fluke and bluefish, striped bass, porgies, butterfish, blackfish, you name it."

Hands's deal: he operates the fuel oil company, does the books for the 59-year-old service station and garage that is operated by his son and son-in-law, and pumps gas for them when help is needed or the urge strikes. He also fishes.

"I like to take the boat out maybe three times a week," said Hands, but his son, William III, overhearing, grins and suggests that *Froggy III* is a more frequent voyager on Gardiners Bay.

"I really do enjoy it," says Hands, "but not just the

fishing. I just like being out on the water. I'll confess: I wouldn't mind becoming a charter boat captain one of these days. Years ago, you know, it was pretty easy to take the captain's license exam and pass it. I'm not so sure now, with all of the regulations. I'm not talking about running a boat. Anybody can run a boat, and a lot of people shouldn't be. I'm talking about really knowing what's going on out here."

Was it as simple as taking off a ball cap and putting on a captain's hat?

"Not really," says Hands, cutting the engines about a mile and a half offshore and allowing *Froggy III* to drift. "I was living and working in Jersey, where I grew up. I'd worked for this oil company every year during the off-season, and it worked out well because winter was always the busiest time. I started as a truck driver, then a salesman, then moved into the office and basically became general manager of the company. Finally two other fellows and I bought this oil terminal, where I worked in the wholesale end of the business for three years.

"But I was supposed to be the guy running it. My partners had other businesses. I got disenchanted though, because I had too many people telling me what to do. They didn't think I was making the right decisions. I guess I just couldn't put up with the bullshit it takes to become a millionaire. At my age then, 43, I was more interested in my leisure time. I didn't care much about going to meetings for political reasons or burning the midnight oil. I'd done plenty of it just to get ahead in the business world and make money. So when the opportunity came, I was more than ready to sell my percentage of the company, come out here, take my baseball pension, and do other things."

Opportunity? Buying Joe's Garage on a finger of land sticking into the Atlantic Ocean?

"Well, that's where my son comes into the picture. My family had been coming out here for years in the summers. Actually, I had relatives living out here before the turn of the century, but only my son's children will be considered natives. Nobody else. You have to be born here. You can't just move into this kind of town and say you're a native.

"Anyhow, here's a kid, my son, who graduated summa cum laude from college as an English major, and he's got a girlfriend and they want to get married, but she's got six months to go before graduation, right? So instead of getting a job he's just hanging around, working at the garage, and going back and forth to see her. Finally he says, 'Pop, I've thought this over, and I've had job offers but none of them worth more than $14,000, and I can't afford to live in New York City on that. What I really want to do is get married and live out here and work at the garage.'

"Summa cum laude, right? So I said, 'Okay, but you'd better get a piece of the action.' That's when we made an offer and bought the whole thing. We all moved out here. Left New Jersey, bought a house on the ocean, and I started the fuel oil business from scratch. The kids run the gas station. And it's really worked out well. They're hard-work- ing kids. My daughter, Heather, and son-in-law live in that six-room apartment above the garage, and we'll soon have a grandchild. I've got another daughter, Heidi, living in New York City trying to find her way. She's 21.

"I just decided this was where I wanted to live. My wife, Sandy, loves it too. And I got tired of fishing rods, so about three years ago I finally bought the kind of boat I wanted. I'd had a couple before, but this one I keep it in the water all year around.

"We hardly ever go into the city. I'm not a city person, I don't even like people calling me a New Yorker because it makes it sound like you live in New York City. Not me. I live in the state of New York. We have to go through Manhattan, of course, to get to Jersey to visit the folks, but otherwise I stay away. I'm not a theater-goer. I fish. And I play golf at that club just back down the road."

And does Bill Hands ever think of baseball?

"Oh yeah, I watch the games on TV. I know what's going on."

Does he ever think about 1969?

"You mean like how we folded? Sure, let's talk about it."

First, remember this about Bill Hands, nicknamed Froggy because his pitching style resembled a Froggy of another era, Don Larsen. Hands was a right-handed pitcher who won only 111 games and lost 110 during a major league career that spanned 11 seasons, 1965 through 1975. But during three of those years with the Cubs (1968–1970), Hands was as effective as his boyhood hero, Sal Maglie; he posted records of 16–10, 20–14, and 18–15, starting 113 games and finishing 41.

During 1969 he was the stopper. During the month of July, for example, when the Cubs won only two of six from the Mets, Hands won them both. He won another five games in August, and when the club was absolutely staggering in September and October, winning only ten of twenty-eight, Hands won four of those.

What made him tough? His temperament. Certainly it wasn't his body. He was the least athletic-looking of any Cub, never to be mistaken for a long-distance runner or weight lifter. Hitters, however, didn't have time to worry about his muscles; they had to concern themselves with his two money pitches, his fastball and his slider, both of which looked the same until the final split seconds.

Hands can say whatever he pleases about 1969 with a clear conscience.

"First," he says, "you gotta understand that over the years certain plays are magnified . . . like the slide play at home in September at Shea Stadium, and that ball Selma almost threw out of the park a couple of days later in Philly.

"But we were already going dead. We were already playing horseshit baseball. We weren't scoring runs, and we weren't pitching that great either. Somewhere from the middle of August on, we just weren't making it. And all that time the Mets were playing unbelievable.

"So we had so much pressure on us that we folded. It's that simple. We folded. I don't want to hear all the bullshit about day games and the guys being tired. I don't buy that crap. I thought it was such an advantage to play in Chicago it wasn't even funny. Biggest home-field advantage in baseball, no question about it. Here we were, home with our families getting normal meals and a normal night's sleep, and here are these other guys down on Rush Street beatin' their brains out with three hours of sleep. And we were at a disadvantage because of the day baseball? No, thank you.

"On paper, positionwise we were better than the Mets. But even with Fergie and Holtzy and myself they still had an edge in pitching. Hey, I pitched 300 innings that year and had an ERA of 2.49. I was very proud that year. I never expected to be a 20-game winner. But the losing was just a terrible, terrible letdown for all of us. It was awful.

"Now I'm living here in New York, and I still have to listen to everybody talk about the Mets. That's OK. You have to give them credit when it's due, and in 1969 they had one great year. They were lucky as hell too, but did you ever think of this? Did you ever think that maybe we weren't really quite as good as everybody thought we were? I can't say we would have repeated. I can't say that. Even back that far, you didn't see many pennant winners repeating."

Hands was paid $31,000 to win 20 games for the Cubs in 1969. He then negotiated a two-year contract worth $50,000 in 1970 and then $56,500, the most he ever earned, in 1971.

"God knows I wasn't the most talented pitcher," he says, "but they just weren't paying big money then. There was no free agency, none of us had any agents, and multiyear contracts were just beginning."

With "mediocre" talent, then, why did Hands win?

"Oh, somewhere along the line I finally learned how to pitch. We all grew up trying to throw the ball past somebody. You live with your fastball in high school and the low minor leagues. But all of a sudden it doesn't matter how hard you throw."

And how hard *did* Hands throw?

"I don't know," he grins. "We didn't have radar guns back then either."

Hands was a New Jersey kid—born in Hackensack, he later lived in Parsippany and could recite the starting lineup and uniform numbers of the New York *baseball*

Giants before they moved to San Francisco. His father, William ("I was Bill II, my son Bill III"), was in the wholesale bakery business and also had a band, "Bill Hands and His Five Fingers," for 20 years.

"Yeah, my dad played around Jersey for a lot of years," recalls Hands. "Did a lot of weddings and even played with Sinatra. He had me playing piano and drums as a kid, but all I cared about was baseball."

It wasn't until Bill threw a no-hitter for Rutherford High School that he got any notice, however, and the scouts hadn't really come to see him that day anyway. They came to scout somebody else. Nevertheless a couple of scouts from the Cardinals and the Red Sox gave him their cards, and for the first time he began to think of baseball as a career.

"But my parents wanted me to go to college, and we didn't know to ask for a bonus," says Hands, "so we turned a lot of scouts off by telling them I was going to college. Well, I went away for a year [to Ohio Wesleyan University], but I didn't like it. I'm not the book type.

"Now I'm back home and want to play ball, but I don't have a clue. I'm working at this gas station and going to Fairleigh Dickinson, which is in my hometown, and one day this scout from San Francisco named Chick Genovese comes in for gas. True story. He says, 'Aren't you Bill Hands, and what the hell are you doing here?' Next thing you know, he's offering me an all-expense-paid trip to Florida so Carl Hubbell could see me pitch. But my dad wouldn't let me go until Easter break at college."

"So I go there over Easter, scared to death, and they were running guys in and out of training camp by the busloads. Somehow, though, I got offered a contract.

"But I'm a sharp kid from Jersey, right? So I ask, 'What about a bonus?'

"No bonus.'

"Well, what about a car?'

"No car.'

"Jesus,' I said, 'you're offering me a salary of $200? That's only $50 a week.

"Yes, but think of the opportunity you're getting.'

"So I signed the contract."

It would be another seven years before Hands, by way of Hastings, Fresno, Eugene, Springfield, and Tacoma, would find his way into Wrigley Field. He came to the Cubs in one of John Holland's greatest trades—Hands and Hundley from the Giants for pitcher Lindy McDaniel and outfielder Don Landrum on December 2, 1965.

"My initial reaction was, 'Oh my God, the Cubs. All that garbage with a different revolving coach every month.' Then I considered the opportunity. I was mired in the Giants organization anyhow, so what the hell?"

He finally got to pitch for the Cubs in 1966 (for $10,000), and he remained with them until 1972, when he was traded to Minnesota along with pitcher Joe Decker and a minor leaguer for left-handed reliever Dave LaRoche.

"They wanted to break up the Cubs," says Hands. "No doubt about it. They murdered the ballclub. I mean, Dave LaRoche? A mediocre high-fastball relief pitcher in Wrigley Field? I just couldn't understand it. Why get rid of me?"

LaRoche posted ERAs of 5.83 and 4.79 before the Cubs shuffled him back into the American League, to Cleveland. Hands, meanwhile, lost his zest, having become disgusted with having to haggle over pennies with Twins owner Calvin Griffith ("To me he was cheap and dirty"), who tried to cut his salary after the trade. Hands eventually maneuvered a trade to the Texas Rangers after the appearance of the Minneapolis newspaper headline HANDS CALLS GRIFFITH STUPID.

"But after leaving the Cubs I just never did much. I lost the enthusiasm. I had a back injury too. So after the 1975 season I told the Rangers that unless they could work out a trade to get me back home to New York I was finished. So they made a conditional trade to the Mets for George Stone, but during the off-season I was at home trying to get into shape—pitching with a high school team during the players' strike actually—and both my back and arm were killing me. So I said, 'I've had it. It's just not worth it.'

"Besides, I didn't want to pitch for the Mets anyhow."

Hands turned *Froggy III* back toward the marina, pointing toward a ferry headed toward New London, Connecticut.

"Takes them about an hour and a half," says Capt. Hands. "Helluva way to commute, huh? A lot of people don't realize what we've got out here, and I'm glad."

Does he keep track of the others from the 1969 team?

"Oh, sure. I go to Randy's camp once a year. I love it. I never thought the thing would last, but he's got repeat customers now and it's absolutely great. I mean, let's face it. We go because it's a chance to get together again. We're not fooling anybody. It's an excuse for the guys to get together. It's not going down there for $1,000 to get sore muscles and beat the hell out of some 50-year-old businessman. We just like to get together and tell our old war stories and sit around the bar at night. There's something we had that just can't be stolen from us.

"We had some guys come along later who weren't good influences on that club. Milt Pappas was a very bad influence. So was Joe Pepitone. And I used to get a little upset with Santo with all of his ego and emotions and everything, but I also give Ronnie an awful lot of credit. God, what a fierce competitor.

"Basically though, what a terrific bunch. I wanted to go back to Chicago last summer for the Equitable Old-Timers Game, but I wasn't invited. But I'll see them all in Arizona at Randy's next camp."

Froggy III's captain then fiddles with the instruments and decides to head in. "Guess I'd better check in at the station," says Hands, grinning. "Hey, I was on my own there this morning . . . had to fix a clutch plate."

AUGUST 31			
East	**W**	**L**	**GB**
Chicago	82	52	—
New York	76	54	4
Pittsburgh	70	60	10
St. Louis	71	62	10½
Philadelphia	52	78	28
Montreal	41	93	41

11
August

"What is our record in doubleheaders? It just seems like they've been our downfall all season, and for the life of me I can't understand why."
—Billy Williams

The month was August, and the Cardinals were coming.

Not into Chicago, just coming. The music and lyrics had already drifted north via the air waves and the mouth of longtime St. Louis radio announcer Harry Caray, who was singing after each Cardinal victory, "The Cardinals are coming, tra la, tra la . . . the Cardinals are coming, tra la."

Caray *was* St. Louis. No announcer in major league baseball was more closely identified with a team than Caray with the Cardinals, for whom he had been announcing and selling beer since 1945. Indeed, long before Harry was a "Bud Man and Cub Fan," he was a "Griesidieck Bros./Falstaff/Busch Bavarian Man and Cardinal Fan."

153

Later, of course, he also became a "White Sox Fan." That Caray has since been embraced so warmly by the current generation of Cubs fans is testimony to his unusual public appeal and ability to transcend the lines of fan loyalties.

In 1969, however, he was All-Redbird and warbling at the top of his regenerative lungs about the defending champions who had won 20 of 28 games in July.

Now it was August and getting hot. The Mets trailed by 6, the coming Cardinals trailed by 8½, and manager Durocher was considering the grueling dog days ahead. He had rested Banks and Hundley two days earlier.

"Randy didn't like it very much when I sat him on the bench," said Leo then. "These guys want to play so badly it's hard to say no to them, especially Hundley. But I wanted him to rest. I may do more of that, depending on how the club is going."

Santo, already with 22 homers and 90 RBI, responded, "He'll have to send me home. I couldn't stand sitting in the dugout and watching."

Kessinger, who had played every inning of all 105 games and with a .296 average led the Cubs in hitting, responded similarly: "The only real way a player can rest is to have an open date at home. You can't relax on the road, whether you're playing or not. But I can remember having only one day off at home in the last two months."

Nevertheless, with the patsy San Diego Padres coming into Wrigley Field for the first three days of August, the Cubs were breathing more easily. The last weeks of July had been difficult and so had enemy pitching. Everybody, it seemed, was saving their best for the Cubs—Don Sutton, Claude Osteen, Bill Singer, Don Drysdale, Juan Marichal, and Gaylord Perry. It had been a struggle.

The magic number, however, had been reduced to 55, and Hands, Holtzman, and Selma were poised to pitch against the Padres, whom the Cubs had already beaten six out of seven. The rotation had been set to accommodate Holtzman, on weekend military pass from Camp McCoy, Wisconsin ("I'm getting used to pitching on weekend passes," says Kenny. "I've done nothing but play catch every other day since checking in there anyhow.")

Banks was his customary self. After being appointed to the CTA board (for $15,000 annually) by Governor Richard Ogilvie, Ernie entertained writers by pulling a sign out of his locker and slapping it across his face. It read:

Want to Wake Up Each Day with a Smile?
Sleep with a Hanger in Your Mouth.

And Hundley, back in the lineup with a .274 average, was lamenting (and nobody could lament better than Hundley) his recent batting slump, blaming the recent visit to Washington, D.C., and the All-Star Game.

"I was just standing around the batting cage watching all those home-run hitters," said Hundley. "Man, they were killing the ball . . . Hank Aaron, Willie McCovey, Boog Powell. And I noticed that these guys, and a lot of other All-Stars, would 'wind up' as the pitch came. You know, they'd pull their arms back a little and really tighten up for that power swing. So I figured why not me? Why not add two or three home runs a season by just tightening up a little?

"Well, shucks, I went into the doggonedest slump by changing my swing. Now I'm taking extra hitting and just going for line drives like I oughta be."

The Cubs swept San Diego, then traveled into Houston to sweep the Astros, thus greeting the month of August with six straight wins. The Cardinals were no longer coming, and now the singing was coming from the Cubs clubhouse, where a tape player was blaring "Pennant Fever," a number recently recorded by Willie Smith and the two Olivers, Nate and Gene, accompanied by a six-piece musical group. A record company had reportedly already ordered twelve thousand platters for distribution.

The Cubs were soaring, as was *Mariner*, an unmanned spaceship that had passed across the south pole of Mars and sent back 91 photographs. The nation was mesmerized. Read one newspaper photo caption, "It's Still Hard to Believe."

Pittsburgh's number-one draft choice, Big Joe Greene (later to be known as Mean Joe Greene), said he'd rather play on the sandlots for $120 than accept the Steelers' offer; and 26-year-old Chisox left-hander Tommy John, usually a blithe spirit, was complaining that a sore elbow might shorten his career, which would actually last another two decades.

In Las Vegas, the King, Elvis Presley, gave his first live performance in more than nine years.

And, over there, another 750 troops had departed Vietnam. A total of 11,800 had now come home since President Nixon began his pullback in June. More than 500,000 remained.

Highlights of that rare Astrodome sweep: (a) Jenkins ran his record to 15–9, (b) Beckert went five for six in the opener, raising his batting average to .302, (c) Santo got the news from doctors that his little finger, struck by a pitch, wasn't broken, and (d) the entire team was taken on a VIP tour of the NASA space center.

August would not be tranquil. As the Cubs continued westward into Los Angeles, Leo made an announcement that stirred a storm: six of the Cubs—Santo, Banks, Beckert, Kessinger, Hundley, and Williams—would not be in uniform for the upcoming charity game against the White Sox on the night of August 19 in Comiskey Park. Leo's reasoning: the club was fighting for a pennant and having just returned from a road trip would need the rest.

Indeed, the Cubs were scheduled to complete the twelve-game, four-city road trip with a doubleheader in San Francisco on August 17, necessitating a late-night flight back to Chicago. Nevertheless, new Chisox general manager Leo Breen went public to say, "The White Sox would never do a thing like that. I think what Durocher is doing is bad for the fans. In the years the White Sox were fighting for a pennant, we never pulled a bunch of players out of a benefit game like this."

Then came the cruelest blow of all. The phone rang in

the *Chicago Today* sports department and the low, ominous voice said:

"The Curse of the White Sox is on them."

"What curse? On who?" sputtered a shocked reporter.

"The Curse of the White Sox," said the voice again. "The Curse is on the Cubs. Their bats will be heavy, their arms will be sore, their feet will be slow."

"Who is this?"

"Just say I'm Joe White Sox Fan," said the voice, "and I'm speaking for all White Sox fans. We're putting the Curse on the Cubs because Leo Durocher won't play his stars in the benefit game. We want the Cubs to lose anyway, because we know the Cub fans used to root for the Yankees against us.

"It's no use. Don't argue. The Cubs are doomed."

On that very day, it was revealed that Kenny Holtzman had bumped into a tree at Camp McCoy, Wisconsin, thus injuring his eye.

Coincidence or Curse?

How little we knew.

The Cubs lost two of the three in Los Angeles with Hands pitching a six-hit shutout in game two to avert a Dodger sweep. It was his eighth win in his last nine decisions. Of other significance: Don Sutton, 24, snapped a personal 13-game losing streak by beating the Cubs in game three.

Few, however, were reading about baseball in Los Angeles newspapers that weekend. The Cubs awoke to headlines screaming that the bodies of actress Sharon Tate and four others were discovered in and about her estate at 10050 Cielo Drive. It would be another four months before Charles Manson and members of his nomadic hippie cult were indicted for the bizarre murders.

Elsewhere, Minnesota Twins manager Billy Martin was trying to explain his parking-lot knockout of Dave Boswell, a pitcher on his own team; football coach Allie Sherman was fired by the New York Giants; hard-throwing Bears quarterback candidate Bobby Douglass declared he was developing a change-up; and in Atlantic City, New

Jersey, legions of young women, striking a blow for women's liberation, threw away their brassieres along the Boardwalk.

The Cubs, one-to-seven favorites to win the NL East championship (according to Jimmy the Greek) continued on to San Diego. Odds against the Mets were fifteen to one.

Chicago blanked the Padres 4-0, in the opener behind Jenkins's 16th victory, but there was a price to pay. Hundley severely bruised his right index finger sliding head-first into first base and was replaced in the eighth inning by Bill Heath. Santo raised his batting average to .304, Beckert was hitting .296, Kessinger was hitting .292, and Williams, breaking an 0-for-17 slump, still led them all at .305.

In game two the Cubs completed their season of mastery over the San Diego club with their 11th win in 12 meetings, despite being victims of a triple play when Williams lined up the middle into pitcher and ex-teammate Joe Niekro's glove. Niekro quickly doubled Kessinger off second and Beckert off first to complete the triple play. Regardless, Hands won his 15th, and the Cubs Big Three now had 44 of the team's 73 victories—Jenkins, 16; Hands, 15; and Holtzman, 13.

The Cubs' magic number was 39, and although the club lost another day of rest by flying into Tacoma for an exhibition game, the standings showed the Cubs leading the Mets by 9½ games.

But on August 15, 1969, two events began, both of which would prove to be historic.

First, more than four hundred thousand young people gathered for the Woodstock Music and Art Festival on a 600-acre farm near White Lake, New York, and one of the organizers, 24-year-old Michael Lang, said, "Today is a time to think about what is happening here—the youth culture has come out of the alleys and streets. This generation was brought together and showed it was beautiful. The peace they are screaming about is what they really want—they're living it. They value each other more than material things."

And on the same day, in San Diego the Mets defeated the Padres in the first of two back-to-back doubleheader sweeps—four victories within 48 hours—and it marked the beginning of an incredible 38-of-49 stretch for the New York club.

The Cubs, meanwhile, acquired a new pitcher from the Yankees, 36-year-old knuckleballer Ken Johnson, and demoted rookie catcher Ken Rudolph to Tacoma. Durocher, when asked by baseball writer Enright how Johnson, the team's 11th pitcher, would be used, replied in typical Durocher form, "I might play him at shortstop."

In San Francisco the Cubs split the first two games, winning 3-0 behind Holtzman but losing 3-0 when Marichal outdueled Jenkins. Then came the doubleheader, with Hands losing the opener but Selma running his record to 10-2 with a victory in the nightcap. The West Coast road swing had been a success (8-4), and as the Cubs headed home with a 7½-game lead over the Mets (8 over St. Louis), they also had a new hero in Jim Hickman, who led the team during the Western trip with 13 hits, including three doubles, four home runs, and eight RBI. Another second-liner was also trying to make his presence felt: utility infielder Paul Popovich, who had been acquired when the Cubs traded away Adolfo Phillips in mid-June, was hitting .343 with a pinch-hitting percentage of .500 (7 for 14), yet he was being used sparingly.

And what of that controversial benefit game against the White Sox on August 18? Durocher relented to media and public pressure, and the Cubs stars *did* appear, if only briefly, to the delight of an audience of 33,333 (the largest paid attendance of the year on the South Side). The Cubs won 2-0 on early home runs by Banks and Williams.

Now the Cubs were home—ah, those Friendly Confines— where they had won 40 of 57 games and would play 24 of their final 43. Even the schedule maker during this first year of divisional play had been kind.

And while Hurricane Camille, the worst storm in history, was devastating the gulf coast of the United States leaving

131 dead and 2,000 injured, there was a different kind of storm rising at Wrigley Field.

The place had become a madhouse. Thousands of fans were showing up at 8 A.M., not only to stand in line for tickets but simply to stand outside the enclosure where Cubs players parked their cars. They didn't even have to touch— just see, or shout encouragement. Chicagoans had lost all restraint. They had gone crazy over this team that surely couldn't lose now, and everywhere could be heard the song:

> Hey, Hey, Holy Mackerel,
> No doubt about it,
> the Cubs are on their way.

Cub Power T-shirts (99 cents) were hot. So were autographed drinking mugs (29 cents), pictures, posters, and autographed balls. And if you could snare one of the Cubs superstars—any Cubs player, for that matter—for a personal endorsement or appearance, you were guaranteed success.

Behind it all, believe it or not, was one man, entrepreneur Jack Childers, a 38-year-old who had once flown jets in Korea and was now soaring to success with the Cubs. Childers had fashioned himself an exclusive marketing arrangement with Cubs players, creating a "pool" fund in which all monies generated by him would be accumulated (minus Childers's 15 percent, of course) and eventually divided equally among players. These were the days, remember, when *none of the players had agents*, and Childers, ahead of his time, had filled a void.

He would later be severely criticized for this endeavor; he was, in fact, called on the carpet by Marvin Miller, czar of the Major League Baseball Players' Association. Childers, though, was and still is strongly supported by all Cubs players.

Childers, who has since expanded his Skokie company, Talent Network, Inc., to include his sons, Mike and Mark, and 12 other employees, recalls those extraordinary days:

"It all started on Opening Day when Willie Smith hit that home run. I saw the fans going nuts, and I started thinking. Then about a week later I went to another game with a friend from Jewel Tea, and we started talking about how to merchandise Cub items. Well, I had an entree with Ernie Banks because we had worked on some things. I also knew Santo and thought I could get Phil Regan and Holtzman, but what I really wanted was the entire team. So through Banks I got to Regan, who was the player representative, and I gave them my ideas.

"Regan loved it. He saw it as a 'one-for-all, all-for-one' endeavor which would help draw the players together. Instead of the superstars like Santo and Banks making all of the money and being deluged with requests they couldn't handle, this plan would include everybody and take away some of the pressure, which would surely grow.

"So Phil talked with some of the players and with Leo Durocher, and two days later I went into the clubhouse and made a presentation to the entire team. This was in early May. Well, the players gave me complete freedom. Anytime somebody wanted a Cub player for anything—speech, endorsement, whatever—they would channel the request through me. They signed forms and everything. And from then on I only dealt with Regan. He was the quarterback, I was the coach."

It was Childers who created the Cub Power bumper stickers and even hired a studio band to cut the record by Willie Smith and the two Olivers.

"I would come to Wrigley Field every day to talk with Regan," recalls Childers, "and I would leave after the first inning, go back to my office, and place calls to all those people seeking something from the Cubs. A vast majority of the deals didn't work out. Some, like the guy who wanted to make Cub masks, did prove profitable. The main thing was that I was keeping all those people away from the players and making money for them too."

How much money?

"We cut two checks during the 1969 season," says

Childers. "Eventually we had more than $150,000 in the pool; all of the regulars made about $4,000 each, while some of the younger players made less. But remember, some of those guys were only making a salary of $12,000. It meant a lot of money to them."

Regan, who had taken over the player rep duties from Hundley ("Leo thought it was taking too much of his time"), recalls how the Childers plan worked:

"It actually kept pressure off the players. Later I read criticism of the Cubs for all their outside activities, but they really weren't doing anything. It was all being done by Childers."

Everyone connected with the club didn't agree. Joey Amalfitano, then a coach, says: "It's hindsight now, but I felt the same way then, that the team was starting to lose sight of things. Instead of looking down the road, we were looking at the end of our noses."

By midsummer Childers was more recognizable in the clubhouse than some of the 41 players Durocher kept unloading from his personal truck. When International Harvester came out with the Cubs tractor, Childers made a deal: farmers Hickman and Regan would do TV commercials and each receive new tractors in return. When Walgreen's needed more autographed baseballs, Childers hired a Brinks armored truck to back up outside the clubhouse where clubhouse man Yosh Kawano and players loaded the balls into the truck while cameras whirred.

"I had free run of the place," says Childers. "I didn't need a pass. I was in and out of the clubhouse without challenge. All of the ushers knew me. I was like the owner."

Not all of Childers's deals were complete successes. He negotiated a $14,000 book contract for Banks, for example, which had to be aborted when the chosen author, Brent Musburger, a former newspaperman then with WBBM radio, begged off the deal because he had an opportunity to replace Paul Hornung on Channel 2 and wanted to devote all of his energies toward a potential TV career. After the season Banks did do a book, with baseball writer Enright, but Childers was not involved.

From it all, however, Childers firmly established himself within the Chicago business community as someone who could represent athletes successfully. He expanded into the area of representing and negotiating for individual athletes in other sports.

And on the final day of the 1969 season at Wrigley Field, Childers was summoned into the clubhouse by the players and presented with home plate, which had been pulled from the earth after the final out, cleaned, and autographed by each player. It was their way of saying thanks for those "pool" paychecks.

He also had another interesting experience on that day. "I was called into Leo Durocher's office," recalls Childers, "and, of course, Leo had been included in the pool. So now he puts his arm around me, signs home plate, and thanks me for everything. I go home with a pat on my back, and he's got an extra $4,000 in his pocket.

"The next day I pick up the *Tribune* and read where Leo has criticized his players for 'outside activities' and specifically criticized me. Next thing I know I'm being called by Marvin Miller [Executive Director of the Major League Players' Association]. So I go into New York and he asks me, 'Are you the reason the Cubs lost the pennant?' I suggested he talk with some of the players, which he did, and that was the end of the investigation. Needless to say, we didn't have a pool the following year. But I've still got home plate with Durocher's autograph on it."

The afternoon of August 19 was euphoric. It would be one of the last such days at Wrigley Field that summer.

The scene through the eyes of Childers:

"I had gone to the ballpark, like any other day, but I was back at my office working by the third inning. Now it's the eighth inning, and I get a phone call from Regan, who says, 'You'd better get over here, quick . . . Holtzman is pitching a no-hitter.' So I jump into my car and race back toward Wrigley Field, listening to the game on the radio. It's about a 15-minute ride from Skokie, and by the time I get there the game is over and the clubhouse is bedlam. So while Kenny is on one side of the room being interviewed by reporters, I get on the only phone in the old clubhouse and I'm calling the Pontiac dealers association, trying to put together a deal for Kenny. Well, they go for it right away. They agree to use Holtzman in a commercial in exchange for a new car. So I say to the guy, 'Hold it,' and I put my hand over the phone and yell to Regan across the clubhouse, 'I just got him a new car!' And Regan yells back, 'For free?' And I nod my head, all the time with this guy on hold, and I'm tying up the only phone in the clubhouse."

Holtzman needed just 112 pitches to blank the Atlanta Braves 3–0 in that first no-hitter by a Cubs pitcher since Don Cardwell faced the Cardinals on May 15, 1960. It was a no-hitter without strikeouts, with Henry Aaron grounding out to Beckert to end the game. Earlier, in the seventh, Aaron had driven leftfielder Williams deep to the vines to catch his drive into the wind.

"Without the wind," said Holtzman then, "that ball would have landed in Evanston. But don't forget one thing. The no-hitter is secondary to the victory." Nevertheless, the Cubs management donated an extra $1,000 to the players' pool in the name of Holtzman.

Cub Power was running rampant. Then the Cubs lost three straight and seven of the next nine, all at home, to the Braves, the Astros, and the Reds. It was as if somebody, somewhere, had pulled the plug.

Jenkins and Hands were sent reeling by the Braves, who had a lineup featuring Aaron, Rico Carty, and Orlando Cepeda; then Selma was beaten by Larry Dierker and the Astros before Holtzman won again thanks to a pair of Hickman home runs, including a grand slam, and a pre-game clubhouse threat by Durocher to shakeup his light-hitting club.

It was at that point, for the first time, that Chicago reporters began to wonder in print if perhaps the Cubs weren't starting to wilt from the August heat, which had consistently been in the high 80s and low 90s during the home stand.

That was also the day when it became evident to convalescing catcher Hundley that the Cubs' situation was getting serious.

The situation: Randy had been sidelined for 12 days with the bruised finger he had earned sliding into base ("I almost tore it off"), but to complicate matters he had gotten an ear infection in San Francisco ("I was flat-sick on the plane coming back to Chicago"). Ten days later he was in Wesley Memorial Hospital with a temperature and an infection.

"I'm on Demerol for the pain, and they've got a wick in my ear for the infection," recalls Hundley. "They had me hospitalized for four or five days. So now it's Saturday, about 7 o'clock in the morning, and they give me another shot for the pain before I check out. My wife picks me up and I say, 'Let's drive past the ballpark so I can at least see what's going on before we go home.' Well, I walk into the clubhouse and Leo is having a meeting. As soon as I walk through the door he says, 'Randy, can you play?' Well, I've got the whole danged ballclub looking at me, so what was I supposed to say?

"I say, 'Well, my hand feels pretty good, Skip,' and before I can say anything about my ear he says, 'You're in the lineup.' Well, I think I felt fine. The pain medication was keeping my finger from hurting, so I go on bloomin' national TV, for cryin' out loud, with my bloomin' hand so taped up I can hardly put the ball in it. I had no more business playing that day than anything, but I played."

Hysteria continued on Sunday, August 25, as the Astros and Cubs concluded their series with another doubleheader. More than 41,000 jammed into Wrigley Field to see the Cubs trail 8–3 in game one only to battle back and win 10–8 on a Banks eighth-inning homer, the 19th of the season and the 493rd of his career. In my column, I described the scene:

While Banks was trotting around the bases, I watched the fans. They didn't have horns or they would have blown their heads off. No balloons either. No confetti. No tubs to thump. So they just jumped in place and screamed and screamed, fists clenched and thrust toward P. K. Wrigley's sun. Cushions, programs, and beer cups flew through the air, and those people with enough strength picked up their chairs and held them triumphantly above their heads. It was enough to bring tears, and there were probably some of those, too.

"It was the greatest team effort I've ever seen," said Santo. "Have you ever seen a team like this?"

It was also on that Sunday afternoon—a day when people paid the exorbitant price of $3 to park their cars near the ballpark and another $1.50 for a standing-room-only ticket—that the guy from Pontiac showed up with Holtzman's gleaming white convertible, his reward for pitching the no-hitter and the result of Childers's clubhouse phone call.

"I wonder how much of that car is mine," said teammate Beckert as the car was wheeled onto the playing field. "Maybe two wheels?" Then he grinned, shrugged, and added: "No, singles hitters don't get new cars."

The Cubs lost the second game of that doubleheader, but it marked the 948th consecutive game played by Billy "Ironman" Williams, who looked exhausted afterward as he said, "What is our record in doubleheaders? It just seems like they've been our downfall all season, and for the life of me I can't understand why."

Dateline: Saigon. A company of American soldiers refused to go back into action after six days of fighting. And over North Vietnamese radio the voice of "Hanoi Hannah" constantly harangued Americans: "Don't be the last GI to die in Vietnam." Another soldier, Pvt. Lyn Hess, 20, was court martialed for refusing to return to the front and received a dishonorable discharge and three years in jail. Meanwhile, the young lieutenant who couldn't get his men back into battle—Lt. Eugene Shurtz, Jr., 26, of Davenport, Iowa—was relieved of his command.

And in Washington, D.C., President Nixon announced

plans to withdraw an additional thirty-five thousand U.S. troops from South Vietnam by December 15. Said the president, "I realize it is difficult to communicate across the gulf of five years of war. But the time has come to end this war."

The Cincinnati Reds were in town for a three-game series, and Durocher was playing the role of ringmaster, perhaps to divert attention from his sputtering ballclub, which lost the first two games. In that second defeat, Leo kicked dirt onto umpire Shag Crawford and got ejected from the game.

"All I did was kick dirt on him.' " lamented Leo afterward, "and if he says I kicked him he's a goddamned liar. Then he draws back his fist like he's gonna hit me. I wish he had. Nobody is gonna challenge me in the middle of the diamond. I just said, 'Be my guest. I dare you. Go ahead. I'll spot you the first punch.' So now he's gonna send in his report that I kicked him, but he's a liar. I just called him a dummy. I only kicked two umpires in my life. Once on purpose [Jocko Conlan] and once by accident [Bill Stewart], and that time I apologized. So now Shag says I'm a liar, and I say he's a liar. It's a Mexican standoff. No way I can win. You think I'm gonna win over umpires?"

Then Leo turned entertainer and began telling stories about his experiences as a gambler. "You can't beat the horses," said Leo. "I know. I once had the ring in my nose. One race a day, that's all you can win. Maybe just one a day. I once lost $8,000 two days in a row. But I finally learned. You can't beat the horses.

"I used to play golf every morning in L.A., then go over to the Friars' club for lunch and gin. Some days I win maybe $600–$700 at gin, but some days maybe I lose $600. Now, when I lose $600 I go to the bank, write a check, and give the guy $600 cash. But when I win $600 what happens? Well, he gives me cash, and it goes into my pocket, and I spend it, but I never put the $600 back into the bank. So you figure out what happens to your bank account. That's why I quit playing gin at the Friars' Club."

Now the manager was warmed up. Nobody was asking about the Mets, who had pulled to within three games. He continued, "It was 1941, and we're winning a pennant for Brooklyn, and we're playin' in Cincinnati. I've got Whitlow Wyatt pitching against Paul Derringer, but I get kicked out of the game in the third inning. Well, in those days you could sit in a box seat near the dugout, and there I was, sitting, still running the club, when this creepy little guy comes down in the aisle and sits beside me.

" 'You gotta win,' he said. 'Sleepout Louie can win $100,000.'

" 'Get outta here, you slimy creep,' I said out of the corner of my mouth. I didn't even look at him. So he leaves, but now I start to worry a little. You don't know what those guys might do. We won 2–1 but I had two of my starting pitchers warming up in the bullpen. I wanted to make damned sure we won!

"Now a week or two later I got this phone call from Sleepout Louie. He said I should bet this horse, Anzac, who was running in Detroit.

" 'How much?' I asked, and he said, 'Just bet it, and keep betting.'

"So it's already 4 o'clock and the race is at 4:20 P.M. and we're in Pittsburgh. I call a friend in New York, and he gets down $2,000. He takes half and I take half. Charlie Dressen and a lot of the players made bets too. But we don't know anything about the race. It wasn't till later that we found out it was a boat race [fixed]. When our horse came down the stretch the other five horses just backed up to make room. Our horse won and paid something like 30 to 1, and I never won so much money on a race in my life.

"But that was Sleepout Louie for you. You know, a gambler."

The Cubs started Oscar Gamble in center field the next day but lost to the Reds, the fourth defeat in a row. The club was making mechanical errors, and Chicago pitchers had allowed 23 runs in the last three days. So frustrated was Santo after the most recent loss that he savagely pulled a package of paper cups from a locker top and somehow injured his left wrist, which had to be soaked in a bucket of ice water. And suddenly there were new clubhouse rules: no tape recorders allowed and no photographers allowed. Meanwhile, the Mets had won 12 of their last 13 and trailed by only 2. Surely if Sleepout Louie had been in town, he would have known which way to bet.

On the final day of what had become a nightmarish home stand (3-7), Fergie Jenkins beat Cincinnati as the crowd of 29,092 pushed the season's attendance to 1,502,222, breaking the club record set in 1929. "This one was like winning two," said coach Pete Reiser as the team prepared to fly to Atlanta.

But the Cubs were definitely shaky, and Chicagoans were definitely worried. One fan wrote Beckert and threatened to bring the FBI to Wrigley Field to investigate why the team was slumping. Another put through an "emergency" phone call to broadcaster Brickhouse, and when Jack came onto the line he heard the guy say, "All of the Cub players need eye examinations immediately. They're taking too many pitches." And there was another man who told Brickhouse this story:

"At 3:15 P.M. somebody on the Cubs hit a home run, and you yelled so loud on television that it woke me up. Then, because I was awake, I decided to have a cigarette. I lit a match, but there was a gas leak in the house, and everything exploded. Now I've got burns on 70 percent of my body, and it wouldn't have happened if you hadn't yelled so loud."

Opposing player Pete Rose even offered this advice as the Reds departed Chicago: "Leo Durocher is an excellent manager, but the Cubs have got to put a little faith in their gloves and bats and not so much in Durocher. He can't swing their bats for them."

Judy Garland was dead. Bobby Hull of the Black Hawks was threatening to ask for a trade unless the team met his salary demands. And the FBI, unable to do anything about the Cubs, had arrested Bobby Seale.

The Cubs and the Mets were tied in the loss column.

And P. K. Wrigley was showing his class. The Cubs owner had decided to pick up the tab for 100 Bleacher Bums to travel to Atlanta to watch the Cubs in the upcoming three-game series. Wrigley was arranging a charter flight and 30 rooms at the same hotel where his ballplayers would be staying—not necessarily a good idea but certainly a generous one. The only problem: Bums president Ron Grousl was faced with the difficult job of deciding which Bums should go, and the folks from over there in the right-field bleachers were feeling downright left out. And since this was before "Left field sucks!" and "Right field sucks!" the two factions couldn't even shout it out.

Perhaps the presence of the Bums in Atlanta helped. The Cubs swept the Braves with one Bum trying to lasso the Atlanta mascot, Chief Noc-A-Homa, another trying to burn down his teepee, and another being hospitalized after taking a 22-foot plunge off the railing of the left-field stands. One other historical note: Lynda Morstadt, intrepid woman sportswriter for the *Chicago Today*, was temporarily banned from the Fulton County Stadium press box—women sports-writers? Unthinkable!—while veteran writers struggled with their rules and prejudices. She was eventually admitted but kept under surveillance.

More importantly, the Cubs had survived August with a record of 18-11, their best one-month mark of the season, and had an overall record of 82–52.

September lay ahead, and the Mets trailed by four.

FERGUSON ARTHUR JENKINS
B. Dec. 13, 1943, Chatham, Ont., Canada

YEAR	TEAM	W	L	PCT	ERA	G	GS	CG	IP	H	BB	SO	ShO	Relief Pitching W	L	SV
1965	PHI N	2	1	.667	2.19	7	0	0	12.1	7	2	10	0	2	1	1
1966	2 teams			PHI N (1G 0-0)		CHI	N (60G 6-8)									
1966	total	6	8	.429	3.32	61	12	2	184.1	150	52	150	1	2	5	5
1967	CHI N	20	13	.606	2.80	38	38	20	289.1	230	83	236	3	0	0	0
1968		20	15	.571	2.63	40	40	20	308	255	65	260	3	0	0	0
1969		21	15	.583	3.21	43	42	23	311	284	71	273	7	0	0	1
1970		22	16	.579	3.39	40	39	24	313	265	60	274	3	0	0	0
1971		24	13	.649	2.77	39	39	30	325	304	37	263	3	0	0	0
1972		20	12	.625	3.21	36	36	23	289	253	62	184	5	0	0	0
1973		14	16	.467	3.89	38	38	7	271	267	57	170	2	0	0	0
1974	TEX A	25	12	.676	2.83	41	41	29	328	286	45	225	6	0	0	0
1975		17	18	.486	3.93	37	37	22	270	261	56	157	4	0	0	0
1976	BOS A	12	11	.522	3.27	30	29	12	209	201	43	142	2	1	0	0
1977		10	10	.500	3.68	28	28	11	193	190	36	105	1	0	0	0
1978	TEX A	18	8	.692	3.04	34	30	16	249	228	41	157	4	0	1	0
1979		16	14	.533	4.07	37	37	10	259	252	81	164	3	0	0	0
1980		12	12	.500	3.77	29	29	12	198	190	52	129	0	0	0	0
1981		5	8	.385	4.50	19	16	1	106	122	40	63	0	0	1	0
1982	CHI N	14	15	.483	3.15	34	34	4	217.1	221	68	134	1	0	0	0
1983		6	9	.400	4.30	33	29	1	167.1	176	46	96	1	0	0	0
19 yrs.		284	226	.557	3.34	664	594	267	4499.2	4142	997	3192	49	5	8	7

12

Fergie Jenkins

---

*"The biggest drug problem is with alcohol,
and it's legal."*
—*Fergie Jenkins*

On August 25, 1980, Canadian customs officials opened the
luggage of Texas Rangers pitcher Ferguson Jenkins and
found a very small amount—three grams, to be exact—of
cocaine, along with similarly small amounts of hashish
and marijuana, total street value of $500.

Jenkins admitted that the luggage belonged to him and
was eventually charged with simple possession. The charge
was dismissed five months later by His Honour Judge G. L.
Young in Provincial Court at Brampton, Ontario. Said
Judge Young in his judgment:

"It seems to me that a person who has conducted himself
in such an exemplary manner that he is held in high
account in his community, and indeed in his country, there

comes a time when he is entitled to draw on that account. This is one of those occasions. Especially, and particularly, when the potential ramification of a conviction would be so severe. I therefore find that it would not be contrary to the public interest to grant [an absolute] discharge."

Translation: Fergie beat the rap.

Bowie Kuhn, then commissioner of baseball, decreed that Jenkins should contribute $10,000 to a drug education program in Texas aimed at young people. He also ordered Jenkins to make public appearances, both in person and on educational film clips, supporting the aims of drug education programs and to "express deep regret for the mistake that led to involvement in the drug charges that were recently disposed of in Canada."

But other ramifications ran deeper.

There was the Hall of Fame thing. Would Fergie Jenkins, one of the great pitchers of the modern era, be denied admittance into Cooperstown because of three grams of cocaine?

Considering all the rotgut booze Babe Ruth consumed, it would hardly seem fair. And Jenkins's statistics certainly made for an overwhelming argument for his induction: in a career that spanned 18 seasons, he accumulated 284 victories, struck out 3,192 men, and walked only 997. He completed 267 games, threw 49 shutouts, and in seven seasons won 20 or more games. Twelve times he was beaten 1–0, five times in 1968.

George Raft and James Cagney would have loved him too. He clammed up and didn't rat on anybody else.

Let's go back to 1980, August 24, the night the Texas Rangers baseball team took a charter flight from the Dallas–Fort Worth airport to Toronto. When the plane landed Fergie couldn't find his luggage. Neither could Mickey Rivers, Frank Lucchesi, or a batboy. Four bags were missing. Fergie made his report to the airlines and caught the bus downtown to the team hotel.

"I was told later that my suitcase was left on the loading dock, and since they didn't know who it belonged to it was opened," says Fergie today. "That seemed strange to me, since it had a big Texas Rangers logo on it and my name on an identification plate."

After the luggage still hadn't been found the next morning, Jenkins went to the ballpark, worried. He knew about the drugs because he had been the "mule," the guy chosen to carry the stuff for the teammates who were planning a party in Toronto. Presumably Jenkins, because he was a Canadian citizen, was considered the safest traveler.

"I was out on the field the next day when the batboy came out to get me," recalls Jenkins. "Inside the clubhouse with [Rangers manager] Pat Corrales were two narcotics officers. I knew right away what had happened. When I went into the shower before changing into my street clothes, one of the officers almost came into the shower with me. I guess he thought I was going to try to escape through the drain."

Upon return to the hotel, Fergie discovered that his room had been ransacked. The officers then began asking whether he had a clothes carryall, which he did not. Then they took him back to the airport for more interrogation.

"I need a lawyer," said Fergie, and by then teammate Rusty Staub had called one—the eminent Edward L. Greenspan of Toronto.

"The problem I had was that they were trying to portray me as some kind of drug pusher on the club," says Jenkins. "It wasn't true. They kept wanting me to name other teammates and tell them where they were getting the drugs. They were questions I couldn't answer."

Attorney Greenspan defended Jenkins in an interesting manner: rather than emphasize Jenkins's prominence, he produced character witnesses from his hometown of Chatham, Ontario. Wrote Greenspan later in a Canadian publication, "I did not want Jenkins to be let off for being a great baseball star. I just didn't want him to be penalized for it."

Jenkins, after all, was a recipient of his country's highest civilian decoration, the Order of Canada. At his trial he was depicted as a man who had raised funds for numerous boys' charities back home in Chatham, population forty thousand, once auctioning off his boots at a charity luncheon for $150 and walking home in stocking feet.

The defense worked. First-time offender Jenkins was given an absolute discharge.

But key questions remained: Was Jenkins carrying the drugs for others as well as himself? Were there other Texas Rangers involved?

"Yes," says Jenkins.

"But I'm not going to implicate others. I respect their families who probably didn't know. What if some guy has an 18-year-old daughter in high school and she reads her father's name in the newspaper? I just won't do it."

Jenkins's stance somewhat perplexed his attorney, who said, "I would have hoped Fergie might have gone farther [in explaining his own role]. Maybe one day he will tell the whole story."

"He told me that someday I could tell everything and make a million dollars," shrugs Jenkins today. "But I won't."

Significant addendum to the Jenkins case: Commissioner Kuhn tried to suspend Jenkins ("Kuhn spoke like Alice in Wonderland," wrote Greenspan. "Sentence first, verdict later."), but the suspension was overturned by an arbitrator, marking the first time a decision by a baseball commissioner had ever been disallowed.

"It is taught at all law schools that a man has a right to remain silent," attorney Greenspan told *Sports Illustrated*. "Kuhn must have missed that lesson."

Through it all, Jenkins missed five starts with the Rangers. He finished the 1980 season at 12–12, and since 300 victories was a consuming goal, the incident cost Jenkins dearly.

He has since gone through a divorce and the loss of his 190-acre farm in Ontario. Although Fergie has been out of baseball for less time than any other member of the 1969 Cubs—barely five seasons—the transition has been bumpy.

Bottom line in his drug case: he made a costly mistake.

He was hurt in salary negotiations, lost endorsement money ("American Express backed out of a deal"), and suffered public embarrassment. In retrospect, considering the continued exposure of drug abuse without censure within professional sports, Jenkins paid a stiff price for his three grams of cocaine. It was never even suggested that he undergo drug rehabilitation.

"There are still so many drugs in sports that I hesitate to even talk about it," says Jenkins. "A lot has happened in baseball and other sports since I had my trouble. I guess the thing that surprises me is that so many players didn't pay attention. The other thing that boggles my mind is that the biggest drug problem is with alcohol, and it's legal."

Then there is the other "drug problem" in sports that Jenkins encountered and that many professional athletes continue to endure. As Jenkins wrote in his own autobiography 16 years ago (*The Fergie Jenkins Story*, Regnery) when still pitching for the Cubs, "I was taking a lot of drugs near the end of the 1972 season for the pain [of a sore arm], and I was higher than I wanted to be. After every game I felt like I was a foot off the ground."

Beyond that, did Jenkins use drugs on a recreational basis during the 10 seasons (1966-1973, 1982-83) he pitched for the Cubs?

"I smoked some marijuana."

In 1989, this 50th anniversary year of the Hall of Fame and Jenkins's first year of eligibility, he ran into a backlog, finishing 5th in balloting, getting 234 out of 447 ballots (52%). The favorites, Carl Yastrzemski and Johnny Bench were easily inducted. Other deserving cadidates included 314-game winner Gaylord Perry, Tony Oliva, Jim Kaat, Jim Bunning, and former teammate Ron Santo. By win percentage, the contending pitchers: Jenkins, 284-226 (.557); Bunning, 224-184 (.549); Kaat, 283-227 (.544); and Perry 314-265 (.542).

But anyone who ever witnessed Jenkins in Chicago would have had no problem marking the ballot. Perhaps of all his statistics the most impressive is his six consecutive 20-game-winning seasons in Wrigley Field, where he ignored the wind and concentrated on the corners. Beginning in 1967 Jenkins achieved successive records of 20–13, 20–15, 21–15, 22–16, 24–13, and 20–12, winning the NL's Cy Young Award in 1971 and being named Pitcher of the Year by *The Sporting News* in 1967, 1971, 1972 and 1974 (when he was 25–12 with the Rangers).

Impressive too were the 267 complete games.

"My mother told me, 'Once you start something, try to finish it,' " says Jenkins. "I always knew my job. I was a starting pitcher. My job was to stop losing streaks, to pitch consistently, and to pitch well."

He was Durocher's workhorse, especially in 1969 when he started 42 games, a career high, and completed 23, relieving in another.

"If a man had a slight injury or was just plain tired," Jenkins wrote in his book, "Leo didn't want to hear about it. He just rubbed a man's nose in the dirt and sent him back out there. You played until you dropped."

But there was the day in 1969 when Durocher called Jenkins a "quitter" in front of teammates during a team meeting. The situation: Jenkins watched a fly ball drop between leftfielder Williams and centerfielder Young, and he got so upset that later in the dugout he said something like, "C'mon, you guys, I'm doing my job, and I expect you to do yours." Santo then got involved and tried to cool Fergie. But it was too late. The Pirates KO'd him the next inning.

One day later Leo unleashed his fire.

"I remember it," says Fergie, "but it was because I quit challenging the Pirate hitters. I have to admit they owned me. Willie Stargell, Manny Sanguillen, Roberto Clemente, Rennie Stennett . . . those guys would send a limo for me. That's all it was. And the thing to remember about Leo: the next day the slate was clean.

"I can honestly say, looking back, that I never had a problem with Durocher. He was just like Billy Martin [Jenkins's manager in Texas]. He just gave me the ball and didn't take it away from me until I didn't pitch right. I knew that faith was there, and that's one reason I had so many complete games. I knew that if I could get past the first or second inning it was my game to win or lose.

"I gave up a lot of home runs too, but that was because I wouldn't walk people."

Jenkins also reveals that he was throwing the so-called split-fingered fastball long before it gained such prominence in the major leagues.

"I just never told anybody about it," says Jenkins. "We called it a forkball, but it was the same thing. The late Fred Martin taught the pitch to several of us. Bruce Sutter threw it, and I threw it. Maybe a few others. I used it as a change-up more than an 'out' pitch. I'd throw it about 70 miles per hour, and it was very effective. I just didn't know I was supposed to be calling it a split-fingered fastball."

Randy Hundley, Fergie's catcher during most of those salad days in Chicago, offers his analysis of Jenkins's pitching:

"We had a special kind of pitcher-catcher relationship. He was young and green at first, and he actually learned a lot more about pitching after he left the Cubs, if you can believe it. But he had outstanding ability. His body [6'5", 205 pounds] made him very deceiving to the hitters. He'd throw those big, long arms, and here comes the ball, and the hitters just couldn't pick it up. Good fastball, good slider, good curve . . . the slider was awfully good, and he could really pinpoint the fastball. I could sit there and catch him with my eyes closed. Sure he gave up home runs, but an awful lot of them are solo home runs."

Jenkins carried no excess emotional baggage from 1969.

"I did all I could do," he says. "I pitched well. Maybe I could have won some more games toward the end [he was 19–11 on September 2 and lost four of his last six decisions], but I do know we didn't score many runs and blew some games in September.

"People don't talk to me much about that season because I've spent so much time in Canada it just never comes up," he says. "Not that I don't remember or relate to the guys. This was my team. My career started here, and when you play that many years with the same men you develop strong friendships.

"I'll tell you something else about that team. We had Canadians, Latinos, Puerto Ricans, Italians, Germans, Scandinavians, whatever you wanted. We had a team of nations, different cultures and religions and backgrounds, and we never had problems with each other. I'd had trouble with racism in the minor leagues. I never said much about it, but I played in Little Rock, Arkansas, and remember I was a Canadian. I'd never seen separate facilities. I'd never seen the Ku Klux Klan or marches or people throwing eggs.

"But with the Cubs, well, I keep coming back to Leo. He was up-front, especially back there in 1969. We all lost touch with him later, I'm afraid, but he was a man who would tell you what he thought to your face. He didn't talk behind your back."

Why, in Jenkins's opinion, did the Cubs falter in 1969?

"The Mets," he says. "They had our number. Al Weis hitting a home run? We would crush other people and lose to the Mets. I think we were short a pitcher too. We needed one more good, sound stopper from the bullpen. Leo kept backing up the truck and trying different kids, but he never found what he wanted.

"The Mets had remarkable pitching. I don't think it was a miracle team, but when you look at their pitching you begin to understand what happened."

What about pitching in so many day games? Did it affect his career?

"Sunshine never bothered me. I've had hitters tell me though that they could see the ball better in the daytime. They claim the ball has a halo around it at night, sort of a fluorescence, and sometimes they see just half the ball. I felt the same either way. I enjoyed the heat. They said I'd die in the heat of Texas, but the first year down there I won 25 games, and sometimes on Sunday afternoons it was 105 degrees."

Ask him what has happened to him since that 1969 season, and Jenkins laughingly says, "I won a lot of games."

That's true. He won 115 games in the American League with the Rangers and the Red Sox from 1974 to 1982 before returning to, of all places, Wrigley Field at age 38.

"The first day I walked into the Texas Ranger camp," says Jenkins, "Billy Martin came up to me and said, 'Fergie, I've heard two things about you. One, you've got a bad arm and, two, you're a clubhouse lawyer.' Well, I just looked him in the eye and said, 'You're wrong on both counts,' and that year I won 25 games."

Jenkins didn't duplicate his 25-win season in 1975, however, and he attributes that to a hockey fight. That's right, hockey.

"I went home to Canada during the off-season, and I was playing hockey in an old-timers league. I had played hockey since I was a kid. It was my first love. Anyhow, I broke my hand in a fight. Here I was, 32 years old, and some guy speared me in front of the net and then laughed at me. Well, I hit him so hard it knocked off his helmet. Then I hit him four or five more times and broke a small bone in my pitching hand.

"I didn't tell the Rangers though, and I won only 17 games in 1975."

Then, after being traded to Boston and back again to Texas, Fergie confounded skeptics by returning to the 1982 Cubs and winning 14 games with a team that was 73–89 under manager Lee Elia. He walked to the mound again in 1983 at age 39, but finally the Wrigley Field magic was gone.

"I would have won more games for the Cubs even if we'd had any kind of bullpen," says Jenkins. "For that matter, I could have won some games for the 1984 Cubs. Unfortunately Jim Frey didn't agree with me. They released me in the spring, and that was the end of my quest for 300 victories.

"You know, it's funny about that 1984 team. That was the year they were finally going to dislodge the hatchet from the back . . . finally win a pennant for the Cubs. But it didn't work. They couldn't get the hatchet out."

Finally, for the first time since first being signed by the Phillies back in 1962, Jenkins was out of baseball. He took off the uniform and went home to Canada to grow soybeans and wheat and feed cattle on the farm he had purchased in 1974. Unable to give up the sport completely, though, he also pitched for a semipro team in London, Ontario ("I think I was 11–1"), and gave the money to a cancer charity.

As a farmer, however, Jenkins felt the same crunch that many farmers were feeling across the continent. Costs were up, prices were down, and so was Fergie's family life. Divorce from his wife, Kathy, was on the way, and his daughters, 19-year-old Kelly, 18-year-old Delores, and 12-year-old Kimberly, were caught in the middle.

Fergie struggled with his identity. He coached the Canadian National baseball team for a while and almost got them into the 1988 Olympic Games in Seoul. He also applied for the vacant Cubs announcing job with WGN radio in 1988, but ex–American leaguer Dave Nelson got the nod instead.

Finally, Jenkins has returned to professional baseball, this time as the pitching coach for the Rangers' Triple-A team, the Oklahoma City 89ers.

"I've found that I can teach pitchers," says Jenkins, now 45 years old. "It's been a learning experience but enjoyable. I keep having flashbacks of my own career and trying to relate my experience to the kids. It's amazing what they don't know, the things you just take for granted. I've learned to be more patient, less judgmental, and to repeat myself just in case they weren't listening the first time."

Would Jenkins attempt to parlay his own prestige and teaching ability into a major league managerial job?

"I don't think so. I'd like to be known as a good pitching coach. Maybe after moving up with some organization, sure, I'd think about managing. But it's certainly not something on which I've been focused."

Fergie Jenkins has done a lot of growing. There were

times during his remarkably productive years with the Cubs when he alternated among anger, arrogance, and cynicism. He once said, "I'm in a class by myself," and when someone suggested that his attitude didn't endear him to Chicago fans, he replied, comparing himself with Joe Namath, "I don't need the fans, and I don't care what they think."

A favorite Jenkins memory: It was 1966 and Fergie, then a free-spirited rookie, was standing on the mound at Wrigley Field blowing bubble gum. Meanwhile owner Phillip K. Wrigley was watching the game on television at his home in Lake Geneva, Wisconsin. One day later Durocher called a team meeting.

"Who owns this team, Jenkins?"

"Mr. Wrigley?"

"That's right. Mr. Wrigley. And what does Mr. Wrigley do for a living?"

"Sells chewing gum?"

"That's right, chewing gum. *Not bubble gum!*"

One day later Jenkins found that equipment man Yosh Kawano had filled the top of his locker with Wrigley's Spearmint gum.

"So I chewed it," recalls Jenkins. "But it wouldn't make bubbles."

Five years later Jenkins became the first Cubs player to hire an attorney, sending general manager John Holland into near-apoplexy during salary negotiations and a three-week holdout prior to the 1971 season. After stringing together four consecutive 20-game seasons, Jenkins was earning only $60,000 and had been offered an $8,000 raise. Fergie, in turn, was asking for $100,000. He didn't quite make it that year, but one season later he got a two-year contract worth $125,000 annually.

Ironically, it had been Holland who had suggested to Durocher that Jenkins be made into a starting pitcher. He had come from the Phillies as a reliever in another of those believe-it-or-not baseball trades. The truth: the Cubs got Jenkins in early 1966 only because Durocher was unable to get Orlando Cepeda to play first base instead of Banks.

How it was supposed to work: Banks's knees were starting to bother him in 1966, Leo's first season, and the Cubs manager had already decided he wanted to dump Ernie. First he offered left-handed pitcher Dick Ellsworth to San Francisco for Cepeda. Owner Horace Stoneham of the Giants balked, however, and swapped Cepeda to St. Louis for another southpaw, Ray Sadecki. That's when the Cubs turned to Philadelphia seeking first baseman John Herrnstein. Holland offered pitcher Bob Buhl for Herrnstein, but at the last minute the Phillies suggested the trade be expanded to include other players.

OK, said Holland, and tossed in another frontline pitcher, Larry Jackson, in exchange for Herrnstein, the young Panamanian outfielder Adolfo Phillips, and reliever Jenkins. Durocher, who admittedly had never heard of Jenkins, made a lot of noise about how great Phillips was going to be.

And what happened to left-handed-hitting Herrnstein? He played nine games for the 1966 Cubs, hit .176, and was traded to Atlanta for first baseman–outfielder Marty Keough, who hit .231 for the balance of the season and was then released.

That kept Banks at first base and gave the Cubs a new starting pitcher named Ferguson Jenkins, who stuck around until finally being sent to Texas after the 1973 season in exchange for Bill Madlock and Vic Harris.

One can only wonder how baseball history would have been reshaped had the Giants agreed to send Cepeda to the Cubs.

Somebody once said that baseball was "an island surrounded by a sea of statistics," and when trying to assess a man's baseball career that is true. Numbers, however, cannot tell you about the art of setting up a hitter or the science of delivering a baseball at 90 miles per hour to the outside black of home plate. Ferguson Jenkins was truly a Hall of Fame–caliber pitcher.

Indeed, while perusing *The Great All-Time Baseball Rec-*

ord Book, I came across this thought-provoking category: "Great Players Who Never Played in the World Series." The analyst-author, Joe Reichler, listed the names of only 13 men, with years of service in parentheses: Luke Appling (20), Ernie Banks (19), Jim Bunning (17), Rod Carew (14), Mel Harder (20), Harry Heilman (17), Billy Williams (18), Ralph Kiner (10), Nap Lajoi (21), Ted Lyons (21), Gaylord Perry (19), George Sisler (15), and Ferguson Jenkins (19).

Criteria for determining a "great player" were not detailed, but it is revealing to note that of all the thousands of men who have played major league baseball during 120 years, Reichler came up with only 13 "great ones" who never reached the World Series.

And 3 of the 13—Banks, Williams, and Jenkins—played with the 1969 Cubs.

JAMES LUCIUS HICKMAN
B. May 10, 1937, Henning, Tenn.

YEAR	TEAM		G	AB	H	2B	3B	HR	HR%	R	RBI	BB	SO	SB	BA	SA
1962	NY	N	140	392	96	18	2	13	3.3	54	46	47	96	4	.245	.401
1963			146	494	113	21	6	17	3.4	53	51	44	120	0	.229	.399
1964			139	409	105	14	1	11	2.7	48	57	36	90	0	.257	.377
1965			141	369	87	18	0	15	4.1	32	40	27	76	3	.236	.407
1966			58	160	38	7	0	4	2.5	15	16	13	34	2	.238	.356
1967	LA	N	65	98	16	6	1	0	0.0	7	10	14	28	1	.163	.245
1968	CHI	N	75	188	42	6	3	5	2.7	22	23	18	38	1	.223	.367
1969			134	338	80	11	2	21	6.2	38	54	47	74	2	.237	.467
1970			149	514	162	33	4	32	6.2	102	115	93	99	0	.315	.582
1971			117	383	98	13	2	19	5.0	50	60	50	61	0	.256	.449
1972			115	368	100	15	2	17	4.6	65	64	52	64	3	.272	.462
1973			92	201	49	1	2	3	1.5	27	20	42	42	1	.244	.313
1974	STL	N	50	60	16	0	0	2	3.3	5	4	8	10	0	.267	.367
13 yrs.			1421	3974	1002	163	25	159	4.0	518	560	491	832	17	.252	.426

13

Jim Hickman

---

*"In all the years I played baseball, we never realized
how tough it was for other people to make a living.
Then we lost everything."*
—*Jim Hickman*

Any motorist driving north from Memphis, 48 miles up
Highway 209 past the Hatchie River, will eventually be
greeted by a pair of home-built signs at the edge of an
inattentive Tennessee community, population 600.

WELCOME TO HENNING, CHILDHOOD HOME OF ALEX
HALEY, reads one sign, decorated by a hand-painted portrait of the author of the bestselling book *Roots.*

Four feet to the left is another sign: WELCOME TO HEN-
NING, HOME OF JIM HICKMAN, CHICAGO CUBS PLAYER.
And below, attached to a painted picture of a kneeling
ballplayer, is an added reminder: HOMETOWN OF JIM HICK-
MAN.

Finding Hickman's house isn't very difficult. Just ask the corner gas station attendant.

"Yeah, down to the light, take a left, Poplar Grove Road, first brick house on the right."

He pauses, takes a long sip of his cream soda, and says, "But he's in Florida."

Looking is allowed though. "Go ahead. People drive by there all the time."

You might also want to see the only bank in town, People's Bank, the one that took away Jim Hickman's farm. It's right there, several blocks down the street from the Museum for Alex Haley, even though Haley didn't really *live* in Henning but just visited during the summers.

People's Bank is the most modern building in town. It's the building with all the money.

Hickman's story is the story of the small American farmer, and it is a tragic one—the kind about which they make movies like *Country* and *The River* and *Places in the Heart*. It's also the kind that makes you want to scream out loud and drive a pickup truck right through the paneled doors of People's Bank. But there has been no Hollywood ending for the Hickmans, Jim and Anita, no Willie Nelsons to sing a song, no Farm Aid miracles. The 250-acre Hickman farm now belongs to People's Bank, as does the house on Poplar Grove Road in which Hickman still lives.

Hickman, 52 on May 10, still straight (6'4"), lean (205 pounds), and silent (as if Gary Cooper or Sam Shepard were playing the part), doesn't hang his head while telling what happened. Occasionally, however, he will wake in the middle of the night with claustrophobic horror, unable to sleep again in darkness.

It was still happening as late as 1988, when Hickman came to Tempe, Arizona, to instruct in one of Hundley's baseball camps. He woke at 3 A.M. feeling like "tearing off his clothes" and went downstairs to the lobby to "walk it off" for three hours.

"But he's better," says his wife, Anita, who travels regularly with her husband now that he has returned to organized baseball for the first time, as a minor league hitting instructor for the Cincinnati Reds organization. "I was really worried about him for a while. The depression got pretty bad. So did the anxiety attacks. Sometimes I'm afraid to turn off the lights. Without Randy's camps I really don't know what we would have done. They were our saving grace."

The farm was Hickman's new career after he got out of baseball in 1974. "It's all I ever really knew how to do, play baseball and farm," says Hickman, "so this farm was for all of us, me and the four boys, after I got out of baseball. So I went home the first years, and the farming was great, soybeans mostly. And I must say this: I'm no financial wizard. In all the years I played, we never realized how tough it was for other people to make a living. Then we lost everything.

"At first things just started slowin' down. From 1980 on, it was tough. It was a combination of things, I guess. Prices went down, my income went down to nothing, costs were huge. Then land prices went from $1,500 an acre to $5 an acre, and we lost all of our equity. Everything I had borrowed had land for equity, I borrowed to buy two tractors, one in 1979 and another in 1980, and one cost $35,000, the other one $40,000. Well, two years later they called and told me they were worth about $8,000 or $10,000 combined, and I still owed the balance of the note.

"We had three bad years in a row. The real dry year was 1980, and so was 1983. It just wiped us out. The only farms around Henning that survived were the old family farms which had been passed down and weren't extended at the bank. They hadn't had to borrow on their land. We had other neighbors like us though who just lost everything.

"And I won't lie—those years were tough. Things are still tough. Without my baseball pension I couldn't have survived. I had to take it at age 45, about $1,000 a month at first—now it's about $1700—but I really should have waited. It cost me a lot of money.

"It all came down during the winter of 1982. You see, here's the way it worked. Every year around Christmas I'd take all my soybean receipts from that year into the bank, and they would total the books and then loan me operating money for the upcoming year. So a week before Christmas 1982, I go in with all my money. I had no savings. So when they're finished counting the receipts the banker says, 'I can't give you any money for this year.'

" 'But I just turned in all of my receipts,' I said. 'How will I live?' "

"And the banker said, 'Oh, you'll find a way.' "

"That's the hell of it. People think that just because you played major league baseball, you've got this fortune hidden away somewhere. Well, you can believe I didn't. One of my sons was living in a small shack where we once kept the fertilizer.

"Anyhow, we somehow got through Christmas that year and into January on $500, but that's all we had."

Then came a call from Hundley—better than a Willie Nelson concert any day. He was holding his first adult baseball camp in Arizona in January and was asking Hickman to come as an instructor. All the other guys from the 1969 team would be there, and didn't it sound like fun?

The Hickmans could have cried. They probably did.

"I sold an old truck for $500 to have some spending money," recalls Hickman, "and Randy sent me the air ticket. I didn't take Anita. We just didn't dare any extra expense. When I got there Randy paid me $700 for the week. Well, I stayed in the hotel room every night and took that whole $700 home because that's what we lived on for the rest of the winter. Ever since then, Randy's always asked me if I need any extra money to come out."

Hickman got some temporary relief from a Federal Housing Administration loan that April of 1983, but the farming didn't get any better. And People's Bank dropped the other shoe and took the land and house.

"But they let me stay in the house and pay them rent," says Hickman. "So that's what I'm doing. I've thought about filing for bankruptcy—I don't see how I can ever pay back the note to the bank, it's so big—but I just haven't been able to make myself do it. It's just not my way. The bank has nothing to gain if I go bankrupt either. There is nothing else for them to take. It's a catch-22 situation.

"They say it all builds character," says Hickman, "but I've got about as much character as I want."

Hickman got back "into baseball," as those who have ever played the game phrase it, because of the death of Ted Kluszewski, the onetime Cincinnati Reds slugging star who had been serving as minor league hitting instructor for the Reds. Sheldon (Chief) Bender, vice president of the Reds who had served as coordinator of the Cincinnati minor league system for 20 years, was Hick's contact through the good ol' boy network.

"When I broke into baseball with the Cardinal organization back in 1956," said Hickman, "Chief was my first manager. We had always kept in touch."

The timing couldn't have been better. The Reds needed someone to relate to their young hitting prospects, and Hickman needed a job badly.

"We always had four kids and a dog around the house," says Hickman, "but now I looked around and it was just the two of us. My mother was 80 with Alzheimer's disease so we couldn't really talk about moving away from Henning. We needed to look after her. So this seemed like the best alternative, particularly with the Reds farm clubs, Nashville [Triple A] and Chattanooga [Double A] so close.

"With all the financial problems, it seemed like we were just sitting at home and getting old. Back in baseball, whether helping at one of Randy's camps or traveling through the minor leagues, you feel so much younger . . . back in life again."

When Hickman first realized how much he'd be traveling, he went into People's Bank and asked if they would issue him a credit card to use just for checking into hotels. The bank officer had him fill out forms, then three days later rejected the request because Jim still owed "so much money" to the bank.

"They made me feel like I borrowed the money to steal it," recalls Hickman.

Hickman would be a perfect coach on the minor league or major league level. He commands respect. Some men do, some don't. Men of all ages find Hickman comforting to be around. Ready to go into battle? Let's go, Hick. We're with you.

"I think I have something to offer the kids," says Hickman. "It's not so much showing them how to hit, although I can help there, but it's helping them with career experiences. I had to fight to make it, and I know how some of them feel. It all came tough for me. I learned as a kid playing ball in Tennessee, and I wouldn't have gotten into the big leagues if some scout hadn't been from that area and seen me in a high school game.

"As a kid I had a good arm, some power, and pitched a little. I never thought about college, just farming and baseball. But when I got out of the game in 1974, I wanted to get away and just farm. Now these camps have rejuvenated my thinking.

"Now I've got the baseball bug again. I'm just like the rest of the guys, I guess. The game is in my blood."

One of those smart-aleck New York magazine writers once wrote that Jim Hickman was his nominee for "underdog of the '60s" because he had been an Original Met (1962–1966) under Casey Stengel but then was playing with the Cubs in 1969, when the team was vanquished by the Miracle Mets.

It was Stengel, with his weird kind of wisdom, who said about Hickman, "He's tall, so I don't know why he don't hit with power."

Hickman, perhaps growing taller in Chicago ("We didn't like living in New York. The kids hit the ball over the fence one day and the neighbor called the police"), certainly found that power. After being traded from the Dodgers to the Cubs on April 23, 1968, along with Phil Regan (in

exchange for Ted Savage and Jim Ellis), Hickman languished in Tacoma for much of the season.

In 1969, however, Hickman was platooned in right field with Al Spangler for the first four months of the season. Finally, on August 3 Durocher made him a regular. Not that the Spangler-Hickman tandem hadn't been productive. Early in that season, when Spangler was hitting .370, he was asked if he didn't feel he should be playing every day. Answered Spangler, "No, because Jim Hickman is too good a player to sit on the bench."

Hickman's power carried the Cubs during the final two months of the season as he delivered 14 of his 21 home runs. Then in 1970 Hickman had his greatest year, hitting .315 with 32 home runs and 115 RBI at age 33.

What happened? Hickman claims his late development is still a mystery, but he is being modest. What happened was that he learned to master the strike zone, and he shortened his swing. He simply quit swinging at bad pitches.

Hickman only wishes things had been different in 1969.

"I don't have the answers," says Hickman. "I do think the tag play at home plate in New York in September was crucial. [Hickman's perfect throw appeared to have nailed a sliding Tommie Agee, but home-plate umpire Satch Davidson saw it differently.] And, to be honest, all of those big games we lost to the Mets made the difference. Al Weis hitting a home run to beat us?

"Then we couldn't bounce back. It's hard to understand why you can't win once you start backward. That's the bad thing about it. We could all see what was happening, but nobody could do anything about it.

"I think about 1969 all the time. It's hard to forget, and I won't lie—it's still sad to think about. But a lot of happiness came from it too. It was a great bunch of guys. We get along as well as any team I've ever known. I guess what happened makes us the best-remembered second-place team in baseball."

Hickman's four sons have all remained near Henning. The oldest, Jim, Jr., 30, spent four years in the U.S. Marines and was a crew member aboard the first helicopter to fly wounded comrades out of Beirut, Lebanon, in 1983.

"He told us how one of the boys died on the helicopter on the way to the hospital ship," says Hickman. "I guess it was a sobering experience for all of those kids. He's had some trouble since, some drugs, but he's better adjusted now. He's working over in Ripley, the town about five miles from Henning."

Two other sons, Bill, 28, and Mike, 24, also work in the Henning area, as does Joey, 26, who graduated from the University of Tennessee at Martin and plays golf almost well enough to try the pro tour. The boys have also been "share-farming" a neighbor's land, and with soybean prices back on the rise there was optimism within the Hickman clan in late 1988.

"I regret sometimes that I didn't push my kids more into sports," reflects Hickman. "Maybe it would have made a bigger difference in all of our lives. But it just wasn't my way."

Hickman's way: quiet, unassuming, competitive, loyal, uncomplicated, gracious, with a wry sense of humor. There were times in the 1960s when he wondered if there was a place in cities like New York and Chicago for a man from Tennessee.

"Opening Day 1970, and I was walking out of Wrigley Field, and this kid came up to me and asked if I wanted to join some Cub fans in a party just down the street.

"I thought that was pretty nice of him, and I asked, 'What kind of party?'

" 'Oh, just a bunch of groovy Cub fans who smoke pot,' said the kid. 'You wanna come?' "

Hickman politely declined and explained that he didn't smoke pot.

"Really?" asked the kid. "Well, how about Glenn Beckert? Does he smoke pot?"

Hickman replied that Beckert didn't smoke pot either.

"Well," said the kid, "who *does* smoke pot on the Cubs? Doesn't anybody?"

Billy Williams moves toward the bat rack while comedian Jack
Benny exits the dugout following a pregame ceremony.

Banks celebrates his birthday with the late John Holland,
general manager of the Cubs.

Santo and Durocher during a mid-winter press luncheon prior to the 1969 season.

Ron Santo (left) and Glenn Beckert display Golden Glove trophies after being honored for defensive excellence during the 1968 season. It was Santo's sixth in a row, Beckert's first.

Don Kessinger
demonstrates
his left-handed
batting style.

Ron Santo displays
his batting stance
for a baseball card
photographer,
circa 1969.

Teammates pummel
Willie Smith after
a game-winning home
run on opening day,
1969.

Ron Santo clicks his heels with joy after a victory.

Tommie Agee of the Mets begins his fateful slide on September 8, 1969, as catcher Randy Hundley prepares for the tag.

PHOTO COURTESY CHICAGO TRIBUNE

PHOTO COURTESY CHICAGO TRIBUNE

Umpire Dave Davidson observes from a distance before making the controversial ruling that Hundley missed with the sweep tag.

Leo Durocher (left) rages during a 1969 discussion with the umpires, the Cardinals' Lou Brock (20), and St. Louis manager Red Schoendienst (right).

A black cat approaches the Chicago dugout during a crucial September game against the Mets at Shea Stadium.

Tickets for the first ever National League Championship to be held at Wrigley Field in 1969 were priced at $7 but were unused.

The Cubs make the long trek to the old clubhouse entrance in left-field corner after a losing day at Wrigley Field.

Herman Franks (left) and boss Durocher yuk it up in the
Wrigley Field dugout after Franks joined the club as a coach in
1970, replacing the ailing Joe Becker. Franks later served as
both manager and general manager of club.

Owner Phillip K. Wrigley's
signs says it all in 1970
(Anyone Who Remains
Calm in the Midst of all
this CONFUSION Simply
Does Not Understand
THE SITUATION.

Ernie Banks connects for his 500th home run against the Atlanta Braves (above) at Wrigley Field in May 1970 and displays the baseball (arrow) after rounding the bases (below).

Billy Williams leaps high to snare a drive below the bleachers' basket, which was installed in 1970.

Ernie Banks (left) and Billy Williams are honored during ceremonies at Wrigley Field.

PHOTO COURTESY ANDY MCNALLY

Companion celebrity signs greet motorists outside Henning, Tennessee.

Same smiles, different waistlines for Ernie Banks (left), Randy Hundley (center), and Billy Williams during an Arizona adult camp.

Ferguson Jenkins
(left) and Ernie
Banks still enjoy
wearing Cubs
uniforms at the
adult camps
in Arizona.

Author Rick Talley (left) and
Bill Hands pose in front of
Hands's service station on
Long Island.

PHOTO COURTESY AP LASER PHOTO

During the Hall of Fame induction ceremony, Billy Williams suggests that baseball's hierarchy has still failed to successfully involve blacks in management, 40 years after Jackie Robinson broke the color barrier.

Ernie Banks acknowledges the applause after being chosen by fans as the greatest Cub of all time in June of 1969.

During the Hall of Fame induction ceremony, Billy Williams suggests that baseball's hierarchy has still failed to successfully involve blacks in management, 40 years after Jackie Robinson broke the color barrier.

Ernie Banks acknowledges the applause after being chosen by fans as the greatest Cub of all time in June of 1969.

"No, I don't think anybody does," said Hickman. "I'm sorry, but thanks anyway."

The kid shrugged his shoulders and departed. Hickman headed for home.

DONALD EULON KESSINGER
B. July 17, 1942, Forrest City, Ark.

YEAR	TEAM		G	AB	H	2B	3B	HR	HR%	R	RBI	BB	SO	SB	BA	SA
1964	CHI	N	4	12	2	0	0	0	0.0	1	0	0	1	0	.167	.167
1965			106	309	62	4	3	0	0.0	19	14	20	44	1	.201	.233
1966			150	533	146	8	2	1	0.2	50	43	26	46	13	.274	.302
1967			145	580	134	10	7	0	0.0	61	42	33	80	6	.231	.272
1968			160	655	157	14	7	1	0.2	63	32	38	86	9	.240	.287
1969			158	664	181	38	6	4	0.6	109	53	61	70	11	.273	.366
1970			154	631	168	21	14	1	0.2	100	39	66	59	12	.266	.349
1971			155	617	159	18	6	2	0.3	77	38	52	54	15	.258	.316
1972			149	577	158	20	6	1	0.2	77	39	67	44	8	.274	.334
1973			160	577	151	22	3	0	0.0	52	43	57	44	6	.262	.310
1974			153	599	155	20	7	1	0.2	83	42	62	54	7	.259	.321
1975			154	601	146	26	10	0	0.0	77	46	68	47	4	.243	.319
1976	STL	N	145	502	120	22	6	1	0.2	55	40	61	51	3	.239	.313
1977	2 teams		STL N (59G — .239)				CHI A (39G — .235)									
1977	total		98	253	60	7	2	0	0.0	26	18	27	33	2	.237	.281
1978	CHI	A	131	431	110	18	1	1	0.2	35	31	36	34	2	.255	.309
1979			56	110	22	6	0	1	0.9	14	7	10	12	1	.200	.282
16 yrs.			2078	7651	1931	254	80	14	0.2	899	527	684	759	100	.252	.312

14
Don Kessinger

"I knew my body was trying to tell me something."
—Don Kessinger

When people speak of the September collapse of the 1969 Cubs, whether with passion or with logical analysis, the name of shortstop Don Kessinger is inevitably invoked.

This is a man who played 2,078 major league games over 13 seasons but finds himself inexorably fused to those frenzied few contests at the conclusion of his greatest season.

Kessinger, 46, dressed in white dress shirt and tie, a graying portrait of success in his Memphis office, tilts comfortably back in the soft chair while looking at memorabilia on the wall. Life is good. His businesses, brokering investments and representing athletes, are flourishing. His sons, Keith and Kevin, are educated and talented; his wife of 23 years, Carolyn, is an attorney and full-time professor of business law at Memphis State University.

Now the door half opens, and his youngest son peeks inside.

"C'mon in, Kevin, I'd like you to meet somebody. This is Mr. Talley. He's writing a book on the '69 Cubs."

"They choked," says Kevin, softly closing the door behind him.

Kevin wasn't even born until two months after the 1969 season ended.

"Yeah, Carolyn was pregnant with him while we were out there choking," says the indulgent father. "But we didn't choke. We wore out. At least I know *I* did."

Until mid-September leadoff man Kessinger played every inning of every game in 1969. He had 664 official at-bats and another 61 bases on balls, and when you throw in sacrifice flies and bunts Kessinger perhaps strode (or staggered) to the plate 750 times. He was hitting .306 on May 30 and catching everything in sight. He was hitting .299 on July 4 and headed for the All-Star Game.

He finished the season at .273 headed for Zombie Land.

During the cruelest days of the Cubs' plummet, from September 4 through September 23, Kessinger hit .148 and played shortstop as if he had been hypnotized. The statue to his left, second baseman Glenn Beckert, hit .203 during the same period and handled grounders like a man trying to extract gophers from their holes.

Kessinger, in fact, had only 10 hits in 65 at-bats after September 7, not many for a man who two seasons later went six for six in a single game.

Kessinger knows all of this. And in the years that have passed, he has been consistent in his opinions, which are:

- The Cubs might have won that pennant had there been lights at Wrigley Field. No guarantee but a live shot.
- Leo Durocher should not have been criticized for overplaying his regulars.
- The Cubs became exhausted nevertheless, mentally and physically.

"It was a very hot summer in Chicago," recalls Kessinger

in his office at Athletic Research Management (ARM), the lesser of his two business priorities; he is also a licensed securities broker. "And as great as the Chicago fans were they added to the problem we had with fatigue. Don't misunderstand—I wouldn't change a thing. It's hard to describe how wonderful those fans were, showing up before the gates opened, hanging over the walls during batting practice begging for autographs. But there was simply no time to relax from the time we left the clubhouse to the end of the game—until we got past them and got home actually. God bless them, but over the course of the summer it wore us down."

Kessinger, a lithe 6'1" 175-pounder who played basketball at the University of Mississippi (where he currently moonlights as a radio-TV analyst), literally lost 20 pounds during the 1969 season, falling to 155 by October.

"Yet I had my best year," he says with pride. "What did I have, 38 doubles, 109 runs scored? I just can't blame Leo. First, we were on a roll all summer. Sure, it's easy to say now that we should have been rested. But if he had come to me in August and asked, 'Do you want a day off?,' I would have said no. If he had come in July I would have said no, I was playing great and felt good. I don't think any of us had a clue what might happen.

"Sure, I would have understood, but I can't blame Leo, and I'm not saying that because I've mellowed or anything. I'm just telling you that managing isn't easy."

Kessinger speaks from experience, however brief. He is the only former player from 1969 to have managed in the major leagues, having served as the player-manager of the White Sox for 106 games in 1979.

Did Kessinger realize 20 years ago that exhaustion was affecting his play?

"Part of it was the switching back and forth from night games on the road to those hot, humid day games at home," he says. "Part of it may have been my military obligation in the [U.S. Army Reserves]. I spent a lot of early mornings, weekends, and off-days in Chicago with the Reserves. Mainly though it was just cumulative fatigue. I first noticed

I was getting tired when I was sleeping past noon on the road. I knew my body was trying to tell me something.

"I've followed the whole campaign since then to get lights for Wrigley Field with great interest. Whether I'm right or wrong, it became my opinion that to compete for a championship the Cubs had to have lights. Personally, of course, I wish everybody played every game in daylight. But because they don't the Cubs needed lights to be competitive.

"Let me give you an example: if you play three hours of tennis during the middle of the day all summer and somebody else is playing three hours every evening at 7 o'clock, who's going to be the most tired after two months? The sun takes its toll."

He pauses to look at pictures of former teammates on the office walls—not an uncommon practice for most of those teammates as well.

"I look at those pictures and realize how fortunate I was to have played with so many great players. There are already two Hall of Famers [Banks and Williams] on that wall, and you know they have to induct Jenkins. Then there's Santo and Beckert . . . what a group of guys. I keep remembering that home run by Willie Smith on Opening Day and how it set the spirit of the summer. We became a team that never thought we were beaten. Even when three or four runs behind, we always thought we could win."

Until September?

"Several things happened. We lost momentum. We went bad at the wrong time. Then it became a mental thing. Every day we'd go out and look at the scoreboard, and those suckers had won again.

"And the first game of that series we played in New York in early September was as important as any game we played all year. The next day Tom Seaver just beat us. A great pitcher can do that to you anytime. But when the umpire missed that play at home plate on Agee and we lost that game, it took a lot out of us.

"It was a strange summer. We didn't have many days off at home, that I remember. And so many things happened—

Leo taking off for that boys' camp, the Don Young flap at Shea Stadium, Willie Stargell's home run, Dick Selma throwing that ball over Santo's head in Philly . . . sometimes it's hard to believe all that stuff happened in one summer."

Kessinger stole only 11 bases in 1969, but that is perhaps the most misleading of all Cub statistics. He explains why:

"I had enough speed, but we really didn't try to steal because of Beckert. He handled the bat so beautifully that you just knew he would make contact. That's why we ran the hit-and-run so often. I was seldom doubled off first base, and I was moving a lot. Beck could do just about anything he wanted to do with a bat.

"We used the hit-and-run so often that everybody expected it but couldn't do anything about it. They'd try to pick up our signs, but many times Leo would give the sign when I was at the plate and Beckert was still in the on-deck circle. What it meant was simply that if I got on base, we'd hit-and-run on the first pitch. I'd get on first, and everybody'd try to pick up a sign from coach Pete Reiser, but it had already been given.

"Beckert worked hard on defense too. We'd spend 20 to 30 minutes a day in spring training working on double plays, just Beckert and I. We'd go out when there was nobody else on the field so we wouldn't have to worry about dodging line drives from batting practice. We had only one practice field in Scottsdale."

Kessinger, the best defensive shortstop of the National League during the late 1960s and early 1970s, surely also ranks as the most consistent and remarkable in the history of the Chicago franchise. Banks played the position for nine seasons but spent ten at the first base, and the fleet Kessinger roamed farther, threw more accurately, and danced an adagio when turning the double play. Indeed, his .252 lifetime batting average was bonus. Teams who bid for championships need shortstops like Kessinger. During the early stages of the 1969 season he established a major league

record for consecutive games at shortstop without error (54),
yet he finished the season with 20 miscues, most of them
coming in late August and September.

That he learned to switch hit so effectively made him an
All-Star. Some of the credit for that significant move has
gone to Durocher, some to coach Pete Reiser. More should
go to Kessinger, whose explanation of the transition should
be heeded by all youngsters with switch-hitting aspirations:

"It was late in 1965, my rookie year, and as a natural
right-handed hitter I was hitting about .200. So I said to
Alvin Dark, one of our coaches. 'I think I can switch hit.'
He said, 'OK, here's what we'll do. You go home this winter,
find yourself a gymnasium, and get somebody to throw
tennis balls at you all winter. Have them throw them hard
and some of them right at you. You've got to find out
whether you can get out of the way of the ball. Sometimes
hitters have a tendency to freeze when they switch to the
other side, and you've got to find out.'"

So during the winter of 1965–1966, Kessinger dodged
tennis balls. He also swung at thousands of them from the
left side. It felt natural, and he was enthusiastic about it.

Something else had also happened that winter, however.
Durocher had been hired as manager of the Cubs, and when
a select group of young players was sent to Escondido,
California, for early spring training, 23-year-old Kessinger
was invited.

"I remember it was late February 1966," says Kessinger,
"because Carolyn and I had just gotten married, and we
drove out. In those days, you can be sure we drove."

During that early camp, Kessinger went to batting instructor Lou Klein, who was running the camp ("Leo just
showed up in civilian clothes to observe for a few days"),
and told him he wanted to switch hit.

"But you have to understand the situation," recalls Kessinger. "Leo was the new boss, and everybody was a little
afraid of Leo. So Klein said, 'I don't know. Let me get back
to you.' Then a couple of days later he said, 'Let's just stay
on the right side for a while and work hitting the ball to

right field.' So that's what I did. I figured the orders had come from Leo.

"Now in May of that season I'm playing regularly but hitting only about .225. And you know what kind of team we had. Leo had predicted we wouldn't finish eighth, and we were headed for tenth. Anyhow, we were playing at home one day against Houston, and Leo came to me during batting practice and said, 'I just heard that you had wanted to switch hit this spring. Is that true?' I told him it was, and he said, 'Let me see you take some swings.'

"Well, I hit a few, ran around the bases, and when I came back he said, 'You look better swinging that way than you do right-handed. Let's try it for a few more days in batting practice and see how it feels.'

"Of course, I had never really hit baseballs from the left side, just tennis balls. But for the next two days I batted left-handed in practice. On the third day we were ahead something like 7–0, which was very unusual for us that year. Leo came to me on the bench and said, 'It's OK with me if you want to hit left-handed this next time up,' which I interpreted to mean, 'Go up there and hit left-handed,' so I did. First, though, I said to Houston's catcher, John Bateman, 'Listen, I'm serious about this. I don't want you to think I'm up here foolin' around just because we're ahead 7–0.' So he laughed and said, 'OK,' and I batted left-handed twice in that game. I hit the ball well twice but both times for outs.

"After the game Leo said, 'Let's stay with it,' and the whole thing sounded wonderful. There was only one problem: while I was staying with it my batting average was heading south. I was hitting the ball but making nothing but outs. I think I was down to about .190. Finally I went to Leo and said, 'Hey, Skip, why don't we wait until next spring? Man, I'm really struggling up there.'

"But I've got to give Durocher credit here. He said, 'No, let's stay with it. Don't worry about what you hit this year. Keep going as a switch-hitter. Now is the time to learn.'

"Well, I hit over .300 for the rest of the year, finished the season at .274, and I was a switch hitter from then on. In fact, I became better left-handed than right-handed. Even now, when I go to Old-Timers Games, I prefer to hit left-handed. I think it's because once you start you get so many more swings left-handed because there are so many more right-handed pitchers."

Did Kessinger ever learn whether Durocher had vetoed that early suggestion to switch hit, back in the spring of 1966?

"I honestly don't believe he ever knew about it," says Kessinger. "I don't think Lou Klein ever said anything to him."

Don Kessinger grew up in Forest City, Arkansas, a small town across the Mississippi River from Memphis. His wife, three years younger, grew up nearby. They had their first date when she was a senior in high school and he was playing basketball at the University of Mississippi. And when they moved to Chicago the Kessingers lived in suburban Northbrook. The transition to the majors hadn't taken long: Kessinger spent only six weeks in the minor leagues, having accepted less money to sign with the Cubs organization because he saw opportunity. The shortstops before him had been Andre Rodgers and Roberto Pena. Enough said.

Even then, at the beginning, Don was straightforward about his priorities. "Mine are, in this order: Jesus Christ, my family, and my vocation, which is baseball," he would say when speaking before Fellowship of Christian Athletes groups. "The FCA has given me an arm for outreach. I'm proud to be a Christian who happens to be an athlete, not an athlete who happens to be a Christian."

Kessinger says his priorities haven't changed.

"I'm not as outwardly active in FCA," says Kessinger, "but I still participate in their charity events like golf tournaments and help them try to raise funds. But there has been no change in priorities—God and family. We go to the Bellevue Baptist Church, and we go together."

The oldest Kessinger son, Keith, is a major league baseball prospect eligible for the June 1989 draft. He's a 6'2", 185-pound senior shortstop with junior baseball eligibility at the University of Mississippi.

"I saw Keith play on television one day and did a double take," says ex-teammate Beckert. "It was like looking at a ghost. He had the same moves as his father at shortstop."

"Except that Keith is a lot bigger," adds Kessinger, "and he's a right-handed hitter with power."

Son number two, Kevin, is finishing his freshman year at Ole Miss and plays outfield.

Carolyn, who went to law school after Don finished his major league career, became a practicing attorney in Memphis before joining the faculty at Memphis State. She was a regular spectator at Wrigley Field during the 1969 season, sitting in the wives' section behind home plate, pregnant with Kevin and with two-year-old Keith in tow. And as the pressure built on the husbands, the wives felt it too. Carolyn said in 1969, "I'm a nervous wreck. I can't relax any more, and I seem to cry at the least little thing. It's horrible."

Six years later, after the Cubs had tried and tried and tried but never succeeded to win a pennant, Carolyn Kessinger's husband was the last one remaining. By 1975 everyone else had gone, everyone but Jenkins and Kessinger. Then, on October 23, 1975, Jenkins was traded to Texas, and five days later Kessinger went to St. Louis for pitcher Mike Garman and a minor league infielder.

"I was the Last of the Mohicans," says Kessinger.

At the end, with new manager Jim Marshall giving Dave Rosello priority time at shortstop, Kessinger asked to be traded. His choices were the Yankees or the Cardinals, and he chose St. Louis because of its proximity to Memphis. In retrospect, he might have reached that elusive World Series if he had chosen the Yankees; the Yanks ended up getting Bucky Dent to play shortstop and won World Championships in 1977 and 1978.

Kessinger was later traded to the White Sox in mid-1977 when the Cardinals brought up Garry Templeton, and Don found himself in a situation he hadn't anticipated. Owner Bill Veeck had named Larry Doby to replace Bob Lemon as manager in 1978 but in midseason asked shortstop Kessinger if he would consider replacing Doby.

"I didn't think it fair to Doby," recalls Kessinger, who did not accept the assignment then "because he hadn't taken the club through spring training."

After the 1978 season, however, Veeck fired Doby and again asked Kessinger to be manager. He accepted the job on one condition: that he continue as player-manager.

It was an ill-fated voyage. The Chisox of 1979 were 46–60 in fifth place when Kessinger resigned and was succeeded by Tony LaRussa.

"I liked Bill Veeck," says Kessinger. "I really thought he was brilliant. But I didn't like the makeup of the team. I preferred pitching and defense. We had a low-budget team made up of designated hitters. Veeck simply didn't have the money to build a winner. We were going nowhere."

So Kessinger in late 1979 got out of baseball, returned to Memphis, and invested in racquetball courts, a business venture that cost him money—"mainly because the guy who bought us out didn't pay." Today one of Kessinger's partners in ARM is former soccer star Kyle Rote, Jr., and although the relationship has been successful and amicable, in late 1988 Kessinger was considering a lesser role with the company. There also remains the possibility that Kessinger may return to baseball in some capacity.

"I feel I've made the complete transition away from the game," he says, "but I do feel I could instruct. I enjoy working in Randy's camps, and I like working with young players. Maybe if the right college or pro job came along, I would do it again."

There are only two more items to discuss before heading northward, up the Tennessee Scenic Parkway, past the Civil War historical markers, scrub timber, cotton fields, church steeples, and billboards (USE YOUR HOTLINE TO GOD. FAMILIES THAT PRAY TOGETHER STAY TOGETHER).

First, there's the cartoon that appeared during spring training 1988 in a Chicago newspaper. It showed a happy Cub riding a giant tricycle, with the caption ". . . Until the Wheels Come Off."

"That's it," Kessinger laughs softly. "That's it."

Then there's the question you can't resist when you're in the heart of Memphis, Tennessee:

"Is Elvis really alive?"

"No, I don't think so," says Kessinger, "but I didn't think we'd lose in 1969 either."

PHILIP RAYMOND REGAN
B. Apr. 6, 1937, Otsego, Mich.

YEAR	TEAM	W	L	PCT	ERA	G	GS	CG	IP	H	BB	SO	ShO	Relief Pitching W	L	SV
1960	DET A	0	4	.000	4.50	17	7	0	68	70	25	38	0	0	0	1
1961		10	7	.588	5.25	32	16	6	120	134	41	46	0	2	2	2
1962		11	9	.550	4.04	35	23	6	171.1	169	64	87	0	1	2	0
1963		15	9	.625	3.86	38	27	5	189	179	59	115	1	2	1	1
1964		5	10	.333	5.03	32	21	2	146.2	162	49	91	0	1	0	1
1965		1	5	.167	5.05	16	7	1	51.2	57	20	37	0	0	0	0
1966	LA N	14	1	.933	1.62	65	0	0	116.2	85	24	88	0	14	1	21
1967		6	9	.400	2.99	55	3	0	96.1	108	32	53	0	5	7	6
1968	2 teams	LA N (5G 2–0)				CHI N (68G 10–5)										
1968	total	12	5	.706	2.27	73	0	0	134.2	119	25	67	0	12	5	25
1969	CHI N	12	6	.667	3.70	71	0	0	112	120	35	56	0	12	6	17
1970		5	9	.357	4.74	54	0	0	76	81	32	31	0	5	9	12
1971		5	5	.500	3.95	48	1	0	73	84	33	28	0	4	5	6
1972	2 teams	CHI N (5G 0–1)				CHI A (10G 0–1)										
1972	total	0	2	.000	3.63	15	0	0	17.1	24	8	6	0	0	2	0
13 yrs.		96	81	.542	3.84	551	105	20	1372.2	1392	447	743	1	58	40	92

15
Phil Regan

"To me, Willie Stargell's home run was just another home run."
—Phil Regan

After leaving baseball in 1972, Phil Regan went home to Grand Rapids, Michigan, to work for a service management company, Service Master, which put him into a training program. The purpose was plain enough. Everybody in the company, including the president, was expected to learn all aspects of the business. Off he went, after 13 seasons in the major leagues, to learn about housekeeping and laundries and others facets of servicing hospitals and plants.

"You had to learn, for example," says Regan, "the seven steps for a maid to clean a room. Then you go to cleaning floors, how to strip a floor, the whole procedure."

One day barely six months since he had been a major league pitcher, Regan was down on his hands and knees, wearing old work clothes, and vigorously scrubbing a floor when a stranger walked past the door, did a classic double take, and said:

"Hey, aren't you Phil Regan who used to pitch for the Cubs?"

"Yeah, I am."

"I'll bet you really miss it, huh?"

Actually, he didn't miss it. After being sold to the White Sox, being released, then saying "no, thank you" to an overture from Japan, Regan found a decade of peace and contentment raising two sons and two daughters, working in a hardware store, and coaching at Grand Valley State College.

Then he got back into baseball as a scout and then a pitching coach for the Mariners and now as a scout for the Dodgers.

Why?

Because he could throw a &%$#@, a.k.a. spitball, a.k.a. sinker.

But that's getting ahead of this crime-in-the-major-leagues-almost-always-pays scenario. Return first to yester-year and Grand Valley State College, where the ballfield had no fence and no scoreboard, but it did have a new coach who had once thrown a great &%$#@.

"I think they were paying me $4,000 at first," recalls Regan, now 52. "I only took the job because I had a friend who owned this huge furniture and hardware store I was working at, and he gave me time off from work to help the school. It really was a rundown program, but we built it up from scratch. I eventually also became head of fund-raising at the school, taught a class, ran a baseball camp, and even managed a semipro team during the summer called the Polynesian Pools and picked up another $3,000 to $4,000 doing that. All in all, I was making about $30,000 outside of baseball and collecting my pension, which was about $23,000, so I really wasn't looking to get back into the game."

Regan loved Grand Valley, a four-year college of about ten thousand, even though the athletic program was far from sophisticated. One spring, Grand Valley's athletic director, ex-Michigan football player Don Dufek, suggested Regan take his team on a spring trip, not an easy task since the uniforms weren't much, there were no games scheduled, and there was no travel money.

"But we came up with some money," recalls Regan "and off we went. Our weather was so bad in Michigan, we just wanted to get somewhere warm to practice. I'll tell you what kind of trip it was: we stopped at one high school somewhere in Tennessee, and I told the athletic director, 'If you'll let us practice on your field, we'll rake it and clean it for you.' So that's what we did. Then after practice he invited us for lunch. We had Beenie-Weenies, and the kids loved it. From there the program just kept growing."

Then the phone rang. Jack Childers, the agent from Chicago, had a client named Al Hrabosky who was having trouble getting hitters out, didn't know how to throw the &%$#@, and would Regan please teach him in order to save his career?

"Sure," said Regan. "Send him on up."

So Hrabosky flew to Grand Rapids, spent three days with Regan learning how to throw the &%$#@, and said, "Would you mind calling some big-league clubs for me to tell them how I'm doing?" So Regan called the Tigers and the White Sox and then tried the Seattle Mariners, who weren't interested in Hrabosky but did have a job to offer Regan.

That was November 1983. Hrabosky, who never did get to try his newly mastered $%$#@, eventually became a broadcaster in St. Louis. Regan meanwhile went to work as a scout for the Mariners in 1984 and advanced to become their pitching coach. When Dick Williams became manager, however, Regan cited "philosophical differences" and landed a scouting job with the Dodgers, for whom he had once pitched.

That's how baseball works. Once a personable ex-player gets a job and doesn't do anything drastic such as buy drugs for the owner's daughter or steal receipts from the concession stand, he can keep jumping from job to job to job.

Regan, with his knowledge of pitching and the National League, will most likely keep advancing on toward a managerial job. He's "well thought of" within the Dodgers organization, and his scouting input was extensive prior to the Pedro Guerrero–for–John Tudor trade in 1988. He also headed south again to manage in the Dominican Republic during the winter of 1988–1989.

"I'm not looking to take Tommy Lasorda's job," says Regan, "but if I have an opportunity to manage within the next three years I'll take it. But it would have to be the right situation."

Regan threw a very fine &%$#@ when he pitched for the Cubs from 1968 into mid-1972. But it didn't do him much good during August and September of 1969, when his arm got tired. That's the crazy thing about a &%$#@. It's really no more than a fastball with "something" on it, whether perspiration or whatever, that makes it drop drastically upon reaching home plate. Those who have mastered the really good &%$#@s, for that matter, don't need anything other than perspiration on the ball. Yet when a &%$#@ loses its velocity, it can also be measured by a hitter.

Regan, age 32, finished the 1969 season with a record of 12-6, and an ERA of 3.70, and 17 saves having pitched 112 innings of relief in 71 games. Yet he won only one game after July 26 and none after August 24.

The standard criticism: Durocher had dialed Regan's bullpen number too often. But had he? Did Regan feel he was overworked?

"I guess I never felt overworked," says Regan, "because I had always pitched in a lot of games, even when I was with the Dodgers. As I think back on it though, I think it is awfully hard to know when you're losing your stuff. After I got out of baseball I gave it a lot of thought. I told myself I was making good pitches, keeping the ball down, slider down and away, good sinker [&%$#@].

"But then I was watching Mickey Lolich pitch with the Tigers, and I realized something. He was getting hit hard and kept saying, 'I don't understand—I'm making good pitches.' So I watched him closely, and he was right—except that those pitches weren't as sharp or crisp as they once were. The slider, for example, would start to roll instead of falling away.

"There is a very fine line between winning and losing for a pitcher. I never *feel* tired. I didn't feel tired in 1969. But I may have lost that crispness. Your pitches aren't as good, but you don't know it."

Ironically, Regan's trouble pitch in late 1969 was his slider, not his &%$#@. Regan had a very good slider, yet when his arm got weary he couldn't pinpoint location and it wasn't breaking as sharply at the plate. Instead it began to "slide" when it left his hand, and hitters were picking it up.

OK, what about the &%$#@?

"John Roseboro always called it a country sinker," said Regan. "What did Hundley tell you I was using? You know I'm not telling. I may want to write my own book someday."

Pitchers who throw &%$#@s are like that. It's part of the mystique. They figure half the battle is keeping people guessing, and they're right. The facts, though, about Regan's &%$#@: he didn't have to hide anything, because he didn't use anything other than "sweat."

"Anywhere and everywhere," says catcher Hundley, "Shucks, when it's hot out there how you gonna keep sweat from rollin' down your arm onto your hands? It just gets there."

"Besides," adds Regan bullpen buddy Hank Aguirre, "Phil had a long forehead."

"I've never said I threw it or didn't throw it," says Regan, "But I had a pretty sinker [&%$#@]. Actually I had it even before going to the Dodgers [in 1966]. I worked on it in Detroit but never used it. Then when I got sent down to Syracuse [1965] I worked on it more there."

The work obviously paid dividends. Regan was 14-1 with an ERA of 1.62 when the Dodgers won the 1966 pennant, and that's when Sandy Koufax gave him his nickname, the Vulture.

"We were playing the Phillies in Los Angeles, Koufax

against Jim Bunning, and they went 11 innings, 1-1, with Sandy striking out 16. Then I came in to pitch the twelfth, we scored, and I got the victory. Now Sandy's next start was in Pittsburgh four days later, and the score was 1-1 in the eighth when Walter Alston took him out for a pinch hitter. He had struck out 10. Well, I pitched the bottom of the eighth, we scored three in the ninth, and I held them in the ninth for the victory.

"Now Koufax had pitched 18 innings, struck out 26 men, allowed two runs, and had no decisions. I had pitched three innings and won two games.

"That's when he called me 'the Vulture,' and it stuck."

With the Cubs Regan had an ongoing battle with National League umpires. On the final night of June in Montreal, for example—the evening Banks's home run was disallowed because umpire Tony Venzon thought it went through Rusty Staub's hole in the fence—Regan was almost made to disrobe on the mound as umpire Dave Davidson stopped play, inspected Regan's arms and uniform, then finally gave up.

Then there was the series later that season at Wrigley Field when Regan entered a game in the eighth to face Mack Jones. After his third pitch, umpire Chris Pelekoudas came to the mound and said, "Don't throw that pitch again." Then out came Durocher, who said, "Did you find anything on the ball?"

"No," said Pelekoudas.

"Then leave him alone," said Durocher.

Pelekoudas, however, had other ideas. After Jones flied out to center field, the umpire called him back and let him hit again. A little later in the game Regan struck out Pete Rose, and the same thing happened. Pelekoudas let him hit again, and this time he got a base hit. (Take note, Ty Cobb fans. It should have taken Pete another at-bat to break that record.)

Durocher got kicked out of the game. So did Hundley and so did outfielder Al Spangler. Regan just got to throw extra &%$#@s.

After the game Leo called Regan into his office and said "Don't talk to the press. Let the umpires do the talking."

And talk they did. They said they didn't kick Regan out of the contest because they "wanted to make him suffer." Needless to say, it made headlines.

A few days later Durocher called Regan into his office and said, "Mr. Wrigley says if you want to sue baseball for what they did to you in that game he will give you his lawyer. That means you'll be suing the Cubs too, since the Chicago franchise is part of baseball, but Mr. Wrigley is willing to do it."

"I don't want to sue anybody," said Regan.

"Well, if you do," continued Durocher, "I've got something I've never told anybody about. When Happy Chandler [the commissioner who banned Durocher from baseball for one year] called me and said, 'Leo, you were innocent, but I have to suspend you,' I got him on tape. And if you want to sue I'll make that tape public!"

Next scene: Warren Giles, president of the National League, calls for an audience with Regan, Durocher, and general manager Holland. Regan remembers it this way:

"I've talked with the umpires," said Giles, "and they will not harass Phil anymore unless they find evidence on the ball or his body. But why, Mr. Regan, if you are so innocent, are you and Gaylord Perry always in the middle of these controversies?"

"Let me tell you something, Warren," interrupted Durocher, not allowing Regan to talk. "I've got a friend at the Mayo Clinic, and he says that anyone pitching in a baseball game is in a stressful situation. Would you agree?"

"Well, yes."

"And he says," continued Durocher, "that if there isn't a little oil on your forehead or on your body during stress, you will die. Now, do this, Mr. President. Touch your fingers to your own forehead. Isn't it a little oily?"

"Well, yes," said Giles nervously.

"Well," said Durocher, "that's what I've been telling you."

Regan looks at the 1969 season through different-colored glasses.

"To me, it was just another year," says Regan, "and we lost. I really don't dwell on it, maybe because it was only my second year with the Cubs. I didn't go way back with Santo and Beckert and Williams and all the others. Not that I didn't think they were terrific. I still do. But I don't look back and feel that my career was ruined or anything like that. I just didn't let it be prominent in my life."

What sticks in his mind about that season?

"I remember Leo taking off for Camp Ojibwa , but the players didn't react. We didn't get upset about it at all.

"And I remember when Leo was angry with the media and would only say 'no comment' for about six weeks. I got the idea that if he ever came to the mound to ask me anything, I'd say 'no comment.' But he never did.

"Playing for Leo, you know, was different than playing for anybody else I ever played under. He was totally different from how I thought he'd be. You picture him as fiery, and he could be at times, but he was only like that when we were winning. Then he would be on everybody.

"But when we were losing he was very quiet. He wouldn't say anything when we were losing.

"All of the young pitchers were afraid of him though. I keep remembering Jim Colborn, who was 22 or 23, in one of those clubhouse meetings when Leo said, 'Anybody got anything to say?' And Colborn very innocently said, 'Well, Leo, we'd like to talk with you, but you're like a viper.' The guys were crackin' up, and I thought Leo was going to choke. I guess he'd never been called a viper."

Even though Regan pitched six years for the Tigers and another two-plus with the Dodgers, he finds himself closely associated with the Cubs.

"Pitching with Detroit hardly exists in my mind anymore," says Regan. "It's like another era. I really didn't have that much success until becoming a reliever in Los Angeles, anyway."

Regan's break in L.A. came because twin holdouts Sandy

Koufax and Don Drysdale missed all of 1966 spring training. That gave Regan a chance to pitch frequently. But so
did Don Sutton, Claude Osteen, Bill Singer, and other
Dodgers youngsters, and when the Big Two returned, Alston
dispatched Regan, with all that perspiration rolling down
his arms onto his fingertips, into the bullpen.

How he got to the Cubs from the Dodgers is one for the
medical journals—one of the truly amazing trade stories in
baseball history.

"It's the spring of 1968, and Ron Perranoski and Bob
Miller had already been traded, so that left me as the only
Dodger relief pitcher with any experience. But just as we
were ready to break camp I got sick. My hands started
swelling and I thought I had the flu, except that they
couldn't find anything. Finally they sent me into a hospital
in Arizona for tests, but by then it had gone away.

"Then after rejoining the Dodgers I started getting sick
again. My knees and legs were swollen, and one morning I
couldn't move my hands. I couldn't even pick up a coffee
cup. So they sent me to Dr. Robert Kerlan, the orthopedic
surgeon, and after the examination, he said, 'You've got
rheumatoid arthritis, and you're going to look just like me.'
Well, I couldn't believe it because Dr. Kerlan, a terrific
doctor and wonderful guy, had been stooped with arthritis
for years.

"So he gave me a shot of cortisone and a bunch of tiny
pills and told me to take six each day. Well, it got worse, I
could hardly get out of bed in the mornings, and my leg
hurt terribly. And I was just 28 years old. But I was taking
the pills and trying to pitch, believe it or not. I also started
reading about arthritis, and somewhere I read about a form
of rheumatoid arthritis that lasted only 30 days. And that's
when an amazing sequence of events came into play.

"Alston, our manager, came down with appendicitis and
went into the hospital, leaving Lefty Phillips as interim
manager. We go into New York for a road trip, and for the
first time in a while I don't have the soreness. I think I
pitched in three of the four games, including both games of

a winning doubleheader. That was on Sunday. On Monday I got traded to the Cubs. [Dodgers general manager] Buzzie Bavasi had gotten rid of me."

For the record: the Cubs got Regan and Jim Hickman, who was playing Triple-A ball, in exchange for outfielder Ted Savage and left-handed pitcher Jim Ellis. Both Regan and Hickman excelled with the Cubs, while Savage hit .206 as a reserve with the Dodgers in 1968 before being traded to Cincinnati. Ellis never pitched an inning for Los Angeles.

But there is more to Regan's medical saga:

"When I got to Chicago the first thing the Cubs did was send me to the hospital. Obviously they had heard about my problems. Finally, after a bunch of tests. Doc [Jake] Suker says to me, 'Phil, we can't find anything wrong with you.'

"It had been exactly 28 days from the time my arthritis started to the day I was traded. And I've never had a problem since. A few weeks after the trade the Dodgers come into Wrigley Field, and here comes Alston walking from the Dodger dugout out to where I was standing. He says, 'I just wanted to tell you that if I had been with the team you never would have been traded.' It turned out that Buzzie had given the Cubs a couple of other choices, including Mudcat Grant, and I was the guy they chose. Hickman was just a throw-in. As a matter of fact, he was having salary trouble with Buzzie and was ready to quit baseball."

Bavasi, seeking to unload one player because of ill health and another because of a salary dispute, had not made one of his better trades.

Regan, who is a strong link between past and present because of his current active major league status, offers these observations:

• The role of the pitching coach has changed considerably over two decades.
• Pitchers are in much better physical condition today than in the past.

- Agents and guaranteed contracts, rather than real injuries, are sending pitchers onto the disabled list.
- The five-man rotation is not good, nor is the theory that starting pitchers should no longer be expected to pitch nine innings.

"Joe Becker was our pitching coach in 1969, but he wasn't really an instructor," says Regan. "He was big on running. The same with Lefty Phillips with the Dodgers: what was he going to teach Koufax or Drysdale? Becker made you do your throwing when you were supposed to do it. He made you concentrate. He was a big, strong guy who loved his pitchers, and Leo drove him nuts. He'd come out of Durocher's office and say, 'I can't understand it. When we're going good, they're Leo's pitchers. When we're going horseshit, he wants to know what's wrong with *my* pitchers.' "

Regan on pitchers today: "They have training methods we never knew about. Nautilus, off-season conditioning programs, the whole program. We never did much in the off-seasons, maybe played some basketball. I really believe I would have pitched longer if I had paid attention to my body like these guys do.

"Yet every time an agent tells them, 'I don't think you should pitch if your arm is bothering you,' another guy goes on the DL. It's really crazy, I remember when Bavasi would offer to give $25 to any Dodger pitcher who could finish running a mile. You think Drysdale would run a mile for $25? Nobody ran it. Yet when I was pitching coach in Seattle we ran anywhere from 1.2 to 1.7 miles every day, up hills. Don Sutton was one of the first pitchers I can remember really running, and look what it did for his career. That body has stayed the same all these years. So how come everybody today is in better shape but more people are on the DL?"

Regan on the five-man rotation: "It's the fault of baseball. We've let pitchers do what they want to do. We tell them, 'Give me six or seven good innings,' and that's all anybody expects to pitch. I think it has hurt the game. Listen, Fergie Jenkins won 20 games six years in a row, and he never had four days of rest. I really think pitchers would be better off with less rest between starts. It's just a matter of them getting accustomed to it again.

"If I manage again, I will seriously consider a four-man pitching rotation."

Regan, who also participates in Hundley's fantasy camps, admits he feels closer to the '69 Cubs than any other team for which he has toiled, maybe because he was the player representative during that bizarre season of "Hey, Hey, Holy Mackerel," maybe because of the makeup of the team.

"There was such a great feeling with that team," says Regan, "and everybody got along so well. If we would have won, I'm sure it would have been one of the best-remembered championship teams in this half-century. But the Mets really played well. Just look back at that pitching staff. They weren't much on the field, but they really did have pitching. In retrospect, Leo probably should have used Ted Abernathy more than he did. Aguirre too, in spot situations. But Durocher just never had any confidence in our kid pitchers. He was always backing up the truck."

And how well does Regan remember the home-run pitch he threw to Willie Stargell on the afternoon of September 7, 1969?

"Oh, I remember it, but I've got to say something about that. I keep hearing it was one of the turning points of the season. But to me it was just another home run. So he hit a home run into a gale-force wind. But that only tied the game, and we lost in extra innings, right? It was a tough loss, but they were all tough at that time. To me it was no tougher than any other loss. Yet years later it has become one of the biggest losses of the season. Why is that?

"To me, Willie Stargell's home run was just another home run."

CHICAGO CUBS AUTOGRAPHS

Ron Santo   Willie Smith

Don Kessinger   "Fergie" Jenkins   Don Young

    Ted Abernathy

Bill Hands   Phil   Regan   Ernie Banks

Pete Reiser   Dick Selma

    Dave Lemonds   Don Nottebart

    Ale Distaso

Billy Williams

Leo Durocher   Randy Hundley

Kenny Holtzman   Hank Aguirre

    Joe Amalfitano

         Nate Oliver

Dean M. Burk   Jim Becker

Glenn Beckert

Jim Qualls   Pat Jacquez   Rich Nye

   Archie Reynolds   Randy Bobb

Terry Bongiovanni

   Verlon Walker   Jimmy McMath

Jim Dunegan   Paul Popovich

       Terry Hughes

   Gary R. Fast

Al Spangler

    Ken Rudolph   John Sung

Jim Hickman   Gene Oliver   Rich Bladt

16

The Bench and the Bullpen

"There is a destiny that makes us brothers, none goes his way alone."
—*Edward Markham*

"I had to sit there and watch all that shit."
—*Don Nottebart*

THE PLAYERS

One is a farmer in rural Illinois, another a carpenter in rural Oregon. The Mexican owns a Detroit company that expects to gross $35 million this year. One Texan teaches school, another runs a rock & roll night club. One sells cars, another sells liquor. One is an L.A. police detective, another a doctor of exotic birds.

One is dead.

One is missing.

223

They all shared the experience of playing with the 1969 Cubs. Mostly though, they just watched—from the corner of the dugout, from the bullpen bench, from the tunnel where one could sneak a cigarette and rage in solitude.

They came and went, 41 of them in total, some who dared not speak too loudly, or throw a strike on zero and two, or hold up the team bus, or unpack.

Ten of them never threw another pitch or swung another bat in the major leagues.

They formed the supporting cast—some, like Jimmy Qualls and Willie Smith, heroic meteors across the sky; others, like Alec Distaso and Rick Bladt, just there for a quick, soon-forgotten glance and good-bye.

They too are alumni of the Class of '69, and they too remember. Some cared, some didn't. Here are their accounts.

Jimmy Qualls is a farmer now. He doesn't own the farm, just "takes care" of 1,500 hogs, a dozen cows, and a feed business in western Illinois about 25 miles north of Quincy, where he has lived since 1971. At age 42 he doesn't think too much about baseball anymore.

"Just every so often. I almost went into Chicago for the Cubs Old-Timers Game last summer [1988]," says Qualls. "Actually, I wasn't invited. I just wanted to watch. They keep sending me literature, but I never send it back. I get a few calls too. Somehow people find me out here. Just over that one deal."

That "one deal" was the line single by Qualls on July 9, 1969, that broke up Tom Seaver's perfect game with one out in the ninth inning at Shea Stadium.

"I've got newspaper clippings, but I don't look at them. I remember I hit a fastball, and I hit it good. I've never heard from Seaver since, but I did see him running in the outfield at Wrigley Field the next trip into Chicago that same year. He ran past me and said, 'You little shit, you just cost me one million dollars.' "

Qualls hit .250 in 1969 playing in 43 games, mostly in center field, but four games at second base.

"I got my chance after Don Young got into the dog-house," recalls Qualls, who was a 5'10" 158-pound switch hitter. "I started the season with the big club, then went down for a month before coming back. They needed somebody at second base after Mike Shannon put Beckert in the hospital in that collision in St. Louis. I was doing OK until one day at Wrigley Field I ran into the wall and jammed my shoulder. By the time it had healed Leo had forgotten me. We had Oscar Gamble by then, and I think Jimmie Hall played some too.

"About us losing, well, I hate to second guess because I've seen the same thing happen to other teams, but our boys were so dad-gummed tired they couldn't walk in September. Bruno [Beckert] couldn't catch a grounder, and the boys on the bench who could have helped just sat there."

Former traveling secretary Blake Cullen tells a story about Qualls:

"He was headed off for two weeks of military duty, and we had to send the obligatory telegram to National League president Warren Giles telling him to put Jimmy on the military list. Well, it just so happened that singer Dean Martin's daughter, I think her name was Deana, was getting married that same day in Beverly Hills, and Leo wanted to send her a telegram too. Somehow we got the two wires switched. So here is Dean Martin at a party opening this telegram, and he says, 'I didn't even know we had a military list.' Meanwhile, Giles was getting a wire that said, 'Love and Kisses, Leo Durocher'—and he wasn't too thrilled about that either."

Qualls has been farming since. Every so often he sees ex-Cub Paul Reuschel, who owns a farm about 25 miles away. He never hears from Tom Seaver or Dean Martin.

Perhaps at age 55 Al Spangler's nickname is no longer Spanky. Certainly one who teaches algebra, coaches baseball, and serves as the athletic director at Hargrave High School, Huffman, Texas, a suburb of Houston, deserves more respect. "Mr. Spangler" will do nicely.

Spangler, who earned a mathematics degree from Duke

University before turning to professional baseball, played 82 games for the 1969 Cubs, more early than late, hitting .211 with 4 home runs and 23 RBI. His 13-year career (.262) was nearing its end, but he served as a coach with the Cubs in 1970 and 1971 and managed the organization's Double-A team in Midland, Texas, in 1972. He returned to Chicago to coach under Whitey Lockman in 1974, but when Whitey was fired and Jim Marshall ascended Spangler was out of a job.

"That's when I packed up my family and went home to Houston, never to be heard from again," he says.

He once had major league managerial ambitions but dreaded the travel. He says, "I've filed for permanent spectator status."

He does appear in a few Old Timers Games, for he was also an original member of the Houston Colt 45s and played in the first game in the Astrodome in 1965. He also participated in the Dream Game in Arizona when the Mets once again beat the Cubs. "We've now officially lost all over the world," comments Spangler.

These days he has the Hargrave Falcons humming on the diamond, and he even served as the architect and engineer when they built themselves a new baseball facility.

"And I still get five to ten letters a week from people wanting autographs on baseball cards," says Spangler. "Almost all of them are Cubs cards."

Richard Jay Selma, once known as "Moon Man" to Cubs teammates, now lives in Clovis, California, where he works for the Oklahoma-based Fleming Foods as a merchandiser. Dick, 46, works in the nonfoods division and serves a regular route of stores. He had also been serving as assistant baseball coach for Fresno City College but lost that job when there was a change in head coaches.

"I couldn't afford to take the head job, but with this job I make ends meet," says Selma.

Sure, he remembers 1969. Why wouldn't he? He was as memorable as the season. He remembers the pickoff play in

Philly, leading the Bleacher Bums in cheers, and, when it was all finished, getting traded.

"You don't see teams today like the 1969 Cubs. Look back position by position, and that was damned near an All-Star team. Other than Paul Popovich, though, we didn't have much flexibility off the bench, and I think after the season Leo decided he needed one more outfielder. That's when they went after Johnny Callison and I got traded." Along with Oscar Gamble, Selma went to the Phillies.

Selma was a star relief pitcher the next season in Philadelphia, saving 22 games and posting a record of 8–9 with a 2.75 ERA and earning Fireman of the Year honors. Yet with the Cubs, who were short on relief pitching, he had been a starter who faded in the stretch. What happened?

"I could throw harder than Nolan Ryan or Tom Seaver. We didn't have speed guns then, but that's what Johnny Stephenson said after he caught all of us with the Mets [Selma was a Met from 1965 through 1968]. I got off to a great start after coming to the Cubs in 1969. I think when Fergie and Holtzy had 11 wins, both Hands and I had 10. Then two things happened. After the All-Star break Leo looked at the schedule and decided he could use a three-man rotation some of the time. Well, then I would go 10 days without a start. Then we went into September, and he pitched me two days in a row. I got KO'd in the fourth inning of one game, and he brought me back the next day when Fergie's arm was sore. Then he did it again. I got knocked out in the first inning of one game, and he used me the next day. I lost every time."

Selma was 10–8 with the Cubs after coming in April from the Padres but 0–4 in September and loser of his last six decisions.

"I guess we proved one thing," says the man they called Moonie. "There is no such thing as a shoo-in."

Willie Smith has always lived in Anniston, Alabama. For several years after retiring from baseball, he worked for the parks and recreation department in the southern community. Now, however, in Willie's words, "I'm not doing nuthin' much, a little job, a little heavier . . . but I got big bones."

Actually, he works as a foreman in a Magic Chef microwave plant, still plays slow-pitch softball at age 50, and enjoys life with his wife and two children. He retired after the 1971 season but played two more years in Japan with the Nankai Hawks.

"But it was too far from Anniston, so I went home," he says.

Willie Smith was a combination court jester and good-luck charm with the Cubs. After joining them in late June 1968, the team got hot (20-7 in July). His home run to win the 1969 home opener, of course, provided one of the more memorable moments of the season.

And of his life.

"It will always stick in my mind. It played a big part in my life. Nobody will ever let me forget it, and that's OK because I don't want to forget. That's the first thing anybody ever says to me when they know who I am. I've been to a couple of Randy's camps, and they're great. It's just like a good ol' family reunion. That's the closest bunch of guys I've ever been associated with . . . and I've sure got more good memories than bad. The Mets were just unbelievable, that's all."

Willie certainly remembers Opening Day 1969, especially coming to home plate with a man on base in the 11th inning against Barry Lersch. He doesn't remember the count (it was 1-0), but he knew the ball "had a chance" when he drove it far toward Sheffield Avenue, winning the game for the Cubs 7-6. From there it was 155 days of first place, a record album featuring Willie's deep voice, and a lifetime of memories.

"The memories are only good," says Willie. "We were the team that should have won."

Surely in some language *Popovich* means smooth. He came from the rough country of West Virginia, but Popo played baseball with one motion, fluid. And the fact that offensively he had his career-best season in 1969 only accentuates the frustration of what happened.

Or didn't happen.

Paul Popovich should have played more.

He was the only Cub to hit above .300 (.312) but batted only 154 times, appearing in 48 games at second base, 10 at shortstop, 6 at third base, and, yes, even one in center field. ("Pete Reiser put me out there the day Leo took off for Camp Ojibway. I caught one fly ball OK, but I don't think I could have played there regularly.")

Most of Popo's appearances, however, were in mop-up or caddy roles; he also hit .370 as a pinch hitter. As a premier swing man, however, Popo was wasted, a utility man who wasn't utilized. But Popovich is a baseball man through and through—manager, coach, scout, and instructor over the past 11 seasons with the Dodgers organization—and you won't find him criticizing the decisions made 20 years ago by Durocher.

"Leo turned around the Chicago organization," says Popovich, 48, who served as the first-base and the third-base coach for the Vero Beach Dodgers (Class A) during the 1988 season. "So I have nothing negative to say about him. It wouldn't have hurt for him to give some of the guys a few days off, but he didn't. That wasn't Leo's way. My opinion is different than most: I think the Mets had the better team. Nobody wants to admit it, but it was true. Their pitching was awesome. I never felt we lost. The best team usually wins over the course of 162 games.

"I thought the Cubs' success in 1984 would make the '69 thing die out, but it didn't. How many guys are left from the 1984 team?"

Twenty years ago Hank Aguirre pitched for the Cubs.

Ten years ago he borrowed $350,000.

This year his company is expected to gross $35 million.

"I've been blessed," says Henry John Aguirre, 57, president of Mexican Industries in Michigan, Inc., the company he founded and owns.

It is a business success story that transcends his 16-year

major league career—an uplifting, I'll-be-damned tale about a gangly, left-handed son of a Mexican grocer from Azusa, California, who got rich giving jobs to other Mexicans.

Yet the dollars ("I'm making more money than I can ever spend") and accolades (National Hispanic Businessman of the Year) haven't replaced the emptiness left over from what happened in 1969.

"I am left with a lot of sorrow in my heart," says Aguirre, at one of Hundley's adult fantasy camps, where he comes to instruct and enjoy. "I think all the time about 1969 and how we self-destructed."

First, the success story, from the mouth of Aguirre, who never earned more than $37,500 a year as a pitcher:

"Like most ex-ballplayers I was wanting to do something and didn't know how to do it. But the minority entrepreneur system was there. Most people think it's a federally sponsored thing, but it isn't. It's a minority entrepreneurial system; in other words, for any company supplying the government there are set-asides to help minorities get their businesses started.

"We have been, as you know, a white, Anglo-Saxon, Protestant country, and our buddies in the country clubs control it. So there was a business move to help the minorities, and since my dad and mother were both born in Mexico I qualified.

"It was Opening Day of the 1979 baseball season in Detroit [where Aguirre pitched for 10 seasons], and at a party afterward I gave this idea to a friend of mine, a vice president with Volkswagen, to start a legitimate minority company and employ my own people. So he helped me. Volkswagen got me started.

"I went out and borrowed $350,000 through the Small Business Association, and that first year we did about $351,000 worth of business. By the third year I was minus-$290,000, and the bank refused to loan me any more money. We were in deep trouble. But we had just sold some new General Motors jobs, and we convinced the bank to stay with us.

"Well, we went from $351,000 that first year to a $26 million gross last year and a projection of a $35 million gross to June 30, 1989. And I'll tell you one thing, this company is not all owner operated. I've surrounded myself with people who are smarter than I am. We employ about 220 people, and 85 percent of them are Hispanics from the inner city of Detroit. We train some of them, and they run one hell of a company."

Doing what?

"We are what Ford calls a Q-1 company, which is the highest quality award given in the company supplier business. Mostly we make soft trim parts, vinyls, carpets, cloth parts for automobiles and trucks. You can look inside any car in any parking lot, and we've made something. We've been lucky, too, with some hot cars like the Ford Taurus. We also make that spare tire cover saying 'Jimmy' or 'Blazer' for GM's four-wheel Blazer downsize.

"Ford loves us because they like seeing all those Hispanic and black people in the plant. We've shown it can be done with your own people. It's just a super little company, and coming from East L.A. like I did, you're damned right I'm proud. In Detroit in 1974 I was dead busted, out of baseball, with nothing in my savings account. But I had a job, and I survived. Then I inquired about this loan, filled out all the papers, put my house up for collateral, and to this day the little Irish lawyer who helped me says, 'I don't know how we pulled this off.' "

Aguirre grew up in Azusa, in the eastern part of the San Gabriel Valley, and went to Alhambra High School where he was a cheerleader, and East L.A. Junior College, where he majored in music and wore his first baseball uniform. He wasn't good enough to make the high school team; the only baseball he ever played prior to college was with his brother in the backyard.

"The only reason I went to college was to keep from getting drafted into the Korean War. My dad was skeptical because, you know, Mexicans go to work, not to college. But except for books it was free, so he let me go, and I worked in his grocery store after class. Dad wouldn't even let me play semipro baseball on weekends. I had to work in the store.

"After my second year, though, I signed a pro contract for a $5,000 bonus and $200 a month. That was 1951 with the Cleveland Indians, and I was 19 years old. Some scout had seen me and said I had a major league arm. How in the world he saw that is beyond me. Anyhow, in those days you had to climb the minor league ladder; I pitched in Duluth, Bakersfield, Peoria, Reading, and Indianapolis before finally going up to Cleveland in 1955."

By the time the 6'4", 210-pound Aguirre reached Chicago 14 years later, he had pitched 1,317 innings in 389 games with the Indians from 1955–1957, the Tigers from 1958–1967, and the Dodgers in 1968. He was 37 years old but had posted a 0.69 ERA in 39 innings of spot duty the year before. Durocher wanted him. He saw him as a man for specific situations.

"There was no left-handed hitter alive that I couldn't get out. That's why I was always sorry I wasn't pitching to Willie Stargell that day he hit the home run to beat us. I couldn't throw a spitter worth a damn, but I still had a fairly good fastball, a slider on the outside corner, and a big curve. Once in a while I threw the screwball too but always to right-handed hitters. I thought Leo really did a great job of using me and Ted Abernathy . . . except for the last month of the season. That's when he just forgot us and kept going to Regan.

"We lost that pennant in 1969. I know the Mets were terrific, but we lost it. No doubt about that. I kept saying, 'It ain't over, boys,' but everybody was dead.

"We had some other problems too. Leo had a dilemma with Ernie Banks because he was such a hero. Leo felt restricted. Looking back, Ronnie [Santo] should have just zipped up his lip after that Don Young game, but mostly we had no dissension on that club in 1969."

That came later, after Aguirre had been released in mid-1970 but then called back by John Holland in 1971 to serve as the so-called information services coach. Translated, Aguirre was supposed to breach the widening communications gap between Durocher and his players.

"I failed miserably at that job," recalls Aguirre. "We had the talent too. I really think that 1972 club could have been the best of all of them."

He was on the Berkeley campus in the early '60s, talks regularly with animals, roomed with Don Young, makes parakeets and snakes feel better, and is considered an international authority on birds.

In other words, Rich Nye, doctor of veterinary medicine, is just a normal left-hander.

If your pet macaw has a sore throat, send him to Dr. Nye, partner in the Midwest Bird and Exotic Animal Hospital in the Chicago suburb of Westchester. But the doctor works only afternoons and weekends. He can be found in the mornings at the Chicago Mercantile Exchange, where he has membership as a broker ("If I'm ever going to retire, I've got to work hard now").

Now 44, Nye started the 1969 season as a member of the Cubs pitching rotation. The next year he pitched in both Montreal and St. Louis. Two years after that he was in graduate school at the University of Illinois, where he was a 1976 graduate of the College of Veterinary Medicine. Prior to his baseball career, Rich graduated in civil engineering from the University of California.

Obviously, he was overqualified to deal with Durocher, but Nye loved the challenge.

"It got to be a joke the way Leo would telephone the bullpen and tell Rube Walker, 'Get Regan up,' " says Nye. "He had forgotten everybody else. Sometimes Don Nottebart and I would start warming up on our own, just to get mentioned in the press box.

"The way Leo handled his pitchers in 1969 was chaotic. He simply didn't know his personnel. Regan must have gotten up 400 times. Joe Niekro and I actually started the season as fourth and fifth starters, then Joe got traded for Selma after they showcased him in April. I was actually better suited as a starter because I wasn't overpowering and control was my best asset. But I had only five starts all season.

"I remember this insane road trip in June. I hadn't been in a game in three weeks, but Hands got knocked out early in Atlanta and I ended up pitching the last 7⅔ innings, giving up one hit. Well, after that I pitched in almost every game on the trip. That was Leo's way. You didn't pitch at all or you pitched every day. So now we're in Pittsburgh for a doubleheader, and I was supposed to start game two. I was excited about it down in the bullpen the night before.

"Then the phone rings in the eighth inning, and Joe Becker is yelling, 'Nye, get loose!' Well, I threw six warm-up pitches and entered the game with a runner on base and Al Oliver at the plate. Wham, he hits a home run, we lose, and I didn't get to start the next day.

"But don't misunderstand me. I loved it that season. If we just could have won, my confidence would have gotten so much better. I was just 24 and hadn't really spent much time in the minor leagues. But I loved coming to the ballpark every day. The pain still comes to me that we lost. I felt it when we went to that Dream Game and I saw all the Mets with those rings on their fingers. To me that, not the lack of endorsements or money, is the epitome of pain. It would have been nice to have on the back of a bubble-gum card that I played with a winner. And we should have won. We had the horses."

Nye, who roomed on the road with rookie Young that season, still has strong feelings about what happened at Shea Stadium.

"Don shouldn't have been blamed for anything," he says. "Remember, we were still ahead 3-2 after he didn't catch those two balls, and neither one of them was charged as an error. And it wasn't Don Young who threw the next hanging slider to Cleon Jones—it was Fergie Jenkins."

Today Dr. Nye just worries about birds.

"I love my work. I love going to work every day, just like I loved going to the ballpark. But a routine just working with dogs and cats can get boring, so I wanted something unique. I wanted to establish myself as an authority." Dr Nye, a busy man, is also president of the Association of

Avian Veterinarians, an international group of two thousand that conducts research and exchanges information on birds of the world.

"Did you know some of these pet birds cost $15,000?" asks Nye. "There are more than 40 million pet birds in the U.S., and another eight hundred thousand are imported into this country every year. Those birds can also bring in a lot of exotic diseases. That's where I specialize.

"I also communicate well with animals. Especially small ones. We refer lions and tigers to other vets."

Wasn't there a lion named Leo?

For the past 15 winters Nate Oliver has worked as a station manager for Bay Area Rapid Transit (BART), has scouted and given baseball clinics for the Giants, and has done community relations work for the A's in Oakland, where he lives.

In the summers Nate Oliver, 48, gets back into the harness as manager of the Reno, Nevada, Silver Sox, an independent franchise of the Class A California League.

He wants to manage in the major leagues.

"I just need to find someone with the gall to hire a black, somebody to make the decision like Mr. Rickey did when he hired Jackie Robinson," says Nate. "The whole myth could be easily dispelled. Our big problem, just like Billy Williams had with the Cubs, is that we don't have anyone inside the buddy-buddy system. Jim Frey got in, and he hired his pal Don Zimmer. We have no clout inside, and that's how the system works."

Nate sang well with the Cubs of '69 ("Willie and I were the stars of the record album"), but the utility infielder didn't play much after coming from the Yankees in an April trade for minor leaguer Lee Elia.

"We had one of the great teams to be assembled in that era, but our problem was that nobody knew what to expect. Phil Regan and I were the only ones with any postseason experience [Oliver's was with the Dodgers in 1966], and when we'd have meetings the other guys would ask, 'What's wrong, what's happening?,' and I would say, 'The problem is that you've been reading everything people have been writing. We weren't as great as everyone said we were, now we're not as bad as that either.'

"The truth is that we ran the flag up the pole too soon. No doubt about it. We celebrated too soon. The entire season was a blast, but when I think about 1969 I think about the agony of defeat."

He was the baby of the team, and answers always come easily to the young. Therefore Oscar Gamble, still just thirtysomething, knows exactly what happened to his '69 classmates:

"No way those old guys could play in that heat that long."

Gamble lives in Montgomery, Alabama, his hometown, and was expecting to work during the spring of 1989 as a hitting instructor with the Auburn University-at-Montgomery baseball team under another ex-Cub, Q. V. Lowe.

"I had a nightclub but got out of that business," says Gamble. "I'm raising a family now and thinking of starting a complex with batting cages. I enjoy counseling kids and teaching them how to hit."

Oscar could hit. In 16 major league seasons with seven clubs, he hit 196 home runs, played in 1,514 games, compiled a lifetime average of .268, and made a lot of money, once signing a then-blockbuster $3 million, six-year contract with the Padres, thanks to free agency.

But in 1969 he was a baby who got into trouble. The Cubs had signed him out of high school, prepared him less than one season in the minors, then added him to the roster in late August so that he would be eligible for postseason play.

"I looked up and I was in the big leagues," he says. "Actually I had a shot during spring training that year, but being just out of high school I think Leo was afraid I wasn't ready."

Yet Durocher went to Gamble in September. Oscar played in 24 games, hit .225, and had one home run with five RBI.

"They told me I was their centerfielder for the next 10 years. Then after the season they sent me to the instructional league, and one day in November a guy comes up and says, 'You've been traded to the Philadelphia Phillies.' I didn't understand. I was young. I sure didn't understand how they could trade me after telling me all that stuff about playing center field for the next 10 years."

Had Gamble heard the rumors that his trade came because he angered both Holland and Durocher by dating white girls?

"No, and I can't imagine that. I just thought it was because Leo needed to make a change after losing and thought getting Johnny Callison would do it. Hey, I was just young and innocent and having a lot of fun. I do remember there were a lot of girls around. I can't lie about that. Billy Williams came to me once and said Leo wanted me to cool it dating all those 18-year-old girls. But I was only 19 myself. I guess Leo was just trying to protect me.

"I've always wondered, what would have happened if I had played all those years in Wrigley Field. I could have piled up some bundle of home runs. But remember that picture they ran of me in one of the newspapers—the new bachelor in town looking out from my terrace over the city? That's what got me into trouble because the article gave my address. Man, that phone never stopped ringing. Every time I walked out the door there was another cute girl.

"But I had never heard that story about why I was traded. I knew they couldn't blame losing the pennant on me. They lost because a lot of old guys got tired in that heat. And besides, if that's why I was traded, how come they sent off Dick Selma in the same deal?

"Was he traded for messin' with some black girl?"

Mark Randall Bobb, known as Randy, was killed in June 1982 in a vehicle accident near Lake Tahoe, California. Bobb, then 34, had gone on a fishing trip to the Truckee River with his father, William, and one other man when the station wagon driven by Randy went out of control and crashed, killing Bobb and his passenger. The senior Bobb had remained back at the campground.

Randy was only 21 when called up by the Cubs in September 1969, and he was zero for two, including a pinch-hit strikeout against Jerry Koosman in the ninth inning of the Cubs' controversial 3–2 loss at Shea Stadium on September 8. His claim to baseball fame: when sent into his first game against Cincinnati on August 18, 1968, Bobb, a catcher, threw out Pete Rose trying to steal second base, and the throw came on the first major league pitch Randy ever caught.

He was traded to the Mets on March 29, 1970, for 33-year-old catcher J. C. Martin. Bobb, a product of San Fernando Valley, California, and the 1967 Arizona State team that won the College World Series, labored in the Mets and White Sox organizations after leaving the Cubs but never returned to the major leagues.

Don Nottebart was a member of what Cubs pitchers called the Dead Man Brigade. Once you gained membership it was difficult to escape. Inactivity, however, did not soften the memory or the opinions of Don Nottebart.

"I won a game in relief for the Cubs on May 14 against San Diego and lost one in Houston on May 17, and that's all I pitched, baby," says Nottebart. "Leo forgot me. He had some guys he would use and that was all. He forgot Aguirre, Nye, Abernathy, Colborn, and me. He tried to win the damned pennant with six guys. I just sat there and watched it go down the tubes. I had to sit there and watch all that shit. I wasted my entire last year of baseball on the Cubs bench."

Nottebart, 53, a nine-year veteran of the major leagues, now lives with his family in Houston (where he once pitched) and owns two retail carpet stores. He admits he once considered staying in baseball as a coach but departed because "coaches have to kiss ass, and I wasn't very good at that."

"I liked Durocher, I really did. He just didn't have a clue about handling the bullpen. Joe Becker was a good pitching coach, but Leo wouldn't listen to him. He got me that spring from the Yankees because he said he needed another veteran in the bullpen. They didn't have to give up much [minor league infielder Jim Armstrong plus cash], but they sure didn't get their money's worth."

Nottebart, whose career record was 36–51, appeared in 16 games with the Cubs, pitched 28 innings for an ERA of 7.00 and a record of 1–1. But the 6'1" right-hander says he had a good view of the season:

"It doesn't leave my mind. I sit here at home year after year and remember. We should have *won it*. What I think you really can't print. I saw some gutless sons of bitches who couldn't handle the pressure, that's what I saw. Banks and Williams were terrific. So were Hundley, Hickman, and Hands. Regan held up too, but you know the guys who folded. It's something those guys have to live with. They weren't winners.

"I especially remember this one clubhouse meeting when Leo was really pissed. A couple of guys were tired and couldn't get to batting practice on time, but they had time to play golf, make speeches, and sign autographs. Leo really chewed their asses. They thought they had it won.

"I didn't do shit to help. I was healthy through August too. Then in September I was running through the outfield and pulled a muscle in my bad leg, the left one, so I wasn't able to pitch in September. But it wouldn't have mattered. He wasn't going to use me. I kept asking myself, 'Why trade for me and not use me?'

"I still remember Aguirre warming up when Leo left Regan in the game to pitch to Stargell. That home run started it. Then we went on the road to New York, and the ump blew that play at home on Agee. We were dead meat."

Gene Oliver ran a restaurant-bar for a while, but that didn't work. He did some radio broadcasting for high school sports, worked in a clothing store, almost bought an automobile agency, then decided just to take his pension and sell cars for somebody else.

Mostly, though, Oliver, 53, is a camp instructor par excellence. He can stand in the middle of a baseball locker room and call bank presidents idiots and make them love it.

Since Randy Hundley began his adult fantasy camps six years ago, Ollie has become a fixture. His ribald humor, confidential manner, and repertoire of anecdotes—not to mention his ability to transmit fundamental baseball knowledge to novices—makes Oliver a natural first lieutenant.

"I've done all but one of Randy's camps, so what's that, 32 or 33? Hey, they helped put my kids through college," says Ollie. "When he called in 1983 I thought he was strokin' us. Dallas Green had just fired all of us . . . Billy, Randy, Ernie, me, because I guess he just wanted to eradicate all memories of 1969. He tried, but he couldn't do it. Anyhow, Randy calls and says, 'Want to go to spring training again?' I thought he was crazy, but I came, and look what this has become. Either they like us or it's a great vacation. Or maybe somehow Randy struck a chord. Maybe the love affair between Chicago and the '69 Cubs is real.

"People who come go back home with different management styles. They learn it's not bad to be a nice guy. They start treating their own people differently. The biggest thing, I guess, is that they learn that everyone puts on their shoes the same way. They leave here with a greater respect for what we did for a living."

Oliver contributed little to the Cubs of '69, and he knows it. A catcher–first baseman with no speed playing the final season of his career, Oliver appeared behind the plate only six times and batted just 27 times, getting six hits and striking out nine times. He was Santo's buddy, though, and tried to become a positive force within the locker room. Finally, on September 2, Oliver was removed from the active-player list and made a coach.

"Being a journeyman you do what you can. All I know is that I didn't lose the pennant."

Oliver still smarts over postseason criticism of his role with the team. He felt it branded him and kept him "out of baseball" at a time when one more year was crucial to his pension status. "If I could have caught on in 1970 and gotten that one more year, I could have waited until I was

62 to take my pension instead of taking it when I was 48. I figured out the difference to be $542,000."

Ollie's thoughts on 1969:

"We knew with 40-some games to play that if we played .500 ball the Mets would have to go something like 30 and 10. Well, they did better than that, and we didn't play .500. I dunno, maybe we got too conservative. If Leo could do it over again, I'm sure he would have utilized his bench differently.

"I do know this: The Mets were a lot younger. I don't think we realized how much until we played that Dream Game a few years ago. I looked around and thought, 'This isn't fair.' "

Cubs fans, pay attention. Of all the people in this book, Jim Colborn may play the most significant role in the *future* of the Cubs franchise.

Colborn, 43, is minor league coordinator of instruction for the Cubs organization and sees shining light at the end of the tunnel. An oncoming train? Colborn doesn't think so.

"Our minor league teams are solid all the way down to the Midwest League [the Class A team in Peoria]," he says. "We have a lot of good young players on their way up. I can see at least two new players being ready for the major leagues during each of the next four or five years. And we've already sent some good ones up."

Colborn, a psychology graduate in college, is in his sixth year with the Cubs organization and believes he will stay in baseball. Indeed, he should be listed among those with strong managerial credentials.

"I do think I'd rather stay in uniform on the field. I already tried it as an owner."

Colborn, former Dodger Ken McMullen, and one other partner owned the Ventura County Gulls in the California League a few years ago, but, unable to secure a field where they could play games at night, sold the team, which now performs in San Bernardino.

Colborn, then a 6'0", 185-pound right-handed rookie

pitcher, played a minimal role with the 1969 Cubs (1-0 in six games, including two starts, with an ERA of 3.00). Yet past is prologue, and surely Colborn's unhappy experiences as a young player contribute to the sensitivity and understanding he takes into his own work today.

After three frustrating and nonproductive seasons under Leo (1-0, 3-1, and 0-1), Colborn went to the Milwaukee Brewers and in 1973 posted a record of 20-12. In fact, he won 68 games in five seasons after leaving Chicago in the trade that brought Jose Cardenal to the Cubs.

Colborn stood for everything Durocher couldn't understand and hated.

"Leo tried to bury me. I can remember after the trade saying to myself, 'What a load off my mind.' It's hard enough playing baseball, but when you have to overcome another obstacle, a man on your own team trying to run down your confidence and ego, it's really hard. I was beginning to wonder if baseball had closed me out."

Even today Colborn has difficulty putting 1969 into perspective.

"As a baseball man, I can say this: a lot of people in baseball learned a lesson from 1969 and have paid attention to what happened. The day games in the heat, utilization of the bench, everything. Playing with the Cubs was a different world. I remember Billy Williams once telling me that he had to be in bed by 9 o'clock at night to keep up his strength.

"And I remember in September when word came that the Mets had just beaten Pittsburgh in a doubleheader, both Don Kessinger and Ernie Banks said to me, 'We're beat. We can't win it.' And we were only 2½ games back at the time.

"Now I realize just how much sacrifice it takes to wear a championship ring. But you can't say those men in 1969 were losers. You just can't say that. How can some people be winners and some losers? I'd say 95 percent of major league ballplayers are winners."

Colborn has never forgotten when he first reported to Durocher in the Cubs clubhouse. The conversation went like this:

"OK, kid, where do you keep it?"

"What?"

"Where do you keep it? I've got to know if I'm gonna protect you."

"What are you talking about, sir?"

Durocher then turned to one of the coaches and asked in stage whisper, "Isn't this the hard-throwing reliever up from Tacoma who throws a spitter?"

Already Colborn, who did not throw a spitter, was in trouble. And the animosity grew—even before Colborn called Leo a viper during a clubhouse meeting.

"Once I was standing near the end of the dugout cheering for the guys on the field, and Leo came down and stood in front of me. So I moved two feet and he moved two feet. Finally he bumped me, acted like it was an accident, and said to somebody, 'Get this kid hurt.' He was mad because I was cheering. I got into trouble one other time in the Houston Astrodome because I caught the infield warm-up ball. Leo was superstitious, you see, and nobody on the bench was supposed to catch the infield ball except Nate Oliver. Well, I reached up instinctively and grabbed it, and he started yelling, 'Tell that fuckin' kid to drop that ball.' Well, I dropped it and went down to the end of the bench, and, one by one, the veterans and coaches came down and said, 'You didn't really catch that ball, did you?' They were giving me the treatment.

"My trouble, I guess, was that I was so young and sensitive. I could see the dissension growing on the club over the next two seasons . . . first the little snips of conversation, then the whispering, then open conversation against Leo at dinner, then on the field during batting practice, and finally the outbreak in the locker room. I thought it was tragic, but now as I look back I guess it was all pretty normal."

Ted Abernathy's trademark was the submarine pitch, an unorthodox, up-from-the-shoetops, right-handed delivery he developed in the minor leagues in 1956 after an elbow injury. And by the time he reached Chicago in 1969 for his second tour of duty with the Cubs, relief specialist Ted Abernathy had already been a professional ballplayer for 17 years.

Today, at age 56, he is a "receiving man" for Summey Products, a Dallas, North Carolina, company that makes module homes and roof rafters. Abby lives in nearby Gastonia, just 16 miles from Stanley, the North Carolina community where he was born and raised.

"At one time I tried to get back into baseball as a coach, but I failed," says Abernathy. "I tried for about five years, calling everybody I knew, but finally gave up and decided to stay home. Now I don't want to go back, but I enjoy Old-Timers Games.

"Doggone, the 1969 season was the closest I ever came to the World Series, and it was really tough. But in those days the players had no say in anything. Everything had to be Leo's way, and he just wore poor ol' Phil Regan out. He plum forgot Hank Aguirre and me the second half of the season. I pitched my best when my arm was real tired—that's when the submarine sinker worked best, and I also had mastered the rising fastball—but my arm sure didn't get very tired that year."

Abby, who came to the Cubs in January 1969 in a trade from Cincinnati for catcher Bill Plummer, first baseman Clarence Jones, and a minor league pitcher, appeared in 56 games, pitching 85 innings for a 4-3 record, three saves, and a 3.18 ERA.

"I saw what was happening in 1969. I was Don Kessinger's roommate, and he was hitting .300 most of the year. Then he just plain wore out. Leo should have used his bench, but it wasn't his way and he was the boss. I'm not mad at Leo though. Heck, I saw him at that Dream Game, and we were laughing about the time I got so mad at him. He had insisted I throw a 3-2 fastball to Willie Stargell—I called him Cousin Willie because he hit me so hard—and when I did, fastball low and away, Stargell hit a double that went about 400 feet. When the inning was over, Leo yelled at me in the dugout: 'It was the right pitch. You just threw it in the wrong place!' Then Randy Hundley piped up and said, 'No he didn't, Leo.'

"Well, after the game Leo called me into his office and apologized and said, 'Go out to dinner with me tonight,' so I did. Leo was like that."

Bill Heath broke his finger in the last major league game he caught ("the twilight of a horseshit career"), the 1969 no-hitter by Ken Holtzman. Since then almost everything has gone considerably better for William C. Heath, certified financial planner. His is another story of success.

Heath, 50, chief executive officer and president of the Center for Financial Planning, was a graduate of the University of Southern California who studied accounting through a correspondence course while playing major league baseball. He then became an auditor for Price Waterhouse & Company, attained his MBA from the University of Houston, and in 1972 founded his own Houston firm with California branch offices in Sacramento and Fresno.

"In the profession of financial planning I'm probably one of the leaders," he says. "We have a different approach at our company. We start with a fee."

Does he do financial planning and tax work for athletes?

"I try not to. They're worse clients than doctors. I remember what I was like when I was young—irresponsible and egotistical. One of the biggest problems you have with athletes is they're pampered all the time. In recent years, though, I have worked with some Houston Oilers players on planning second careers."

Heath was not a great catcher (four teams, four seasons, a .236 batting average) but did pride himself on calling pitches.

"That's what was so frustrating about breaking my finger in the seventh inning of that no-hitter. I'd been in the lineup quite a bit since Hundley hurt his thumb on August 12, and our pitchers hadn't allowed many runs. I always thought if Randy had any weakness it was calling pitches. I was mainly kept around as a left-handed pinch hitter and backup catcher. Now I was finally getting to play, and damned if I didn't break my right index finger on a foul tip. Gene Oliver had to come in and finish catching the no-hitter."

Heath, who remained with the 1969 club for the balance of the season without being activated, recalls what he saw from the end of the Cubs' bench:

"I watched the whole gory thing. It wasn't sad, it was stupid. You could see what was happening, everybody getting tighter and tighter and nobody doing anything about it. Leo Durocher went into a trance.

"Somebody should have kicked butt. It was really sad to see somebody like Kessinger missing those ground balls; Beckert too. It's not that they didn't want to win, but the harder we tried the worse we got. Sometimes I think it was tougher on those of us on the bench who had to watch.

"I know I wasn't there long, but I would love to see those guys again, all of them. But they never invite the rinky-dinks to Old-Timers Games or fantasy camps. I'd just like to see them, not to get back on the field, just to see the guys."

Archie Reynolds never won a game in the major leagues. He tried hard, he really did, over parts of five seasons with the Cubs, the Angels, and the Brewers. But the big (6'2", 205-pound), affable right-hander from Tyler, Texas, never won a game (he was 0–8), and if you want a free drink at his nightclub don't bring up the subject.

Archie, 43, lives in Burleson, Texas, about 14 miles south of Fort Worth, but his club, Archie's, is located in Azle, northwest of Ft. Worth.

"It's in the boonies, but a lot of people go there," says Reynolds. "I also own some land with my dad in East Texas, so I go there some and piddle too. But my wife and I are sure proud of Archie's. It's not one of those country-western places. We're real rock & roll."

Archie has done other things.

After leaving baseball in 1972, he struck out on his own in the Louisiana oil fields, eventually landing a job with

Otis Engineering, a division of Halliburton, testing oil and gas wells in Saudi Arabia, where he spent five years.

"That was nothin' after tryin' to pitch for Leo."

Archie started two games for the '69 Cubs, pitching only seven innings and acquiring a 2.57 ERA before being returned to Tacoma in mid-June. He never came back that season and was traded the following July to the Angels for Juan Pizarro.

That winter Archie (nickname: Wahoo) told the Cubs he wanted to be traded.

"I just wanted to go anywhere to get away from Leo. I couldn't get out of his doghouse. I could never get a straight answer from him. We all compared him to George Allen of football because he'd rather go with a 40-year-old veteran than a kid with potential. I was warming up once in 1970 to start a game against Nolan Ryan of the Mets, and he walked past and said to Joe Becker, real loudlike out of the side of his mouth, 'If the first guy gets on, go to the bullpen.' "

That was enough for Reynolds, who headed for the oil fields.

Now he says, "Tell all the guys about Archie's. It's a family-type night club, not your big-type club like Billy Bob's or Gilley's. And we don't have any trouble. I'm the bouncer too."

After considering Adolfo Phillips, Don Young, Jimmy Qualls, Rich Bladt, Oscar Gamble, and even Paul Popovich (for one game) and Jim Hickman for center field, the Cubs tried Jimmie Hall, a left-handed-hitting journeyman acquired on September 11, 1969, from the Yankees.

That didn't help either. Hall played in 11 games, hit .208, and was sold to Atlanta in early 1970.

Hall, 51, is now semiretired in Wilson, North Carolina, where he works some for a trucking company but mostly finds himself "takin' life easy."

"I haven't done much of anything since leaving baseball in 1971," he says. "When you're done, you're done. I hunt and fish a lot, and I watch a lot of sports on TV. I wouldn't go back to baseball if I was offered a coaching job. I'd hate to be telling some kid on the field what he was doin' wrong and have him say, 'Who the hell do you think you are?' I don't begrudge these kids the money they're making today, but a lot of them don't know how to play the game. At least I knew what I could do."

Hall played eight seasons in the major leagues with the Twins, the Angels, the Indians, the Yankees, the Cubs, and the Braves—a left-handed hitter with power (121 homers), defensive ability, and an average bat (.254).

"But I came too late to help the Cubs in 1969. They had a pretty good club, I guess, but the Mets were better, and that's what counts."

The thing Dave Lemonds remembers most about 1969 is the number he wore, 48.

"It must have been the uniform which fit all sizes," he says, "because I wore it, and Jim Colborn wore it, and Archie Reynolds wore it. One would come up from the minors, another would go down, and uniform number 48 was always there waiting for the next guy. I always figured that Durocher felt that whoever was wearing number 48 couldn't pitch."

Lemonds, 40, lives in Charlotte, North Carolina, and works as a regional sales manager for Marion Laboratories, the pharmaceutical company founded by Kansas City Royals owner Ewing Kauffman. Lemonds, who has been in the "medical business" since 1975, covers the eastern portion of the United States.

The left-hander had been signed by the Cubs out of the University of North Carolina and spent less than a full season in the minor leagues before getting his call in 1969.

"I came up on the first day of June and sat on the bench for 20 days. Finally, on the last day of June I got to start a game, the night Ernie Banks hit a home run that didn't count because the ump said it went through a hole in the fence. Well, I got the loss in that game, and three days later I was sent back down and somebody else got to wear number 48."

For the record: Lemonds pitched five innings in two games, had an ERA of 3.60, and never pitched again for the Cubs. He was traded in 1970 to the White Sox, where he finally got to pitch some in 1971 before his career was ended prematurely by a freak injury.

"Following the 1972 season I was in Ponce, Puerto Rico, pitching in winter ball, and one day I was taking out the trash from my high-rise apartment, pushed open the metal door, and it swung back to hit me on the elbow. The ulna nerve was damaged, and I never made it back.

"I really can't identify with what happened to the '69 Cubs, but I always thought I had something to offer that they didn't accept. My minor league pitching instructor, Fred Martin, told them I could throw harder than Kenny Holtzman, but Leo had no tolerance for young pitchers. He only trusted experience."

When Leo Durocher "backed up the truck" one day, Rich Bladt got off. When the truck left, Rich got on again. He left with some bitterness.

Bladt, 42, now lives and works in rural Mount Angel, Oregon, as a carpenter. He does not identify with the 1969 Cubs. He says he wouldn't walk across the street to shake hands with Leo Durocher ("Is he still alive?") or Ron Santo. He claims he remembers P. K. Wrigley coming into the Cubs clubhouse to give Don Young a new contract after the Incident in New York. That didn't happen.

Nevertheless, his claim reflects (a) how time can play havoc with a man's memory and (b) how unhappy Bladt's experience in major league baseball was.

He came up from Tacoma in June 1969 when Qualls had to leave for his military obligation (or was it to attend the birthday party of Dean Martin's daughter?). Bladt, a 6'1", 160-pound right-handed hitter, played in 10 games, mostly in center field, and hit .154 (2 of 13). That was it. After the season he was traded to the Yankees organization, where he spent the next six years buried in the minor leagues before getting another shot in 1975, when he played 52 games for the Yankees.

"All in all, I spent 11½ years in the minor leagues, 8½ in Triple A. Then when I finally did get back up, I got caught up in the George Steinbrenner–Billy Martin–Bill Virdon transition. Then I coached some in the Baltimore organization but finally got out after the 1977 season [with a career average .215] while I still had some pride left.

"I guess what I remember most about the 1969 season was Leo Durocher calling Kenny Holtzman a gutless Jew in front of other players. Then when I went back to Tacoma I remember my teammates saying, 'The Cubs are going to make it.' And I said, 'No way, not after the things I saw.' "

Charley Smith batted twice as a pinch hitter with the '69 Cubs and never came to the plate again in the major leagues.

Smith, 51, now works as a senior maintenance man for the streets department of the city of Sparks, Nevada. He also lives in Sparks, a suburb of Reno.

"It's a place I chose to live after playing minor league ball with the Reno Silver Sox," says Smith, a native of Charleston, South Carolina, a true journeyman who played with the Dodgers, the Phils, the White Sox, the Mets, the Cardinals, and the Yankees before finding the Wrigley Field truck stop. Smith, in fact, would provide somebody with an excellent trivia question: What player was traded for Dick Farrell, Joe Koppe, Roy Sievers, Chico Fernandez, Roger Maris, and Ken Boyer?

The answer is Smith, right-handed-hitting third baseman with nine years of major league experience and a lifetime batting average of .239, with 69 homers, who came to the Cubs on March 29, 1969, from San Francisco, where he never actually played. For that matter, he didn't actually *play* with the Cubs either. He had serious knee problems, and the Cubs quickly shipped him to Tacoma, where his professional career came to a close.

Smith has no opinion to offer about how or why the Cubs lost the pennant, and one can understand why.

The assistant baseball coach at Louisiana College, Pineville, Louisiana, does have an opinion. His name is Ken Johnson, and 1969 was his last full season in the major leagues. He was 36 when the Cubs acquired him and his knuckleball from the Yankees in August of that season, Durocher once again turning to veteran help for his bullpen.

His opinion: "Obviously, I don't have all the answers. But as a coach I have to look at one key thing: the head-to-head competition between the Cubs and Mets. When they beat us it gave them the momentum to keep on going. And you saw what it did to us."

Johnson appeared in nine games as a middle reliever for the Cubs, pitched 19 innings for a 2.84 ERA, had a record of 1–2, and was credited with one save. One season later, after being released from the Cubs, he played briefly with the young Expos, then retired from a 13-year career with 91 wins and 106 losses.

How did Johnson end up in Pineville?

"Both of my sons played college baseball here, and after visiting them I fell in love with the area and just stayed as assistant baseball coach at the college. It's an NAIA school of about 1,200 students, but we've done well with our baseball program in the Gulf Coast Conference."

Johnson, 56, has lost touch with members of the '69 team but used to occasionally show up for an Old-Timers Game in Houston, Cincinnati, or Atlanta, all places where he pitched.

"But that was before Equitable took over the Old-Timers Games," he says. "I guess I wasn't a big enough star to be included anymore."

If you're ever driving south on Interstate 5 from Los Angeles toward San Diego and feeling thirsty, take the Santa Fe exit at the sleepy coastal town of Encinitas and pull into the first liquor store in sight. That'll be Santa Fe Liquors, and you'll know it's the right place when you see baseball pictures on the wall.

Gary Ross, 41, owns and operates the establishment, and he needn't apologize that most of the pictures include people wearing San Diego Padres uniforms. After all, that's where the Cubs sent him when they acquired Dick Selma in April 1969.

As a 6'1" hard-throwing right-hander, Ross started one game for the Cubs that year, but it was obviously a showcase appearance on April 22 in a doubleheader against Pittsburgh. Ross and another showcaser, young Joe Niekro, were dispatched to San Diego three days later in the trade for Selma.

Ross, incidentally, compiled a 13.50 ERA in his two innings of work with the Cubs, but things improved. He lasted 10 seasons in the major leagues and compiled a record of 25-47.

"Leo always seemed to be mad at me," he says. "I never understood why. I'll never forget one game in 1968 when I was pitching against the Giants, and he was so mad because I wasn't hiding the ball in my glove. So he kept yelling to the Giants what I was throwing—but they still couldn't hit me."

After the trade did Ross get to pitch against the '69 Cubs?

"Yeah, as a matter of fact, Fergie Jenkins beat me 2-0 in Wrigley Field the next month. But don't forget, I was 3-12 that year, and we were an expansion team. Everybody beat us."

He won 221 games in the major leagues, 1 with the 1969 Cubs, 196 after leaving.

Why was Joe Niekro traded?

"I still don't know," says Niekro, 44, who finally walked off the mound in 1988 to serve as the pitching coach for the Portland Beavers of the Pacific Coast League.

"Leo wouldn't let him throw the knuckleball, and his other stuff wasn't that good," recalls ex-traveling secretary Cullen. "Holland hated knuckleball pitchers."

"I didn't have a knuckleball then," says Niekro.

"Leo got rid of Joe because he always looked nervous on the mound, fidgeting with his cap," says one ex-Cub starting pitcher, "and Leo told Joe Becker, 'Get him out of here.' "

"If that's true," says Niekro, "I guess they would have gotten rid of Gaylord Perry too."

For whatever reasons, Niekro went with Ross and minor leaguer Francisco Libran to San Diego on April 25, 1969, in the trade for Selma. This was not a case of Durocher dealing away an unknown quantity. Niekro had posted records of 10–7 and 14–10 under Leo in the previous two seasons. With the pitiful Padres in 1969, he finished 8–18, and his career didn't really soar until eight years later, when he started winning regularly with his flutterball in Houston, where he won 127 games from 1977 to 1984.

Niekro was using just a fastball and a slider in 1969, when he made three early-season starts for the Cubs, pitched 18 innings, and ended up with a record of 0–1 and a 3.72 ERA. Durocher's five-man rotation when the Cubs broke spring training: Jenkins, Holtzman, Hands, Niekro, and Nye.

Later that season Niekro pitched against the Cubs and lost 1–0 on a ninth-inning home run by Santo. The Padres swapped Niekro to Detroit following that season, and he then pitched for the Tigers, the Braves, the Astros, and the Twins before being released in May 1988.

Knuckleball pitchers, however, are never ready to admit it's time to quit.

"I enjoyed being a pitching coach," says Niekro, "but I won't rule out a pitching comeback in 1989."

John Hairston, 43, teaches school and coaches baseball in Portland, Oregon. He is another who only briefly experienced the 1969 season with the Cubs.

"I didn't even have a cup of coffee," says Hairston, whose brother, Jerry, plays with the White Sox. "I was just the cream in somebody's coffee."

John was called up to the majors in late August when

Jimmy Qualls went on the disabled list with an injured right shoulder; he was returned to Tacoma two weeks later after batting just four times (one hit—a double) in three games.

That was it. Upon return to Tacoma he suffered a serious knee injury that eventually ended his professional career.

"If that hadn't happened I think I would have become Randy Hundley's backup," said catcher Hairston, whose father, Sam, also played briefly in the major leagues (with the Chisox in 1951). "Leo Durocher liked me."

Just two years out of high school, an excited Alec Distaso found himself breaking spring training 1969 as a member of the Cubs pitching staff. But in mid-April the kid from Wilson High School, Los Angeles, hurt his arm pitching during a doubleheader in near-freezing weather in Montreal. Nevertheless, two days later he pitched during another doubleheader again in Pittsburgh.

He never appeared in another major league game.

Distaso, 40, now a detective with the Rampart Division of the Los Angeles Police Department, still refers to 1969 as "the biggest disappointment of my life."

"After I hurt my arm they sent me down to San Antonio, and it kept getting worse," he says. "I bounced around the minor league system for the next two seasons and finally got released during spring training 1971.

"So I came home and became a cop. The old locker-room mentality got me, I guess. I wanted to be outside, part of the action, part of a team. I've been with the L.A.P.D. for 17 years, the last eight as a detective."

The record shows that Alec Distaso, a 6'2", 190-pound right-hander, pitched a total of five innings with the Cubs, allowing six hits, two earned runs, one walk, and one strikeout. That was it. Good-bye, Alec.

"I've never felt any shame not making it, but I really believe I could have stuck around if I hadn't hurt my arm. I remember giving up a double to Roberto Clemente in Pittsburgh. A lot of guys never got that far."

Of the 17 pitchers who walked to the mound for the Cubs during the 1969 season, Distaso is perhaps least remembered. "But I bought a car the other day from a Jeep dealer, and the guy said, 'Didn't you play with the Chicago Cubs?' I was impressed."

On the bench in 1969 watching Randy Hundley strive against the Mets was a 22-year-old rookie catcher named Ken Rudolph.

Eighteen years later Hundley's son, also a catcher, signed a pro contract out of high school with the Mets.

And one more year later, the summer of 1988, Rudolph's son, also a catcher, signed a pro contract out of high school, also with the Mets.

Todd Hundley, meet Mason Rudolph. May both of you win.

"It is kind of interesting," reflects the elder Rudolph, 42, an operations manager with United Parcel Service in Tempe, Arizona. "The Mets drafted Mason and made such a good offer he couldn't turn it down." The younger Rudolph is a 6'1", 195-pound right-handed hitter and was all-everything at Dobson High School in Mesa. His 12-year-old sister, Kelly, is a regionally ranked tennis player.

It's a wonder the Mets haven't also signed catchers named Heath, Oliver, Hairston, and Bobb. Amazingly, the Cubs did use six catchers in 1969.

"I never could figure that one out," says Ken Rudolph. "Other than three weeks away from the club for National Guard and a week to get back into playing shape, I spent the entire season with the big club. But every time I looked around somebody else had a catcher's mitt. Gene Oliver had major league experience, but he spent most of the season in the bullpen with a scorecard and sunglasses."

Rudolph caught in only eleven games that year and played outfield in three others, hitting .206 (7 of 34). He eventually spent nine-plus seasons in the majors with the Cubs, the Giants, the Cardinals, the Giants again, and the Orioles, finishing with a career batting average of .213.

"In retrospect, I was so young I was just glad to be there,"
says Rudolph, "and it wasn't until much later that I realized
what a shame it was that we didn't win."

And why didn't they win?

"Physical fatigue. Our guys just couldn't get it up in
September. Leo had All-Stars at most positions, but they got
tired. Heck, Randy lost so much weight he had to start
wearing suspenders.

"I'm a firm believer that 25 men are on a team for a
purpose. But we didn't serve that purpose with the Cubs.
We just sat there and watched everything happen."

In recent years Joe Decker coached with the Salt Lake
City Trappers and the Boise Hawks, but in 1988 Decker, 41,
finally walked away from baseball. He remained in Idaho
and now serves the Northwest as a sales representative for a
company that distributes videocassettes.

Joe doesn't have a video of the time he was fined $100 by
Leo Durocher—the only fine Leo ever collected from a
member of the Cubs. No audio either: it was X-rated.

The year was 1970, the Cubs were in the throes of a 12-
game losing streak in late June, and when Durocher walked
to the mound in St. Louis to remove pitcher Decker, the
young right-hander responded with what Leo described as
"defiance."

"Eyeball to eyeball," said Leo at the time, "he defied me. I
told him to stand there until the relief pitcher arrived. So
what did he do? He turned his back on me and walked
away."

Decker was an angry young man with the Cubs but a
young man with immense talent.

He appeared in only four games (1-0, 3.00 ERA) after
joining the Cubs in September of 1969, getting one start on
September 18 when the Mets already had a five-game lead.
He lasted another three seasons (2-7, 3-2, 1-0) wearing a
Cub uniform but never came to terms with himself or
Durocher. He was traded following the 1972 season, along
with Bill Hands, to the Twins for Dave LaRoche.

At least in the American League the hard-throwing right-hander got to pitch. He posted a record of 16–14 with the Twins in 1974, but it was his only season in the sun. He finished a nine-year career with a record of 36–44.

And looking back, that mound incident in 1970—an incident that Durocher obviously created to use the rookie pitcher as a scapegoat to detract from the 12-game losing streak, the team's longest in 26 years—epitomized Decker's Cubs career.

Earlier in that same game, before Leo's trip to the mound, as Decker had walked to the plate to hit, the Cubs manager had told him to take a strike. Decker, then 22, turned on his manager, then 65, and said:

"You want me to take a strike?"

"Yeah, take a strike," said Leo.

So Decker took a called ball—then swung at the next pitch.

"The guy was in orbit," said Durocher afterward. Decker wouldn't comment, but one Cubs player confided at the time, "Joe still needs to grow up, but this is too bad. He lacks confidence, and this will kill him with the Cubs."

As it did.

Adolfo Phillips and Leo Durocher both had career batting averages of .247, but it was the only thing they had in common. When the Panamanian outfielder came to the Cubs in April 1966, Durocher heralded him with pre–Cesar Cedeno enthusiasm as the "next Willie Mays."

The love affair soon turned sour. Leo wanted Adolfo to bat leadoff, and Adolfo didn't want to. He said brushback pitches made him so nervous that his stomach hurt.

Phillips, a native of Panama City, could run fast, hit with amazing power for his 6'0", 177-pound frame, and make spectacular catches in the outfield. He was not, however, fond of running in practice.

"[Coach] Pete Reiser was all the time tryin' to rush me, do this, do that," said Phillips a few months after leaving the Cubs in 1969, "and I say, look at my body, I no need to run so much."

Adolfo was traded to Montreal in June of 1969 after he

fractured his hand, and Durocher figured Don Young could play center field.

"The Cubs needed me," said Phillips after the '69 season was over. "No trade me, they no lose. But I was glad to see that man [Leo] suffer. He was no my friend."

For the record: Adolfo played in 28 games, batting .224, with the '69 Cubs before being sent away in the three-way trade that brought Paul Popovich to Chicago. Adolfo played only three more seasons, with the Expos and the Cleveland Indians, before retiring after the 1972 season, his stomach still hurting.

In recent years, Phillips, 46, has worked in New York City as a security guard and as a jewelry salesman and in Panama City as a baseball instructor for the Panamanian government.

THE COACHES

They served as a four-man coaching unit for only three seasons (1967–1969) under Durocher, but each had an illustrious baseball career.

Rube Walker was the wit of the Cubs and often the heart.

He fought leukemia throughout the 1969 and 1970 seasons and died in late March 1971, leaving a legacy of warmth and honesty that touched many. Rube spent his entire professional career in the Cubs organization, first signing in 1948 and catching with seven different minor league teams before beginning his 10-year major league coaching career in 1961.

He was a goodwill ambassador from Lenoir, North Carolina, forever referring to his 19-foot fiberglass boat or his house on the lake back home. As a player he had been just average, maybe less as a pro, but he could tell about how he beat out Rocky Marciano in the low minors and how, when Rocky realized he was a worse catcher than Rube, Rocky got so mad he started beating up people.

Ironically, Rube's older brother, Albert Bluford, who was also nicknamed Rube, served as the 1969 Mets' pitching coach.

The Cubs' Rube claimed to be on speaking terms with the champion hog caller from Lenoir ("He can call the bacon out of a bacon-lettuce-and-tomato sandwich at 100 yards"), and when there was tension within the Cubs clubhouse, it was often Walker who said the right thing to ease the pressure.

And during his last summer, 1970, when there was a free-for-all brawl between the Pirates and the Cubs at Wrigley Field, Rube Walker plunged into the fray.

Why? To shield rival manager Danny Murtaugh, who recently had suffered a heart attack.

There was a time five decades ago when they called Pete Reiser the second Ty Cobb. Reiser was only 19 years old then and had signed with the Brooklyn Dodgers for a bonus of $100.

And one spring day in 1939, when Dodgers shortstop Durocher was rested, the kid nicknamed Pistol Pete got his first look at major league pitching. And he hit a home run in his first at-bat.

But he didn't become another Ty Cobb. Reiser, who kept running into center-field walls—hard, ungiving walls without ivy or padding—was a player who could do everything except stay healthy.

When he was 21 he hit .343 to win the National League batting championship, and by July 1942 he led baseball with a .380 average. Then he crashed into a wall and fell unconscious. Historians claim it cost the Dodgers the pennant and ended Reiser's greatness. He was never the same, suffering from recurring dizzy spells, headaches, and mysterious ailments for the balance of his life.

But Pete was a living baseball legend and somehow remained in the major leagues for another 11 years. He still holds a major league record from 1946: seven steals of home in a single season.

One day he chased a fly ball into another wall and damaged his right shoulder. That winter he learned to throw left-handed, just in case his right shoulder didn't heal. "I never had to play left-handed, but I could have done it," said

Reiser. "If a guy can hit both ways [Pete did], he can learn to throw both ways. I hear ballplayers talking about 'pacing themselves' over a long season. What long season? What is this 110 percent stuff I keep hearing? You can only play 100 percent, and you can't do that every day, but you sure as hell can strive for it."

Reiser became so disgusted with working with Durocher in 1969 that he resigned after the season to take a similar coaching job with the Angels. But after Del Rice replaced Angels manager Lefty Phillips, Reiser returned to the Cubs for the 1972 and 1973 seasons.

By then, however, Reiser's health was deteriorating, and he was forced to retire. He died in Palm Springs, California, in 1981 at the age of 62.

Pitching coach Joe Becker also wanted to quit after the 1969 season but was persuaded to remain one more year. Then Joe had a heart attack, and, in his words, "It was time to put the shoes in the rack and call it a career."

Retired in Vero Beach, Florida, and still playing golf regularly as he nears age 80, Becker offers this concise evaluation of what happened to the 1969 Cubs:

"No offense down the stretch."

Not a shortage of pitching? Not physical exhaustion?

"No way," says Becker. "We quit hitting. It's too bad too. I still say we celebrated too soon that year. There were some egos in that clubhouse."

Joe Becker knew great pitchers. He coached Don Newcombe, Sandy Koufax, Don Drysdale, Bob Gibson, and Fergie Jenkins.

"And we almost won it in 1969 with three pitchers," says Becker, "but you can't take anything away from the Mets. They did get great pitching."

Most of all, Joey Amalfitano remembers the Chicago fans. They got to him.

Amalfitano, 55, now third-base coach with the Los Angeles Dodgers, spent 13 seasons wearing a Cubs uniform as player, coach, and manager. And he specifically remembers the fans of 1969.

"I would be driving down Irving Park and make that right turn onto Clark Street, he recalls, "and there they were, mothers with their children, men carrying brown bags, all headed for the ballpark, and I'm talking about 8:30 A.M. It was unbelievable. The city went crazy over that team. It's such a great city. I always felt that if you hustled in Chicago, I mean gave an honest day's work, you were appreciated.

"The Cubs are their children. That's how the fans look at it. If you attacked the Cubs, you were attacking their children. Being in Chicago was a great time in my life. I'll never be able to replace those memories."

Joey, who coached under Durocher from 1967 to 1971 and under Herman Franks from 1978 to 1979 and then managed the Cubs in 1980 and 1981, says he would manage again.

"I've learned," says Joey. "And it would have been interesting to see what might have happened with the franchise had Franks remained as general manager when the Tribune Company bought the team. He had a brilliant business mind for baseball. I learned an awful lot from him."

He also learned alongside veterans Durocher, Reiser, Becker, and Walker in 1969.

"Becker was tough like an old roofing nail, and Rube was inherited by Leo but really won him over. Durocher thought the world of him. Rube wasn't just one of those coaches who rubbed the baseballs. He was always involved. And Pete was just terrific. It was really something working with all those personalities."

Speaking of personalities, what about coaching under Tom Lasorda, who copies Durocher by wearing #2 on the back of his uniform? Are there similarities between the men?

"On the field, yes. They're similar offensively, and when they get ahead they're aggressive. Their personalities are similar too, and they both get a lot of attention. When Durocher or Lasorda walks into a room, his presence is felt.

The difference, though, is that Tommy is more visible off the field. Leo would stay in his hotel suite until five minutes before the bus left. Tommy likes to be out among people. He has things to do, and he enjoys doing them. He's a people person."

What happened in 1969, Joey?

"Once things started going badly we just couldn't turn it around. I remember that bus ride into New York City after Willie Stargell's home run beat us in Chicago. Some of the guys were saying things like, 'Drive us straight to the ballpark,' positive stuff like that, but after we didn't get Tommie Agee at home plate—I was sure Hundley tagged him—things just stopped working for us.

"Leo, you know, had stopped smoking a couple of months before, but when we got into Philly after that Mets series he lit up and started puffing like a steam engine. Then there was that Selma pickoff play. I don't think that was in Leo's game plan."

Joey never had an opportunity to manage the Cubs for a full season. Not a true full season. After succeeding Preston Gomez late in 1980, he brought a restructured team out of spring training in 1981, only to be struck down like everybody else by the players' strike.

"We made a lot of changes during the first half of that split season," says Joey, "but in the second half we were right there in third place with about 14 days to play, maybe three or four games back, and nobody could figure us out. But it was a young team, and we just couldn't keep it together."

It all came together for Los Angeles Dodger third-base coach Amalfitano, however, in 1988. After 38 years in the major leagues, he celebrated a World Championship.

AND ALSO . . .

At least nine U.S. presidents and twenty-two Cubs managers have paraded through office while Yosh Kawano was doing laundry and cleaning dirt off spikes. Yosh won't confirm anything, including his age, but this much is certain: he has been an employee of the Cubs longer than anyone else.

Yosh is the equipment manager. That means he runs the Cubs' clubhouse. He started running it shortly after the end of World War II, 1948, and it remains his domain today.

Yosh did not cower before Leo. Yosh cowers before no man. He spent his subservient time in a Japanese-American detention camp at the outbreak of World War II. Ballplayers, particularly rich ones, don't scare him. He has seen them come and go, including those heroes of 1969.

When Ernie Banks showed up in late 1953 wearing yellow shoelaces in his baseball shoes (a holdover from his days with the Kansas City Monarchs), it was Yosh who slipped him some black ones and whispered, "Maybe you ought to switch to these to conform with the rest of the fellows."

Yosh was on television before there was color. Cameramen can always find him in the dugout: he's the short guy in baggy khaki pants, white T-shirt, and sailor cap.

He plays golf with his pal Ray Floyd, frequents Binyon's restaurant, owns real estate in Arizona (if the Tribune Company hadn't purchased the team, Yosh probably could have made an offer), and keeps in close touch with his brother, Nobe, who holds a similar clubhouse job with the Los Angeles Dodgers.

If the Cubs ever reach the World Series, Yosh Kawano should throw out the first ball.

SEPTEMBER/OCTOBER

Date	Cubs	Winning Pitcher	Losing Pitcher	W/L	GB	W/L	Mets	Winning Pitcher	Losing Pitcher
					SEPTEMBER				
1					4½	L	at L.A. 6–10	Bunning	Koosman
2	at Cin 5–4	Jenkins	Cloninger	W	5	W	at L.A. 5–4	Gentry	Sutton
	at Cin 8–2	Nye	Arrigo	W					
3	at Cin 0–2	Maloney	Hands	L	5	L	at L.A. 4–5	Mikkelsen	Di Lauro
5	Pitts 2–9	Blass	Holtzman	L	4½	W	Philly 5–1	Seaver	Jackson
					4½	L	Philly 2–4	Wise	McAndrew
6	Pitts 4–13	Veale	Jenkins	L	3½	W	Philly 3–0	Cardwell	Johnson
7	Pitts 5–7	Dal Canton	Johnson	L	2½	W	Philly 9–3	Ryan	Champion
8	at NY 2–3	Koosman	Hands	L	1½	W	Chicago 3–2	Koosman	Hands
9	at NY 1–7	Seaver	Jenkins	L	½	W	Chicago 7–1	Seaver	Jenkins
10	at Philly 2–6	Wise	Holtzman	L	–½	W	Montreal 3–2	Taylor	Stoneman
					–1	W	Montreal 7–1	Ryan	Reed
11	at Philly 3–4	James	Selma	L	–2	W	Montreal 4–0	Gentry	Robertson
12	at St. L 5–1	Hands	Taylor	W	–2½	W	at Pitts 1–0	Koosman	Moose
						W	at Pitts 1–0	Cardwell	Ellis
13	at St. L 4–7	Grant	Jenkins	L	–3½	W	at Pitts 5–2	Seaver	Walker
14	at St. L 1–2	Gibson	Holtzman	L	–3½	L	at Pitts 3–5	Blass	Ryan
15	at Mon 2–8	Wegener	Selma	L	–4½	W	at St. L 4–3	McGraw	Carlton
16	at Mon 5–4	Hands	Robertson	W	–4				
17	Philly 9–7	Jenkins	Champion	W	–4	W	at Mon 5–0	Koosman	Waslewski
18	Philly 3–5	Jackson	Regan	L	–5	W	at Mon 2–0	Seaver	Stoneman
19	St. L 2–1	Holtzman	Gibson	W	–4	L	Pitts 2–8	Veale	Ryan
	St. L 2–7	Torrez	Selma	L	–4	L	Pitts 0–8	Walker	McAndrew
20	St. L 1–4	Carlton	Hands	L	–4	L	Pitts 0–4	Moose	Gentry
21	St. L 4–3	Jenkins	Taylor	W	–4½	W	Pitts 5–3	Koosman	Ellis
						W	Pitts 6–1	Cardwell	Blass
22					–5	W	St. L 3–1	Seaver	Briles
23	Mon 3–7	Stoneman	Holtzman	L	–6	W	St. L 3–2	McGraw	Gibson
24	Mon 6–3	Hands	Renko	W	–6	W	St. L 6–0	Gentry	Carlton
26	at Pitts 0–2	Ellis	Jenkins	L	–7	W	at Philly 5–0	Koosman	Fryman
27	at Pitts 1–4	Blass	Holtzman	L	–8	W	at Philly 1–0	Seaver	Jackson
28	at Pitts 3–1	Hands	Veale	W	–8	W	at Philly 2–0	Gentry	Johnson
					OCTOBER				
1	NY 5–6	Taylor	Selma	L	–9	W	at Chicago 6–5	Taylor	Selma
2	NY 5–3	Decker	Cardwell	W	–8	L	at Chicago 3–5	Decker	Cardwell

17
September

"It was as if someone in my family was dying a slow death."
—A fan

How deceptive the beginning. There was no off taste, no harbinger of misgiving. Not yet, not at the commencement of what would become a month of torment. The Cubs, admittedly fatigued and emotionally on edge, had nevertheless won their final four games of August—at 18-11 their winningest month of the summer—and on the first day of September in Cincinnati, they rested.

On the second day they rejoiced, winning twice, first successfully completing two innings of a game suspended from June, then beating the Reds behind Jenkins's 19th victory. Kessinger hit his fourth home run of the year (he hit only 14 in his lifetime); the rookie centerfielder Oscar Gamble got his first major league extra-base hit, a triple;

and, on the down side, Santo injured his right knee sliding into a base.

"If everything goes according to schedule," said Jenkins afterward, "I can be home by October 20th or 22nd for duck hunting season in Ontario."

He was, of course, allotting time for the first-ever National League playoffs and a possible World Series. The two victories, after all, had given the Cubs a 5-game lead over the Mets and put them 32 games above .500 at 84–52.

Ken Johnson, the 36-year-old pitcher who had been purchased in mid-August from the Yankees recalls that postgame locker-room scene vividly:

"I got the save in the suspended game, and after the sweep I remember the reporters coming up and saying, 'Well, you've just wrapped up the pennant.' Then I don't know what happened. Nobody does."

What happened was that the Cubs lost their next 8 in a row and 11 of 12.

The Mets meanwhile won 12 of 15.

That's where the 1969 pennant was lost. Not before, not after. Right there, September 3 through September 15, when a 5-game lead became a 4½-game deficit. It was a swing of 9½ games, which sent the city of Chicago into trauma.

"It was as if someone in my family was dying a slow death," said one tortured fan. "I'd wake up each morning and say, 'They'll win today.' . . . but they didn't."

There are hundreds of thousands of such memories among Cubs fans. It's not so much what they remember; it's what they can't forget. Certain events, certain spans of time, lock themselves into our brain cells forever. For example, I remember being at a Cub Scout meeting learning to tie a slip knot when I heard on the radio that an "atom bomb" had dropped on Hiroshima, Japan. I can also remember standing over the clacking UPI machine in the newsroom of the Rockford *Morning Star* staring at the inked impressions on the moving yellow roll of paper as the unbelievable, unstoppable words followed the Dallas dateline . . . President John F. Kennedy had been killed.

Baseball isn't World War II or the death of a president, but Cubs fans who are old enough and are real Cubs fans remember Willie Stargell's home run, Tommie Agee's slide into home plate at Shea Stadium, Dick Selma's pickoff throw into left field in Philadelphia. . . .

They remember because they can't forget.

It started on September 3 without warning or worry because the Mets lost on the same night. While Jim Maloney of the Reds was blanking the Cubs 2–0, in the final game of their road swing the Mets were losing in Los Angeles. That's all. Just a loss that didn't hurt anybody because the lead was still 5 games and the magic number had been reduced to 23. Besides, the Cubs now had a day off before opening a three-game home stand with the Pirates at Wrigley Field.

Meanwhile, death was in the news: Rocky Marciano, Ho Chi Minh, Everett Dirksen. The retired and unbeaten heavyweight champ had gone down in a private plane crash near Newton, Iowa. What effect would the loss of 79-year-old Ho have on peace overtures in Vietnam? Could anyone fill the shoes of Illinois Senator Dirksen, to be buried in his hometown of Pekin?

But in Chicago optimism remained. Officials at Hawthorne Race Course requested permission from the Illinois Racing Board to hold night racing in October if the Cubs reached the World Series. The bean counters at Wrigley Field were also optimistic; an all-time Chicago baseball attendance record was on the horizon. The White Sox had drawn 1,644,460 in 1960, the year following their American League championship. The Cubs needed only 142,239 to break that record and had twelve home dates remaining, including two against the "pesky" Mets on October 1 and 2.

First, though, the red-hot Pirates were coming to town for a weekend series and hadn't won a game at Wrigley Field all season. The Cubs felt ready for anything, and why shouldn't they? For the first time since spring training Durocher was in love with his outfield. He still had Williams in left, but, having become less infatuated with Young and Qualls in center, had replaced them with his new phenom, his newest Willie Mays—19-year-old Oscar Gamble. Predictions for Gamble were generous: the Cubs had a centerfielder for the next 10 years. Right field, too, was solidified with Hickman, who had delivered 10 homers and 28 RBI during the month of August.

And while September had yet to be played, many were thinking toward October. The Cubs were being shadowed by American League superscouts Cal Ermer of Minnesota and Jim Russo of Baltimore. In turn, Cubs GM Holland had dispatched scouts Rube Wilson and Buck O'Neil to observe American League clubs.

"And this is the team I'm going to stay with," said Russo about the Cubs, "because this is the team."

Why?

"Because of the lineup," said Russo. "Look at the balance. Who would you name as the Cubs' most valuable player?"

It was a thought-provoking question, for which one could offer several answers:

- Banks, because where would the Cubs possibly be without him?
- Santo, having the greatest run-producing season of his career.
- Kessinger, baseball's best shortstop and a superb leadoff man hitting .286.
- Jenkins, on the threshold of his third consecutive 20-game season.
- Beckert, the best hit-and-run man in baseball.
- Hundley, one of the two best catchers in the business, along with Cincinnati's Johnny Bench.
- Williams, who would finish second in National League MVP balloting over two of the next three seasons.
- Hands, unquestionably the team's best pitcher down the pennant stretch and eventual 20-game winner.

Russo's point was clear: if you had charted daily heroes

during the Cubs' 1969 season, the line would have danced up and down from April through August.

Now it was September, and they would all go down together.

On Friday, September 5, Billy Williams, just back from an off-day fishing trip to Wolf Lake in Indiana with buddy Fergie Jenkins, hit two doubles and two home runs in a single game. Pirates starter Steve Blass, however, blanked everybody else as the Bucs clobbered Holtzman 9–2. By collecting all of his team's four hits in a game, Williams tied a major league record. The Mets meanwhile split a doubleheader with the Phillies and narrowed their deficit to 4½.

On Saturday, September 6, Pittsburgh hammered the Cubs again, this time pounding Jenkins, who was seeking his 20th victory. The Mets' Don Cardwell, meanwhile, was shutting out the Phillies, and the margin was cut to 3½.

Nevertheless, the town was agog on Sunday when Durocher sent Selma to the mound against the Pirates in the final game of this brief home stand. Selma was an interesting choice. He hadn't pitched in eight days, and normally this would have been Hands's start with three days of rest. Durocher, however, had juggled his rotation for the crucial upcoming two-game series at Shea Stadium which would begin on Monday night. Hands was saved for game one with four days of rest. But if Holtzman were to pitch in game two on Tuesday, there would be a problem four days later with him unable to pitch on Rosh Hashanah, so Leo decided to pitch Jenkins in game two with just two days of rest.

Willie Stargell would not send the Cubs into New York in a very happy mood.

Hickman's dramatic two-run homer in the bottom of the eighth put the Cubs ahead 5–4, and Regan needed just three outs in the Pirate ninth to record his 13th victory of the season, all in relief.

He got two of them.

Just one strike away from victory, Regan threw a 2–2

spitball that the powerful Stargell drove into a right-field wind and onto Sheffield Avenue for his 27th home run of the season, tying the game 5-5.

"It's something I have never been able to forget," recalls Santo, who watched the unbelievable shot from his position at third base.

"In retrospect, I guess we should have thrown him a slider," says catcher Hundley. "But Reegs threw him a good pitch. That sucker had already fouled off about eight pitches with a two-strike count. Besides, it was overcast and cool, and with the way the wind was blowin' in at 35 miles per hour, how was he gonna hit it out? I knew Regan was thinkin' the same thing. We just kept throwin' and throwin' those spitters, and he just kept foulin' them off. I just couldn't believe it when he hit the bloomin' ball over the wall."

Regan's reaction 20 years later: "The home run didn't beat us. We lost the game two innings later."

He's right, of course. But it was a home run from which the Cubs did not recover.

Not only did they bungle a great scoring chance in the bottom of the 10th (left-handed hitter Willie Smith, facing a left-handed pitcher, failed to sacrifice runners into scoring position), but they lost 7-5 in the 11th on two unearned runs.

"It was a monumental loss," recalls left-handed pitcher Nye, who had been warming up in the bullpen with another southpaw, Aguirre. "Leo never should have left Regan in that spot to pitch to Stargell. It was a crucial psychological blow to our team. Aguirre should have been in the game."

"Rich is right," says Aguirre. "I've never been one to criticize Leo, but he made a big mistake there. I should have been in the game. One thing I could do at that stage of my career was get out left-handed hitters." Ironically, Aguirre had been perfect against the Pirates that season, allowing no runs in nine innings over six games for an ERA of 0.00.

In New York, meanwhile, they were scoreboard watching. The Mets were beating the Phillies behind Nolan Ryan, and for the first time in the history of the Mets' sad franchise they faced a truly crucial series. The Cubs were coming into New York with a lead of 2½ games, and James Enright of the *Chicago Today* had written prophetically, "Time has come for the Cubs to face reality. Nobody can win the National League's Eastern Division title until the Cubs lose it."

"I remember Aguirre on the bus as we came from the airport to the Waldorf-Astoria," recalls then–traveling secretary Cullen. "He stood up in the back of the bus, threw his wallet onto the floor, and yelled, 'You guys don't have the guts to pick up the money! This team isn't going to win. I've played with winners. You guys aren't winners.' "

The gauntlet was down on the eve of the Cubs' most important game of the season.

It was a drizzly, misty night, but 43,274 came to Shea Stadium to watch Koosman pitch against Hands.

And to watch Tommie Agee hit the deck.

And to watch Koosman retaliate by hitting Santo.

And to watch Agee homer.

And to watch Agee score on the most controversial play of the Cubs season.

And to watch the Mets win 3-2.

First, some background about Hands and the Mets. On May 4 at Wrigley Field, Tom Seaver had sent Santo sprawling with a high inside pitch in the second inning of game one of a doubleheader. Then Hands had hit Seaver between the shoulder blades in the third inning. Finally Seaver had fired a pitch into Hands's midsection in the bottom of the third, both managers had rushed onto the field, and fans had started throwing oranges. That was in May.

In July at Shea, after Agee had ripped a leadoff home run, Hands had nicked him in the left hand with a fastball the next time he came to the plate.

That was Hands. He considered Sal Maglie a pretty good guy. He was meanest when challenged. It's the way he learned the game and the way he played it.

And on the night of September 8 at Shea Stadium, he sent

Agee reeling, blue helmet flying, on the first pitch of the most important game of the year. Almost 20 years later, when asked about "the pitch to Agee," Hands replied, "The one that knocked him down?"

You know which one.

"Well, there was nothing wrong with that pitch. It was the one two innings later that was horseshit. I hung a slider out over the middle of the plate, and he hit a two-run homer over the left-center-field wall."

But what about the knockdown pitch?

"I was not *told* to do it. I just *did* it."

In other words, Hands just decided to get the series off to a good start.

"Right. Let's go, gentlemen. Right on his ass. I didn't hit him, did I? I just did what I wanted to do. And you know, here's the funny thing about Tommie Agee. He had that kind of arrogant swagger about him, you know? All through the minor leagues I owned him. But in the majors I just couldn't make good pitches against that mother. I was constantly hanging sliders over the middle of the plate, and he was constantly hitting the shit out of them."

"I didn't know it was coming," recalls catcher Hundley. "He shocked the livin' pee out of me. I mean that mama was comin' right at Tommie's head. I can still see that ball just missin' his chin. I thought, 'Boy, this is what it's all about, right here!' "

Another gauntlet had been dropped.

But the Mets were not to be intimidated. In retrospect it was the worse thing that could have happened—to the Cubs. When Santo came to the plate at the top of the second, Koosman plunked him with a fastball on the first pitch—drilled him in the right forearm and the damndest thing is that Santo says he wasn't expecting it.

"Everybody on my team knew I was going to get hit but me," recalls Santo, still wonderingly. "I honestly thought that pitch had just gotten away from Hands. I mean we'd been out the night before talking about hitters and everything and he never gave a clue he might do that. And I know

Leo never told him to do it. Nothing was said in any meeting. So here I am, the first guy up in the next inning, and all I'm thinking about is getting a hit. Now he drills me in the arm and I'm thinking, 'Jesus Christ,' but even then I don't think it was intentional. Koosman is a classy guy. A battler, sure, but I guess I just didn't grasp the situation. He got me right in the bone too, and it really stiffened up as the game went along."

There was no question about the intention of Koosman's pitch. He threw it to hit Santo—to retaliate for Hands's knockdown pitch—and although he was cute about it later in the locker room ("I usually pitch Santo low and away, so tonight I started him inside . . . he probably stepped into it"), the left-hander later acknowledged it was a deliberate plunk ("but don't make it sound like I'm bragging because I'm not").

"The thing that really hurt was that they had to spray-freeze my arm, and I couldn't really grip the bat after that," says Santo. "And the second time up I missed a home run by just a few feet, right against the wall. But I just couldn't pop my wrists."

In truth, Koosman's retaliation had far-reaching effect on the Cubs.

For they just sat there. Nobody charged the mound. Nobody screamed or shouted. They just sat there on a silent bench in Shea Stadium while their cleanup hitter writhed in pain at home plate. It was a strange way indeed to battle for a pennant.

"That's when we should have gotten into a fight," says Aguirre. "It really hurt me deeply that Santo just walked to first base, and nobody did anything. That's when I knew we were hurting. Leo or Santo or somebody from the dugout should have started a fight. I wish I hadn't been stuck out in the bullpen or I would have started it."

"We were easily intimidated," says pitcher Nye, recalling the scene from his bullpen vantage point. "It was a degrading incident. I still can't believe Ron didn't charge the mound. The club just folded."

Hundley viewed it as the Mets saying, "Hey, don't fool with us" and adds, "You have to give them credit."

The Cubs catcher, however, was not prepared to give them what came later.

The Cubs got to Koosman in the sixth with three straight singles and Santo's sacrifice fly, tying the score 2-2. Then came the events that no Cubs player or fan can ever forget:

Agee drove a hit past Santo at third base, and when the wet grass embraced the ball in short left field, Agee daringly slid safely into second for a double. Wayne Garrett then singled to right, and Hickman, alertly pouncing upon the ball, threw accurately toward home as Agee tried to score.

Hundley took the throw, and as Agee dodged past, Hundley threw out his left hand, nailing him with a sweep tag. Then, without hesitation, Randy leaped back into throwing position in front of home plate, arm poised to throw out Garrett.

"It never occurred to me that Agee would be called safe," recalls Hundley. "I knew I tagged him. I was just worried about Garrett advancing to second."

But that's not how home plate umpire Dave (Satch) Davidson saw it. He signaled Agee safe, and Shea Stadium erupted. So did Hundley's temper. He did a frog leap that would have made Mark Twain proud.

"It had to be a world record for a vertical jump," recalls Kessinger. "From my position at shortstop there was no way I could tell whether he tagged him or not, but I know Randy well enough to say this: 99 percent of the time when a man reacts as Hundley did, the umpire missed the call."

Hundley still can't talk about the play without getting agitated. "I tagged him so hard I almost dropped the ball," he recalls. "Right up his bloomin' side. It wasn't just a little tag: I swept him right up the uniform. I was really afraid I would drop the bloomin' ball.

"Have you ever seen a player make a tag, miss it, and then instinctively go for another? Sure you have. It's instinct. If I had missed him I would have reacted. Instead my next reaction was to first base. It was a hard tag.

"How in the world could Davidson miss that play? I get

upset right now just thinking about it. The pit of my stomach gets so stinkin' upset I want to go through the wall. It wasn't even close. I couldn't believe it. I just couldn't believe it. I wanted to flatten him [Davidson].

"I tagged him *so hard* the ball was rolling up from the pocket of my mitt into the webbing. That's when I felt so relieved that I turned toward the runner at first. Then I turned around to toss the ball to Hands and I heard this tremendous roar. I guess that's when my quick, analytical mind told me something was wrong."

"Randy made a sweep tag and missed,". recalls umpire Davidson, now retired in Houston. "That's the way I saw it then, and that's the way I saw it later on TV replays."

One play does not a baseball season make, nor does one game, as the Cubs would so graphically prove in the coming days. Yet Hundley says this about Agee's run that won that game 3–2:

"Without question it was the biggest play of the year, and I'll tell you why. When a team like the Mets can win on a play like that, they say, 'Hey, things really are going our way. This is really our year.' Then they start doing things they're not capable of doing. That had to be the most important run of the season for the Mets, and it was an outright gift. That's all it was, a gift."

"But that doesn't mean we still couldn't have come back and won the pennant," offers Santo.

Nevertheless, the effect of that controversial play was devastating to the Cubs. Their clubhouse afterward was a morgue. The Mets had now won five of the last seven between the two teams, the Cubs had lost five in a row, and the next day they were to face Tom Seaver.

Durocher would not answer questions from the media after the game. He had gone into his "no comment" mode but expanded on that phrase somewhat by saying, "I don't say anything after a game—win or lose. You can wait until snow comes over the fucking clubhouse door, and I won't have anything to say. No comment. No fucking comment!"

The Mets now trailed by 1½.

The following night was a continuation of the agony. It

wasn't even a game. An audience of 58,436 stood, waved white handkerchiefs, and sang "Good-bye, Leo" as Seaver beat the Cubs 7–1.

Maybe the black cat had something to do with it. Somebody released the feline in front of the Cubs dugout early in the no-contest, and while some players chuckled as the cat ran back and forth in front of the bench as if trained, Leo the Lion stared straight ahead. Perhaps the King of Beasts knew.

Jenkins, working with two days of rest, was ineffective, giving up four runs while Seaver retired the first nine Cubs. Later there would be criticism of Durocher for allowing Jenkins to remain in the game so long. Even though the score stood 5–1 after four innings and 6–1 after five, Fergie stayed to pitch seven innings, surrendering ten hits, three walks, and five earned runs.

"Before I went to the plate to hit in the fifth," Fergie said afterward, "Leo asked how I felt. I said 'fine' and he said, 'Go ahead.' If there had been anybody on base he probably would have hit for me though."

In the audience, that Mets fan with all the imaginative signs displayed a banner that read: TOOTHLESS CUBS— JUST A LOTTA LIP, and in the Chicago clubhouse, where bags were hurriedly being packed for a trip to Philadelphia, Durocher said to writers, "No comment. No fucking comment."

The Cubs, still in first place after 155 days, had lost six straight and led by the Mets by half a game: .002.

In Chicago the universe had gone on tilt. People were having anxiety attacks. Eyes were turned toward newspaper sports sections and television sets. Taxi drivers grunted and pounded steering wheels while listening to Vince and Lou on WGN radio.

Many will now claim they knew then that the Cubs were dead.

"I'm one of those," admits traveling secretary Cullen. "I knew after the Mets series the Cubs wouldn't win."

But there were still countless believers, even among the ever-cynical writers who were seeing puzzlement and doubt in the eyes of these players who had performed so remarkably most of the season.

This was a team that needed shaking.

"By then we were starting to believe we were jinxed," says Aguirre.

"Nobody knew what to do," says Williams. "I guess that's because we'd never been there before."

Yet outwardly there did seem to be some fight remaining. Durocher, in fact, got off a few growls as the Cubs fought their way past heckling fans to reach the team bus outside Shea Stadium. "Who cares what they think?" said Leo. "And I'll tell you something else, when these fans go after me, they're not goin' after any maiden."

Kessinger, when asked to react to the waving handkerchiefs and objects being thrown against the bus windows, said, "They're going to regret this. They're going to eat their words. All we need now is just·one victory."

So most people didn't see it. They didn't see the Cubs as dead. There was no outward dissension, only plenty of weak hitting, faulty defense, and poor pitching . . . and, although not yet obvious, a strange passivity—a passivity that would devour.

At 8:43 P.M. Eastern Standard Time on Wednesday, September 10, the Mets moved into first place by percentage points. They did it by virtue of beating Montreal in both games of a doubleheader. Then the Cubs lost in Philadelphia, so by morning New York had a one-game lead.

The Cubs never led during this, their seventh straight loss, even though this was a Philadelphia team that would post a season record of 63–99 and finish 37 games behind the Mets. But, as the Cubs would continue to prove, it no longer mattered which opponent was on the field. The Cubs were playing themselves.

Santo's knee was swollen and filled with fluid. He was sleeping with an ice pack and planned to have it drained when the club reached St. Louis. Durocher, meanwhile, was still politely saying "no comment" to writers, particularly those from other cities. The manager, normally a source of information, was unavailable, so the players were increasingly besieged by those seeking information.

With 19 games to play, the Cubs now had a new ambition, to stay close enough to see the Mets come into Chicago on October 1 and 2 for a final, meaningful series.

By the next night all hell had broken loose. Dick Selma had practically sailed a pickoff throw out of the ballpark.

It was an eerie scene in Philly. Only 4,164 spectators had shown up, and you could hear the foul balls banging off seats in dilapidated Connie Mack Stadium. On the scoreboard the Mets were winning again.

In the third inning it became situation comedy.

The Cubs led 1-0 with Phillies Tony Taylor and Johnny Briggs on first and second, two out, and Dick Allen standing at the plate with a 3-2 count.

"That's when Selma decided he was a rocket scientist," recalls second baseman Beckert.

Actually, what Selma decided was that he didn't want to pitch to Allen.

"I would never have tried what I did unless there was a hitter up there I didn't want to face," recalls Selma. "But Roger Craig had taught me this play during spring training that season with the Padres [Selma came to the Cubs on April 25] and this looked like the perfect situation.

"With a 3-2 count, you see, the runners are going. Now instead of me delivering the ball to the plate, I lift my leg off the rubber and fired the ball to third base for an easy out."

Sounds great, Dick. So what went wrong?

"Santo didn't cover third base."

Did Santo know he was supposed to cover third base?

"We had a signal," says Selma. "When I came over from the Padres I explained it to Ronnie. I would give a verbal signal: 'Knock the ball down, Dag' [short for Dago], and he would answer 'OK' to show me he knew the throw was coming."

So far, so good, except that Selma's throw sailed high

over the vacant bag into the darkness of left-field foul territory, allowing Taylor to score the tying run from second base.

"The runners were going, just like I knew they would be," explains Selma, "but when I whirled to throw I could see Santo about 15 feet behind third base, locked in on the hitter, and I'm yelling, 'Ronnie . . . Ronnie,' but I can't keep from throwing the ball."

Santo's version:

"We had discussed this play once. We had never tried it. So now I'm playing deep against Allen, and my mind is really into the game. Allen is a great hitter, and I know I've got to be ready. So all of a sudden Selma is yelling for me to knock the ball down, and that's exactly what I'm telling myself in the first place. I've got to knock it down to keep him from getting an extra-base hit, so I'm nodding my head and saying 'OK, OK' to Selma.

"Do you think I'm thinking about a damned pickoff play in the middle of September we've never even used before? He throws it into left field, the tying run scores, we lose 4–3, and I can't believe what's happening to us."

"The best part was Leo," recalls Beckert. "Those old dugouts in Philly were very small and had tin roofs. Well, when that ball went over third base Leo jumped up and hit his head on the roof."

"In retrospect," says Kessinger, "Dick should have just balked when he saw Santo wasn't covering. That would have meant just advancing the runners to second and third, and we could have walked Allen."

Twenty years later Selma agrees. But he had other troubles on that evening in Philadelphia. He later gave up a two-run homer to Allen, and homers by Banks and Willie Smith weren't enough to save the evening.

Afterward Durocher was livid.

"I'd never seen him so mad," recalls Santo. "I couldn't tell whether he was mad at me or Dick or what, but the veins were about to burst out of his neck. He just couldn't believe what had happened."

"Santo knew it was his fault," recalls Selma, "so I told

him, 'Tell the writers it was my fault. I'll take the blame. Tell them I screwed it up.' I figured Ronnie had enough on his shoulders then."

Coach Amalfitano still chuckles when he recalls the wild locker-room scene: "Leo kept yelling, 'Where's Selma? . . . Where's Selma? . . . Go find Selma,' but nobody could find him. I'm looking everywhere. Then I go upstairs into the training room and there in a locker I see two feet sticking out from under some clothes. It was Selma hiding."

With 18 games to play, the Cubs trailed by two.

Durocher decided to break his silence. Prior to "the Selma game" he had agreed to a private meeting with me in his Philadelphia hotel room. In retrospect, I'm still not sure why.

The day after "the Selma game," with his team in the throes of an atrocious losing streak, Leo began talking about a variety of subjects:

- About how he was thinking about lifting the 1:30 A.M. curfew so the club could "go on a bender and loosen up."
- About how the team had "been playing their hearts out" and had not given up.
- About how nobody was hitting the panic button.
- About how Williams was playing with a bad back, Hundley an injured hand ("You can see him let go of the bat sometimes, it hurts so much"), Santo a variety of bruises.
- About the Mets ("Somebody told me they were already drinking champagne. That might be premature").
- About how the Cubs had almost acquired Al Ferrara three weeks before from San Diego and tried to get Tommy Davis from Seattle.
- About how he had decided to ban card playing in the clubhouse two hours before every road game and one hour before home games.
- About himself. He said, "I admit, that in reality, I'm a tougher winner than I am a loser."

It was an exclusive interview in a highly competitive city

of four newspapers. But Durocher quickly made peace with other writers one day later in St. Louis by holding a press conference, at which time he said, "Now I suppose somebody will make something out of the fact that I'm talking. They'll say, 'Well, Leo's getting beat now, so he's looking for sympathy.' "

Leo's dealing with the press, of course, had absolutely nothing to do with the team's success or failure on the field. Nevertheless, a few players had something to say about him at the time:

"That man has shown me more class in the last three weeks than most managers show in an entire season," said Hickman.

"Many managers would be shouting and screaming at us, but Leo has done just the opposite," said Aguirre.

Ironically, Aguirre now looks back on September 1969, and says, "There became a lot of disappointment around the team as we continued to lose that Leo didn't do something, anything. We were all waiting for him to just close the door and raise all kinds of hell, but he didn't. It's a second guess now, but we really needed shaking up."

By this time, it was obvious that players were dragging, but wasn't it too late for Durocher to worry about exhaustion? Perhaps he should have rested the club more during July and August, but this was September, and were the Cubs going to catch the Mets with Santo, Beckert, Kessinger, or Hundley on the bench?

They weren't going to catch anyone unless the losing streak ended, and on Friday night, September 12, it ended in St. Louis. Hands was the stopper, and afterward Banks was saying, "Happy Rosh Hashanah, it's a new year for the Cubs."

Laughter in the Cubs clubhouse? It was perhaps the happiest any baseball team had ever been following a half-game loss in the standings—for the Mets had won twice in Pittsburgh by identical 1–0 scores, and both New York runs were driven in by the starting pitchers, Koosman and Don Cardwell. Normally this would be cause for wailing, but for the Cubs a bad dream had ended. They had just lost eight games by the scores of 2-0, 9-2, 13-4, 7-5, 3-2, 7-1, 6-2, and 4-3.

"The slump just happened," offered Captain Santo. "And it was horrible. But we've still got time."

"That's right," said Kessinger. "We've just got to win and forget about the Mets."

Forget about the Mets? They had won 35 of their last 41.

And one night later the bad dream returned. The Cubs gave a game away to the Cardinals in all the wrong ways— errors, walks, and runners stranded. St. Louis had broken a 4-4 tie in the eighth on a base hit through the middle that Beckert missed by inches.

"It skipped under my glove," said Beckert, "and I should have had it."

Jenkins, failing to register his 20th victory for the third time, was equally distraught. Behind the hitters all night, he had used more curveballs and sliders than he normally did. Why? Because he felt his fastball had lost its velocity.

And the Mets? They won again in Pittsburgh behind Seaver and led the Cubs by $3\frac{1}{2}$.

On Sunday, September 14, the Mets' 10-game winning streak finally ended in Pittsburgh, but the Cubs didn't benefit. They were beaten in St. Louis in 10 innings, and realistically it was their last gasp. Holtzman pitched one of his best games of the year, dueling Bob Gibson pitch for pitch, yet, because of sloppy fielding and Lou Brock's 10th-inning home run into the lower-right-field pavilion (his first since July 16), the Cubs lost.

"Somebody put a curse on us," said Beckert afterward, but I didn't have the heart to tell about that July phone call from the White Sox fan.

Statistically, the "curse" read this way: over the last 11 games, of which the Cubs had lost 10, they had averaged just 6.63 hits and 2.63 runs per game. Opponents had averaged 5.73 runs per game.

Yet surely relief was in sight. The Cubs were headed for Montreal, where the expansion-team Expos, eventually to lose 110 games and finish 48 games behind the Mets, were waiting. Durocher announced he would start Selma in the opener but perhaps move to a three-man rotation of Hands, Jenkins, and Holtzman for the remainder of the season.

With the brilliant Steve Carlton scheduled to pitch against the Mets that same night in St. Louis, there remained some slight hope among the Cubs. Victory over the Expos coupled with a Mets loss could cut the margin to 2½—and don't forget: the Mets were scheduled to play two in October in Wrigley Field.

That evening of September 15 in Montreal remains a vivid memory, perhaps because of the almost surrealistic setting at Jarry Park. It had rained all day, causing the Cubs to skip batting practice, and there had been a 20-minute clubhouse meeting during which WGN announcer Lou Boudreau was called upon to tell humorous stories about how he managed pitchers Satchel Paige and Jim Bagby.

But they weren't funny enough. In the first inning the Expos hit four balls that the Cubs could have caught but didn't: Rusty Staub's foul pop fly that Banks couldn't reach outside first base; Staub's drive that bounded past slow-starting Williams in left for a double; Ron Fairly's catchable fly-ball double that dropped between Hickman and new addition Jimmie Hall; and, finally, a ground ball by Mack Jones that Beckert booted.

After that it got worse. The Expos chased Selma to win 8-2, and the futility of the Cubs' situation was best exemplified in the fourth inning when pitching coach Joe Becker took five steps out of the dugout only to be called back by Durocher.

"Will you make up your mind?" Becker reportedly said to Leo, although perhaps not so politely.

"Durocher is managing like a man who knows he won't be managing next year, win or lose," said announcer Boudreau during a half-inning break. "Oh, he wants to win, but he isn't taking any drastic action."

The good people of Montreal, understandably, were unable to grasp how the Cubs were suffering. Fernand La Pierre, for example, the Expos' organist and the only one in the league with a backup (the organist he replaced didn't want to leave, so he got $10 a night to sit behind Fernand and keep his fingers limber), said after the game:

"Is it so bad that you lose tonight? Do you lose everything?"

The next morning at the Queen Elizabeth Hotel, Glenn Beckert picked up the newspaper that had been deposited outside his door and smiled. The headline read CARLTON STRIKES OUT 19. Then Beckert read the story. The Mets had beaten Carlton 4–3. Ron Swoboda had homered twice.

He threw down the newspaper, stared out the window, and said, "It's raining."

"I don't care," said roommate Santo. "It's already poured in my life."

Later, at breakfast, Santo said, "I had a dream last night. I dreamed they called me into the front office and said, 'Santo, you've been with the Cubs 10 years and haven't won a pennant. So we're trading you to Philadelphia.' But I wouldn't go. I dreamed I said, 'I won't go.' "

Beckert, toying with his fork and French toast, then started laughing. "Are there any openings for copy boys down at the newspapers?" he asked.

"I know what you mean," said Santo. "I don't want to go back to Chicago. I don't want to face the first guy who asks 'What happened?' "

Now, finally, the Cubs knew they were not going to win. Carlton losing to the Mets after striking out 19 had done it. They now trailed by 4½, and their hearts had been torn out.

By pregame, in Doc Schueneman's training room, they were even laughing, but it was gallows humor.

"Have you heard about how well the Cub Power record album is selling?" asked one player. "It's breaking all sales records. People are using the album covers for dart boards."

"Yeah," answered a teammate, "you can buy two T-shirts, two mugs, a record, and three autographed baseballs for $1.98."

Rain that evening of September 16 would have been considered a moral victory. Instead Hands was again the stopper, beating the Expos 5–4. Over a period of two weeks the Cubs had won only two games, and Hands had won them both. Durocher also finally did something that night. He made his biggest lineup change of the season, benching Banks and Kessinger in place of Willie Smith and Popovich.

"I didn't sleep all night just thinking about what might lift the club," said Durocher.

Now, with some players still saying things like "We can do it," and "We can't get down on ourselves," the Cubs headed home. It would be their first appearance at Wrigley Field since September 7, the afternoon of Willie Stargell's home run.

The bad dream had turned into a nightmare.

Gale Sayers, positive of a comeback from knee surgery, signed a three-year contract worth $75,000 a year, making him the highest-paid Bear in history. Egyptian planes raided Israeli forces in the occupied Sinai, the New York Giants said sayonara to coach Allie Sherman, and, believe it or not, somebody estimated that Jackie Onassis was somehow spending $384,000 a week.

But she wasn't spending it at Wrigley Field. When the Cubs returned home, few people were spending anything there. It had been an amazing transformation. From "Hey, Hey, Holy Mackerel" madness, the cathedral of baseball had become a mausoleum. Only 6,062 showed up for the cool Wednesday afternoon home opener against the Phillies.

Where were the Bleacher Bums? Did they go back to school too? More frightening, were they looking for jobs? Where was the magic number? Any more free tractors or cars out there to give away?

There would be no more heel clicks either. Doctors advised against it, for the Cubs' third baseman had been limping with a sore knee for two weeks. Besides, it had been so long since a victory at Wrigley Field (15 days), did Ron still know how?

Finally, on that first day back Jenkins got his 20th victory, 9–7 over the Phillies, with Nye holding the losers in check for the save. The Cubs, who hadn't hit on the road, delivered 14 hits, including a double by 38-year-old Banks that gave him 100 RBI for the season.

Afterward there was an interesting announcement from Durocher, who said, "You can put it in writing. I'll be back next year. And if we can put together four or five wins, this thing isn't over yet either." Later that evening, however, the Mets did it again: Koosman shut out Montreal, and the deficit remained at four.

There was also a statement from owner Wrigley, who, when asked if Leo's mid-July visit to Camp Ojibwa had anything to do with the Cubs losing, said, "Any connection between that and our slump is ridiculous. As I said at the time, the whole thing was blown out of proportion. When that happened the team was only 4½ games ahead, and one month later they were 9½ ahead. So what kind of logic is that?"

Somebody else was being quoted too. Hall of Famer Jackie Robinson, in Chicago to speak at a luncheon at the Merchandise Mart, said, "I think the Cubs have blown it. I think they've given up on themselves, and I think the fans will probably feel the hurt more than the players. The whole thing is a tragedy."

Durocher, having already abandoned his plans for a three-man pitching rotation, gave 22-year-old rookie Joe Decker his first major league start on September 18, but that didn't work either. The Phillies won, beating Regan in relief on the same day Seaver blanked the Expos 2–0.

This about Tom Seaver: during the month of September Seaver won six games by the scores of 5–1, 7–1, 5–2, 2–0, 3–1, and 1–0. Mets pitchers, for that matter, threw 10 shutouts in their final 25 victories.

And now on September 19, with the Cardinals in Chicago for a doubleheader, the Cubs trailed by five games (six on the loss side) with just eleven to play. The Cubs were walking down an aisle with a shotgun at their backs with no place to escape and full knowledge that marriage to the second-place girl was imminent. Already they were being compared to Gene Mauch's 1964 Phillies who blew a 7½-game lead with only 12 left to play.

Aguirre, who had pitched for the 1967 Detroit Tigers, who lost the pennant to the Boston Red Sox on the final day of the season, considered his fate. "There's a dark cloud hanging over my head," he said. "When we were 9½ games ahead I was a Spaniard. Now I'm just another Mexican."

The Cubs were also feeling the wrath of the fans.

Holtzman, for example, opened a letter, and a piece of paper fell out. It was his autograph. The fan didn't want it anymore, so he had sent it back.

Santo was hearing it unmercifully from the fans along third base, and when three players—Regan, Gamble, and Popovich—showed up to sign autographs at a new automobile showroom, the first guy who saw them shouted, "You guys blew it!"

It even got sick. Santo opened a letter that read, "It's too bad you and Holtzman weren't on that plane that crashed in Indiana."

The Cubs split their doubleheader with the Cardinals on a rare Friday when the Mets lost a pair to Pittsburgh, but time was running out. Even when the Mets were no-hit the following day by Bob Moose, the Cubs couldn't gain. Hands was beaten by Carlton, and the Cubs, having lost 14 of the last 18, still trailed by four games with eight to play.

Fergie beat the Cardinals on Sunday for his 21st victory, but the Mets did it again, sweeping another doubleheader from the Pirates. Then, when Seaver beat the Cards on Monday, day off for the Cubs, the Mets were within sniffing distance of clinching the pennant. The Cubs trailed by five with seven to play.

Willie Mays hit his 600th home run that September 22 as the Cubs rested. Quarterback Joe Theismann was basking in glory after guiding Notre Dame to a 35–10 shellacking of Northwestern. And defendants were making last-minute preparations as the trial of the Chicago Eight was about to

begin, Judge Julius J. Hoffman (who would later gag
Bobby Seale and reduce the number to seven) presiding.

Also defendants, as the Mets approached their inevitable
pennant-clinching victory, were the Cubs. How could this
have happened? There were questions without answers.
And as the Mets moved another step closer on September 23,
clinching at least a tie by beating Bob Gibson and the
Cardinals (New York was in the midst of another nine-
game winning streak), the Cubs, as if in trance, lost again,
to Montreal.

What *had* happened? Only the numbers were there for
scrutiny. From September 4 through September 23, Kessinger hit .148; Banks, .156; Hundley, .188; Beckert, .203;
Hickman, .246; Santo, .262; and Williams, .329. Holtzman
was 1–6 during the month, and Selma failed to finish his
last seven starts, losing five of them. It had been a simulta-
neous collapse, with failures in hitting, fielding, and pitching. It was not enough then, as it is not enough today, to
explain away what happened by applauding the Mets, as
stirring as their finish was. For that finish to happen, the
Cubs had to fall apart—and they did.

But the failures came so unexpectedly, so completely, that
there were no explanations. There was only the feeling of
emptiness that permeated Chicago. Perhaps that is why so
many rushed to grope for reasons.

Some spoke then, and speak now, of exhaustion, ques-
tionable managing, diversions, inexperience, lack of bench
depth, shortage of a bullpen stopper. Everyone had an
opinion. There were no answers. There was only next year.

At precisely 9:07 P.M. E.S.T. on September 24, the Mets
clinched the pennant by blanking St. Louis 6–0. And from
Chicago came this message of concession from Durocher:

"We wanted to win it, and we played like hell. We had an
exciting year in Chicago, and we certainly didn't want to
lose. But if anybody had said during spring training that
the Cubs were going to be in first place from getaway day
until September 10, you would have said he was crazy.

"Two good clubs, St. Louis and Pittsburgh, finished

behind us . . . although we played the worst baseball I've seen in years. But the Mets won 13 of 14 at one stretch. If they had played like Pittsburgh and St. Louis, we'd have had no problem.

"But they had a hot streak that never stopped. It's a credit to them."

In New York, as the Mets celebrated their truly unexpected and extraordinary achievement, Ed Kranepool took time to lift a champagne bottle on high and pronounce:

"Here's to Leo."

It was not an easy celebration for Cubs fans to imagine. There was, after all, an image to consider. As Robert F. Jones wrote in *Sports Illustrated*, "Chicago appears in its true colors. A loser. Not even the Second City anymore, but the one city that has to blow it. For the stale smell of defeat lingers in every dark corner of Chicago, and not even the coarse, cold wind off Lake Michigan can scour it clean."

That "stale smell" was so permeative, in fact, that the 1969 Bears, also playing in Wrigley Field, followed the Cubs' act by suffering their worst record in history (1-13) and later, when stepping forward to claim their college-draft consolation prize, lost the coin flip and watched quarterback Terry Bradshaw go to the Pittsburgh Steelers. Drafting next, the Bears were so confused they swapped their pick to the Packers for linebacker Lee Roy Caffey, running back Elijah Pitts, and center Bob Hyland.

That wind had a lot of blowing to do.

For the record: the Mets did come into Chicago for those obligatory two games in October of 1969, but nobody cared, not even the Mets. Selma lost the opener, but rookie Decker got his first major league victory on the last day of the season, and the Cubs finished at 92-70, their best won-lost record since 1945. Nevertheless, they finished *eight* games behind the Mets (100-62), who had played the months of September and October at a 24-8 clip. The Cubs during that same period were 10-18, the worst in all of baseball.

The record will also show that the Mets swept three from

the Atlanta Braves in the first-ever National League Championship Series by scores of 9–5, 11–6, and 7–4. Then, after losing game one of the World Series to Baltimore 4–1, New York swept the next four, 2–1, 5–0, 2–1, and 5–3.

The story was complete.

Yet every beginning journalism student is taught that no story is complete without answers to six basic questions: who, what, where, why, when, and how?

Who, what, where, and when came easily. You could even make a case for how.

But why?

This observer fell into the same trap as everyone else in Chicago, amateur or professional. I wrote a two-part article in the *Chicago Today* attempting to explain "why" the Cubs didn't win the pennant. Included in the analysis:

- The Cubs didn't have the team fiber or togetherness to regroup after their early September slump. They had time but couldn't cope with the challenge. They tried but didn't know how. Said the veteran Aguirre, "From the beginning of spring training some of us tried to bring this team together. We had parties with our wives, and we tried different things, but we never quite made it. There were still cliques."
- Durocher's bullpen failed, and as manager he should be blamed.
- The Cubs were lionized by an adoring public and press for five months, and when the team's only slump arrived the players couldn't believe it.
- Physically, the team wore down, and for this Durocher should also be blamed.

From there, you could only wonder about the effects of Camp Ojibway, outside commercial activities, the Don Young Incident, Santo's heel clicking, Leo's feud with sportswriters, and even the fact that reserve catcher Gene Oliver had been a card-playing clubhouse lawyer who didn't belong and caused resentment among the fulltime coaches when Durocher kept him on the payroll as a coach to enable him to reach another level on the pension fund. Few writers could forget Oliver's interrupting a newsman's interview with Holtzman following Ken's August 19 no-hitter by saying, "Why give them all of that good stuff when you could sell it to a magazine?"

I wrote about Oliver's remark, and he was deeply offended by the article. In fact, when we first saw each other again 19 years later in the clubhouse of a Hundley Baseball Camp in Tempe—two overweight men in their mid-50s—we started shouting at each other while Jenkins and Beckert sat laughing in a corner.

"How can you blame a guy who batted only 27 times for losing the pennant?" asked Oliver.

"Did you jump off the John Hancock building yet?" I countered, referring to Oliver's infamous statement, made after Seaver one-hit the Cubs in Shea Stadium July 9, 1969. Talking with close friend Santo in the clubhouse afterward, Oliver had said, "If we lose to the Mets we oughta all jump off the John Hancock building."

"Of course some reporter overheard me, and it came out that I said, 'I'll jump off the John Hancock building," said Oliver afterward, who has been munching on his words since.

On the final day of the 1969 season, in fact, when Oliver walked into the Cubs clubhouse, equipment man Yosh Kawano, a gentleman of few words, feigned shock and said, "It's a mirage . . . did you bounce?"

Point of the digression: This observer, then 34, lifetime Cub fan, and full of passion for the team's quest, was just as bereft of answers as anyone else. Indeed, to suggest that Oliver contributed to the team's collapse with his 27 at-bats and quick tongue took an imagination of desperation.

Belated apology then to Gene Oliver (.246 lifetime, 93 homers), who played 10 seasons in the major leagues with the Cardinals, the Braves (Milwaukee *and* Atlanta), the Phillies, the Red Sox, and the Cubs but finds himself indelibly identified with the best team that never won.

One question, though, Ollie: did you use a parachute?

"He must have," said Beckert. "Otherwise they couldn't have filled up the hole."

Two decades later, I believe I have found an answer to "why." It came slowly but decisively as I charted and studied over a period of weeks and months the day-by-day progress of the 1969 Cubs and Mets.

Something new did appear, something I had never considered:

Doubleheaders.

Consider two baseball games in one day. It doesn't happen much anymore. The 1988 Cubs, for example, had *zero* doubleheaders on their schedule. The 1988 Mets had one.

That wasn't the case 20 seasons ago. Franchises hadn't yet figured out that offering two games for the price of one was bad business. Nor was television revenue as married to the schedule as it is today.

Factor in an unusually wet summer of 1969, and the result is startling: the 1969 Mets played 44 games in doubleheaders, winning 30. The Cubs played 30 doubleheader games, winning 13.

The Cubs actually scheduled 14 doubleheaders in 1969 and picked up 1 more because of a rainout. The Mets scheduled 12 doubleheaders and, incredibly, *played 10 additional twin bills because of rainouts.*

So what?

The Mets were a perfect doubleheader team. It was a team without position superstars, and manager Gil Hodges often platooned several positions.

Also, the Mets were one of baseball's first teams to successfully employ a five-man pitching rotation. Because of the quality and depth of New York's young arms—Tom Seaver, age 24; Jerry Koosman, 25; Gary Gentry, 22; Jim McAndrew, 24; Nolan Ryan, 22; Tug McGraw, 24; Cal Koonce, 28; Ron Taylor, 28; and Don Cardwell, 33—Hodges was able to reach deep into the rotation without a harmful dropoff in quality. How deep was the Mets pitching? Nine of the pitchers won six or more games. This is with what Hodges was working: Tom Seaver, 25–7 (2.21 ERA); Jerry Koosman, 17–9 (2.28); Gary Gentry, 13–12 (3.43); Don Cardwell, 8–10 (3.01); Nolan Ryan, 6–3 (3.53); Cal Koonce, 6–3 (4.99); Jim McAndrew, 6–7 (3.47); Tug McGraw, 9–3 (2.24, 12 saves); and Roger Taylor, 9–4 (2.72, 13 saves).

For much of the season Hodges platooned regularly at four positions: right field (Ron Swoboda and Art Shamsky); first base (Ed Kranepool and Donn Clendenon); third base (Ed Charles and Wayne Garrett); and second base (Al Weis and Ken Boswell). Only four Mets enjoyed actual regular status: catcher Jerry Grote, leftfielder Cleon Jones, center-fielder Tommie Agee, and shortstop Bud Harrelson.

The Cubs were the opposite. Whether this was the fault of Durocher for not showing faith in youngsters such as Joe Decker, Jim Colborn, Rich Nye, and Archie Reynolds is an arguable point, as was his utilization of bench personnel. The facts, however, are that the Cubs tried to play with a short, however talented, deck over a long season—a season of doubleheaders for which they were ill-equipped.

In truth, if he could have, Durocher would have preferred to go with a *three*-man rotation of Jenkins, Hands, and Holtzman.

The Cubs swept only 2 of the 15 doubleheaders in which they played. The Mets swept 11—3 in August (all against the pitiful Padres) and 3 more in September. The hard numbers:

	DOUBLEHEADERS					
	Scheduled	Played	Swept	Split	Lost	Record
Mets	12	22	11	8	3	30–14
Cubs	14	15	2	9	4	13–17

Thus the Mets played 30 percent (44 of 162) of their games in doubleheaders and accumulated 30 percent (30 of 100) of their victories during doubleheaders. By contrast, only 14 percent (13 of 92) of Chicago's victories came in double-headers.

Let's play two? Wash out your mouth, Ernie Banks.

FINAL STANDINGS			
East	**W**	**L**	**GB**
New York	100	62	—
Chicago	92	70	8
Pittsburgh	88	74	12
St. Louis	87	75	13
Philadelphia	63	99	37
Montreal	52	110	48

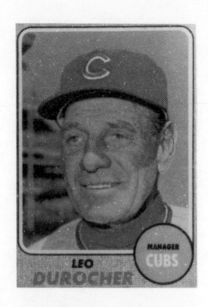

LEO ERNEST DUROCHER
B. July 27, 1905, W. Springfield, Mass.
Managerial Record

YEAR	TEAM	G	W	L	PCT	STANDING
1939	BKN N	157	84	69	.549	3
1940		156	88	65	.575	2
1941		157	100	54	.649	1
1942		155	104	50	.675	2
1943		153	81	72	.529	3
1944		155	63	91	.409	7
1945		155	87	67	.565	3
1946		157	96	60	.615	2
1948		75	37	38	.493	5
1948	NY N	79	41	38	.519	4
1949		156	73	81	.474	5
1950		154	86	68	.558	3
1951		157	98	59	.624	1
1952		154	92	62	.597	2
1953		155	70	84	.455	5
1954		154	97	57	.630	1
1955		154	80	74	.519	3
1966	CHI N	162	59	103	.364	10
1967		162	87	74	.540	3
1968		163	84	78	.519	3
1969		163	92	70	.568	2
1970		162	84	78	.519	2
1971		162	83	79	.512	3
1972		90	46	44	.511	4
1972	HOU N	31	16	15	.516	2
1973		162	82	80	.506	4
24 yrs.		3740	2010	1710	.540	

18

Leo Durocher

"If I'd known we were going to lose eight straight I would have just played nine pitchers every day and let everyone else go home and rest."
—Leo Durocher

It wasn't until after the 1969 season that Leo Durocher was accused of gambling on Cubs games.

No evidence was ever presented to indict or even implicate Durocher, yet while snow whipped through the streets of Chicago during the winter of 1969 and early 1970, the rumors raged within newsrooms and the baseball commissioner's office.

The rumors were about association: Leo had reportedly been seen at a north side Italian restaurant in the company of a known hoodlum, a man suspected in the killing of a sports bookmaker.

There were specifics: Leo had reportedly won $60,000

betting against the Cubs on September 9, 1969, in Shea Stadium, the day he pitched Ferguson Jenkins against the Mets with two days of rest and allowed him to hit for himself in the fifth inning when the Cubs trailed 6–1.

Nothing was ever printed because nothing could be proved. Yet commissioner Bowie Kuhn launched an official investigation, sending two special agents into Chicago and a third to Las Vegas. The IRS was involved. So was every investigative reporter in town.

Nothing.

Clean.

When Leo later wrote about the probe in his autobiography, *Nice Guys Finish Last* (Simon and Schuster, 1975), he called it a setup. He also wrote about the visit to his Lake Shore Drive apartment by three men: one was from the Better Business Bureau, one was from the IRS, and one was the late Bill Jones, later to become managing editor of the *Chicago Tribune*. In their possession was a photograph of the hoodlum in question, and they wanted to know if Leo knew the man.

Leo says his wife, Lynne, chased the unwelcome visitors out the door and immediately contacted her brother, Rob Walker, then chief investigator for the Illinois Crime Investigating Commission. Walker's reaction, according to Leo's book: "It's a setup. There are two things going on right now, and I'll warn you about them right now."

The two things:

• Walker claimed that Governor Richard Ogilvie, a Republican taking office in Springfield, wanted to get rid of the Illinois Crime Commission and was personally out to get Walker who had also reportedly been seen at lunch with the hoodlum, as had Lynne. Supposedly it had been a chummy luncheon foursome.

• "It's the Commission they're really out to discredit," Walker said, "and if they can tie us together, using Leo's name and my name, the press will do the rest of it for them and kill two birds with one stone." Walker was later dismissed from the Commission.

Durocher, in recounting the incident, also suggested: (a) that his feud with Jack Brickhouse was behind the Tribune Company being "out to get him"; (b) that his apartment telephone was tapped; and (c) that during Lynne's previous marriage to Joel Goldblatt, the Goldblatts had been close friends with Mr. and Mrs. Don Maxwell, and Maxwell, then editor of the *Tribune*, had taken Joel's side in the divorce and was also after Leo.

Durocher's paranoia was running rampant. But then so were the unsubstantiated rumors.

When Kuhn came into Chicago that winter for a speaking engagement, I told him I had heard rumors about his investigation and planned to write a story.

He asked me not to print it.

"It will hurt baseball," said Kuhn, "and so far we have no proof."

One can understand why the commissioner was so sensitive about the subject. Detroit pitcher Denny McLain was under suspension for association with a bookmaker, and a national magazine had just published an article by former Chicago sportswriter Bill Furlong entitled "How Leo Blew the Pennant."

I didn't write the column until the following July, after confirmation that Kuhn had personally interrogated Durocher at spring training in Scottsdale, Arizona.

"He had an open file on me," said Durocher when asked about the probe, "but he closed it."

Leo bragged about the confrontation. He exulted in the fact that his wife, Lynne, had lost her temper (reportedly because she got her feet wet walking through the grass) and "told off" the commissioner, threatening to sue baseball unless the allegations ceased.

"His face was red," said Leo about Kuhn's visit. In fact, Leo claimed he could remember everything about the Kuhn interview, held at the Executive House in Scottsdale. Leo's version of the conversation went like this:

"Do you go to Las Vegas?"

"Sure I go to Las Vegas, during the off-season."

"Do you gamble?"

"Of course I gamble."

"Did you gamble and win the last time you were there?"

"Yes, and I won a lot, and it's on my income tax."

Kuhn, according to Leo, then looked into his file, said "I know," and closed the file.

Durocher said later, "I didn't go to school just to eat my lunch. From now on people had better be careful what they write about me. Judge John J. Kelly [Lynne's stepfather] and his lawyers are examining every word."

Then he paused and said, "So be careful. If you find anything new to write, you're Houdini."

Leo had a point; not the unveiled threat, but about his track record. By 1970 he had made more than a few head-lines on and off the field. He had been suspended from baseball in 1947 by commissioner Happy Chandler, for "conduct detrimental to baseball" (translation: Leo was associating with some pretty bad guys). He had been named in divorce suits, alienation of affections suits, and at least three times had been charged by fans with assault and battery. The man did know his law.

Little else was written about Leo and his gambling fol-lowing the interrogation by Kuhn in 1970. Durocher, fired in mid-1972, managed the Houston Astros briefly in 1972 and 1973 (long enough to label Cesar Cedeno the "next Willie Mays"), then retired to Palm Springs, California, where he has lived ever since.

Lynne Walker Goldblatt Durocher left Leo three years later, returned briefly after he underwent open-heart surgery, then left again and divorced him in 1981. They haven't spoken since.

"I left because he started to gamble heavily," says Lynne, sitting in a Chicago restaurant, Lino's, located across from Ditka's, for whom she does public relations.

"He told me when we married, 'I used to gamble, but I don't anymore.' But it was a disease with him. Leo was a degenerate gambler, and I lost all respect for him. He didn't have any money of his own, and he didn't get mine, but he tried. When I realized it could go that way, I got out. I don't believe in gambling, and that was the finish for us."

What kind of gambling?

"Rolling dice, playing gin at the country club. All he wanted to do was play cards."

Was it that way when he managed the Cubs?

"Not like that. Only once can I remember him going to Las Vegas then, and that's when he won $25,000 and reported it."

Did Leo bet on baseball games?

"I'd stake my life against it. I don't think he ever gave information to gamblers either. He had too much respect for the game.

"Leo was capable of almost anything, but he loved baseball too much. He was too much of a competitor. He had too much pride. It meant too much for him to win to take. If he'd been on the take he would have had money. But he never did."

But Leo's gambling wasn't the only reason Lynne left.

"I didn't want to live in Palm Springs either. Our marriage was fun for a time. As long as we were in Chicago it was exciting. My friends and family were there. But after we left baseball and moved from Houston, he wanted Palm Springs. He had wanted to live there all of his life. It was his dream. But I told him, 'If we move to Palm Springs, this marriage will end in divorce or I'll lose my mind.'

"Palm Springs is too limiting. It's a transient community. I was a Chicago girl. I'd lived a little in Los Angeles as an actress, but I wanted something from a town, some culture. It had none.

"But we went there anyway. I bought a place. Leo didn't have any money. He never had any money. He always made a lot and either gave it away or lost it. He was a generous man. But that's when he started to lose a lot gambling too. It was all new to me. I could have been his daughter: I didn't know about his background with Happy Chandler, getting kicked out of baseball, or any of that.

"The other thing about Palm Springs was the Sinatra

crowd. Everything was a command performance night after night. Leo always wanted to be where Frank was. He was always waiting for Frank's phone call. I would go back to Chicago to visit, but he preferred to wait in Palm Springs for the phone to ring. I told him he should be working instead of waiting to hear from Frank."

Of Leo's open-heart surgery in the late 1970s, Lynne says, "I was in Chicago and I got this call from his doctor, Dr. Michael De Bakey, who said, 'He needs you.'

" 'That's a rotten thing to do,' I said. Leo wouldn't call his own family, so he had the doctor call me. He was hoping for a reconciliation. So I went back to Palm Springs for 10 days of his abuse while he was recovering from the operation and staying at Sinatra's house. He was a terrible patient. Mean to me and mean to his nurses. Taking care of Leo was hell. So when he got better I left again, and the last time I saw him was in court. We had some fun times. Some angry times too. But also a lot of boring times."

Then suddenly she becomes the interviewer and poses the question I have been expecting.

"Didn't you make your name in Chicago at the expense of Leo?" she asks, referring to the feud that had erupted between Durocher and me in the early 1970s.

"I didn't look at it that way," I say, "but I did write about him a lot. If it happened that way, it wasn't on purpose."

"I didn't think you were fair. You were attacking my husband."

We talk more about Leo. After a few more semipersonal questions about their much-publicized marriage, she finally says, "Are you asking me how Leo was in bed?"

"Not exactly."

"Well," she says, "he was terrific. After all those years on the road, how could he not be?"

Having already learned more than I expected or wanted to, I reached for the $27 lunch check.

"I think this is the first time I can ever recall a sportswriter buying me lunch," says Lynne.

"I'm not too happy about it, either."

Three months later, upon telephoning Lynne to verify facts surrounding the chronology of 1969, we have another insightful exchange.

"Did you take a road trip with the Cubs into Montreal just a few weeks after you and Leo got married?"

"I don't remember. We got married in April."

"April? You were married in June."

"I was married April 19."

"Lynne, are you sure you weren't married to Leo Durocher on June 19, 1969?"

"Listen, are you trying to tell me when I got married? Don't you think I know when I got married?"

"Well, you've been married a couple of times."

"So?"

"Well, it says right here in this newspaper clipping that you and Leo were married in June."

"April."

"June."

"Are you sure it says June?"

"That's what it says."

Long pause. "Oh, well, what the hell," she finally concludes. "It doesn't matter anyway."

Leo's gambling had been a poorly kept secret.

Bob Glass, a former reporter with the *Chicago Today*, had investigated the connection between Leo and Las Vegas. "I made contacts in Las Vegas and found that P. K. Wrigley paid off Leo's gambling debts," he says. "There was nothing illegal about it. Wrigley just wanted Leo's slate clean, so he paid off thousands of dollars in markers."

"We all knew Leo was a gambler," says former traveling secretary Cullen, "because he was always trying to keep up with Sinatra and before that George Raft and his crowd. But baseball meant more to Leo than anything in the world. There was never any discussion within the Cubs organization that Leo might be doing business with gamblers. Wrigley knew he was in hock financially, but he never suspected him of dumping games.

"Leo wouldn't have been able to control a game anyway. How would you like to have a bet on a game the 1969 Cubs were playing?"

Of course it is naive to suggest a manager can't manipulate or control what happens in a game. Indeed the selection and/or removal of a starting pitcher would be a powerful edge, if not a sure thing, for anyone gambling on baseball.

But despite all the times Durocher may have been guilty in his life without getting caught, this time he was probably innocent. Baseball and winning were all-consuming to Durocher. It's hard to accept the idea that he ever wagered *against* the 1969 Cubs. He had too much to gain by winning the pennant, in both ego and material wealth.

So when making your final sweep search for definitive reasons behind the collapse of the Cubs, throw out gambling. The only sure thing in September of 1969 was Mets pitching.

Even 20 years ago Leo Durocher provided an extraordinary link with the past. Born on July 27, 1905, on the kitchen table of a old wooden house in West Springfield, Massachusetts, he went on to play baseball alongside such legends as Babe Ruth and Dizzy Dean. He fought in the Yankees clubhouse with Ruth and was about to fight Ty Cobb when Ruth came to his rescue. He dropped bags of water out of hotel windows with Dean and other members of the St. Louis Cardinals' Gashouse Gang.

There was also the well-traveled story that Leo once stole Ruth's watch. Leo denies it saying, "If I had wanted Babe's watch, he would have given it to me."

Leo reveled in his own image. Born poor ("We never had a Christmas tree"), raised by French-Canadian parents, he became a kid pool hustler who worshiped baseball player Rabbit Maranville, the shortstop for the Boston Braves.

He learned racial tolerance early in life by bossing a crew of blacks on the Albany railroad (already having been kicked out of high school for punching a teacher), and it was a tolerance he practiced throughout his baseball career.

It was Ruth who gave Leo the nickname "All-American Out," and, over a major league playing career of 17 seasons (Durocher's last year was 1945, a familiar year to Cubs fans), he hit only .247 but at 5'10" and 160 pounds still played efficient shortstop.

Always in debt ("after two seasons with the Yankees I owed money all around town"), often in trouble (baseball commissioner Judge Kenesaw Mountain Landis called him on the carpet for writing bad checks), Leo kept forging ahead, finally finding his niche as the playing manager of the Brooklyn Dodgers in 1939.

He managed for 24 seasons, winning pennants with the Dodgers in 1941 and World Championships with the 1951 and 1954 New York Giants. His career was explosive, almost mindboggling. Leo and Willie Mays, Leo and Branch Rickey, Leo and Dusty Rhodes, Leo and banishment from baseball for one season (1947), Leo and Laraine Day.

Seven times his teams finished second. He was fired, hired, and fired again. Then he coached for the Los Angeles Dodgers from 1961 through 1964 (where he got into trouble for trying to undermine manager Walter Alston), finally becoming a network commentator (hired and fired by NBC) in 1965, then a sports talk show host for KABC radio in Los Angeles.

By the time Durocher arrived in Chicago his name was already legend. He had been recommended for the job by Herman Franks, who coached under Leo with the New York Giants and later became a reasonably successful manager of the Cubs from 1977 to 1979 (238–241).

The situation for Durocher was ideal: slumbering team, right man, right place, right time. He took them, resurrected them, inspired them, and lost the 1969 pennant with them.

Then he destroyed them, or they themselves. Opinions will always vary about what happened to the Cubs after 1969, but this much is fact; they were never the same. The joy never came back. The magic turned to acrimony.

An eastern sportswriter and avowed enemy of Leo Durocher once wrote, "Leo could be standing on a bridge with two other guys. One of them pushes him off into the swirling water, and the other guy dives in to save his life. The next day Leo goes back to the same bridge, sees the same two guys, and they start out even again."

With this in mind, I drove through the desert heat to Palm Springs to see Durocher, the man I hadn't pushed off any bridges but had pushed hard during his final years in Chicago.

From the radio came the shivering voices of Dodgers announcers Vin Scully and Don Drysdale, in New York for the 1988 National League Championship Series. The weather was cold, wet, and falling-down miserable for the ballplayers, but on the left coast girls strolled the streets in shorts and halters, their broad-brimmed straw hats protection against the 100-degree sun.

Few stirred around the pool at the Joshua Tree apartment complex at the corner of Sagebrush Road and East Palm Canyon Drive, where Leo has resided for almost 13 years. It isn't elegant, certainly not by Palm Springs standards, but it's clean and safe and comfortable and rent-controlled (one bedroom upstairs is $570). He lives there on his pension from the Players' Association, which exceeds $50,000 a year.

Leo and I start out even again.

No long interviews, please. It's nothing personal, you understand, but no long interviews at age 83. He had just returned from a one-month vacation in Japan and South Korea ("Of *course* I went to the Olympics, why *else* would I go to Korea?").

Leo is blunt about the 1969 season. "It's one of the sore spots of my entire career that we didn't win at least a division for Mr. Wrigley. He was a great man."

Looking back, would he had have done anything differently during September of 1969?

"It's great to be a Monday morning quarterback," he says, "so I can say now that, sure, if I'd known we were going to lose eight straight I would have just played nine pitchers

every day and let everybody else go home and rest. But I
didn't know that, did I? Everybody played hard, that's all I
can tell people. It was just one of those things. The Mets
just killed everybody. Every time we looked up, the Mets
were winning 1–0 or 2–1.

"It was like being on a golf course standing over the ball
on the first tee and looking up at the scoreboard and seeing
that the guy you've got to beat has just shot 63. Now you've
got to shoot 62, and you haven't even swung the club.

"That what happened to us. It affects you."

Knowing that Leo has kept in touch with some of the
1969 Cubs as well as people such as Willie Mays, Joey
Amalfitano, and Herman Franks, I ask, "Was the 1969 team
the best group of men you ever managed?"

"I can't say that," says Leo, "but it was a great bunch
because of their attitude. After I came to Chicago their
attitude changed, and they became an exciting team. They
gave me 100 percent and tried to give 115 percent, but they
couldn't. They played their hearts out, but the Mets, well,
they ran over everyone, including us."

I once wrote that Durocher was the only amoral man
with whom I had ever been associated, my contention being
that Leo could only differentiate between right and wrong
depending on how it affected him personally. Whether this
description was accurate or colored by personal bias remains for others to judge. But I do know that if not for Leo's
behavior, his name would long ago have been emblazoned
in the Hall of Fame at Cooperstown.

That his seven teams in Chicago won only nine more
games than they lost (535–526) should not detract from
Durocher's contribution to baseball. Before presenting his
case, let's phrase it this way: If the history of baseball were
being written and 100 names were placed on a list, how
soon would Durocher's name be selected? Could the history
be written accurately without mentioning him?

Yet year after year the Veterans Committee of the Hall of
Fame has bypassed the 83-year-old Leo Durocher. Why?

Because he himself pushed too many people into the swirling water? Others don't judge as Leo judges. Others don't start fresh the next day.

"Durocher won't be voted into the Hall of Fame until people on the committee who knew him are dead and buried," observes veteran baseball writer Jerome Holtzman of the *Chicago Tribune*. "Bill Veeck is in the same boat. Baseball executives didn't like either one of them."

At least one member of the committee was more optimistic. Buzzie Bavasi, former Dodgers executive in Brooklyn and Los Angeles, was prepared to "stand up and fight" for Durocher.

"Durocher belongs," said Bavasi recently, "and last year he got 10 votes out of 17 when he needed 14. Umpire Al Barlick got 12. This year I think they both might make it.

"The only reason Leo isn't in the Hall of Fame is because he was banned that one year by Happy Chandler, and that never should have happened. It was ridiculous, I have written documents to prove it, and I'm taking them to the meeting with me. Unfortunately for Leo, Branch Rickey wouldn't appear at the hearings on Leo's behalf. I don't know why. Maybe he wanted to get rid of Leo.

"Nobody in the committee meetings ever really admit that Leo's banishment is the reason they're not voting for him, but this year I'm going to put it all on the table. Durocher not being in the Hall of Fame just doesn't make sense. At least Birdie Tebbetts had the guts at last year's meeting to stand up and say, 'I never liked the SOB, but I'm going to vote for him.'

"Leo never managed for me either, but remember this: he took a Brooklyn team that finished seventh in 1938, and three years later he won a pennant. He took a fifth-place club in New York [the Giants] in 1949 and two years later won a World Championship. He took an eighth-place ballclub in Chicago and almost won the pennant. And of the last five managers who have been inducted into the Hall of Fame, only Walter Alston had a higher winning percentage than Leo."

The idea of Durocher's induction was first suggested by the press within 48 hours after he left the Cubs on July 24, 1972, a concept which caused Brickhouse's blood pressure to rise.

"How can you vote a .247 hitter into the Hall of Fame?" asked Brickhouse.

Here's how. Consider Bavasi's arguments, plus:

- Leo was part of major league baseball for almost half a century, 1925 through 1973.
- He played 20 seasons as an excellent shortstop, albeit at .247.
- He spent 24 seasons managing the Brooklyn Dodgers, the New York Giants, the Cubs, and the Houston Astros, managing 3,749 games, winning 2,019, and losing 1,709 for a winning percentage of .542.
- He won a pennant with the 1941 Dodgers and two World Championships with the 1951 and 1954 Giants in a managerial career that spanned five decades, 1939 through 1973.

For the record: the Veterans Committee must cast 75 percent of its vote for someone in order for that person to be elected into the Hall of Fame. The voting members, equally representing the press, former players, managers, executives, and the commissioner's office are:

Edgar Munzel, Bob Broeg, Joe Reichler, Shirley Povich, Allen Lewis, Red Barber (new member), Ernie Harwell, Gabe Paul, Joe Brown, Buzzie Bavasi, Roy Campanella, Stan Musial, Ted Williams, Monte Irvin, Al Lopez, Birdie Tebbetts, Charles Gehringer, Buck O'Neil, and chairman Charles Segar.

Why the above-mentioned gentlemen have refused to give Durocher 75 percent of their support in the past is a question only they can answer.

Sure he was a rat. Sure he cheated, lied, swindled, used, and abused.

But Leo was baseball at its competitive best. And nowhere

in Cooperstown is there a moral code of ethics. Not under
Ty Cobb's name. Not there alongside Ruth or Dean or
Alexander or Mantle. Try the test. See if you make a list of
100 without Durocher.

Interesting too has been Leo's disregard—at least on the
surface—of Hall of Fame consideration.

"I just don't think about it," he says. "It's not part of my
thinking. If there was something I could do that would be
different. But I have no control. I'm not part of it. It's all up
to the Veterans Committee, and I leave it to them."

Had he heard that Bavasi was to present a strong case in
his behalf?

"I've heard some things, but I have to fall back on an old
cliché when it comes to talk about the Hall of Fame.

"I'll believe it when I see it."

When the subject came up a few years ago, Durocher said
to friend Herman Franks, "I'm not worried about getting
into Cooperstown. I'm more worried about the gates upstairs being opened."

Those gates? The pearly ones?

Durocher has never been more serious. In recent years he
has been a regular parishioner at Our Lady of Solitude
Catholic Church, sometimes even passing the collection
plate. He goes to mass regularly.

Members of the '69 Cubs first noticed Leo's rediscovered
faith when he stood to apologize to Santo at the Randy
Hundley adult camp dinner several years ago.

"It was like he was trying to put everything right,"
observed Hundley.

"Santo deserved the apology," recalls Leo. "I was wrong,
and when you're wrong you should say you're wrong."

There has been incredulity about it all among those who
played under Leo. When someone said, "Leo is laying
bricks on that road to heaven," Billy Williams chuckled,
"He's got a lot of bricks to lay."

Yet by reaching back almost three-quarters of a century
into Durocher's past, one can understand.

Leo was an altar boy. And in his autobiography, published at age 70, Durocher wrote of being raised in the Catholic Church:

> . . . The Church played an enormously important part of our lives. My brothers and I were altar boys. Many a Sunday the four of us were on the altar together in our little white surplices, serving mass.
>
> . . . You don't ever get away from that kind of upbringing. Not that I was ever in any danger of joining the priesthood, but in all the years I was traveling around playing ball I very rarely missed a Sunday morning mass. When I was divorced [for the first of four times], I lost the right to have my confession heard and receive communion, and that hurt me. I found it very painful to sit there and watch everybody else get up and file up to the altar. And so, while I still feel the urge to go to church from time to time, I always leave without a sense of fulfillment.

In the years since, Leo has found new fulfillment at Our Lady of Solitude. "I go to the 5:30 mass every Saturday afternoon," says Leo. "I get there in time to take collection, light the candles, and go to confession."

Then he started to smile and said, "I probably shouldn't be telling you this, but sometimes when I go into the confession the priest says, 'What are you doing here? You haven't done anything,' and I say, 'Well, Father, if you want to go back a few years, I have done a few things.' "

19
Beyond 1969

"If only we could find more team players like Ernie Banks."
—Phil Wrigley's letter to the public

At the time it happened, nobody understood.

Sure, it hurts, that September collapse that cost the Cubs their first National League pennant since 1945. Sure, it was distressing to be overtaken by the Miracle Mets.

But there was always next year, and this was, in Leo's parlance, some kinda team.

This meteor, however, was headed toward an atmosphere of chaos. From their high point of 1969, a record of 84-52 on September 2, Durocher's immensely talented teams played exact .500 baseball (221-221) until he was fired in mid-1972.

Next year ran into next year ran into next year.

In 1970 the Cubs had a wonderful chance to win the pennant but again folded, even though there were no smoking Mets to beat that year.

The season was stressful from the beginning. Leo forced his players to disband their off-season basketball team, yet he signed a $40,000 eight-month contract to do a talk show on radio station WIND. The show lasted until midseason, when Leo suddenly resigned after players complained about learning lineup changes over the air rather than at the ballpark. ("Santo is playing like he's in a fog," Leo told a listener. "Let him sit down.") Newspaper beat writers covering the team were angry too, for they were hearing on the radio which players were to be sent to Tacoma, or from Tacoma, before they could compete in print. Once Wrigley realized what was happening he forced Leo to drop the show.

In late June of 1970 the Cubs lost 12 games in a row, falling from a 4½-game lead (35–25) to 4½ games behind. That's also the season the Cubs added outfielder John Callison, pitcher Milt Pappas, and first baseman Joe Pepitone to the roster. The four starting pitchers were Hands, Holtzman, Jenkins, and Pappas, and the batting order was Kessinger, Beckert, Williams, Hickman (who had his greatest year), Pepitone, Santo, Callison, and Hundley. Presumably all the holes from 1969 had been filled.

But the Cubs were experienced losers by now. On September 4 they were tied for first place with a record of 72–64. But they went 12–14 to finish at 84–78, second place by five games behind the Pittsburgh Pirates.

During the winter of 1970 some of the players tried to shake their doldrums by appearing on stage at the Mill Run Theater in Niles with comedian Milton Berle.

Berle: "How do you hold a bat?"

Santo: "By the wings."

Berle: "How do you handle a high fly?"

Williams: "I keep my jacket buttoned."

Berle: "I understand you're from Dallas. Were there any big men born in your neighborhood?"

Banks: "No, only babies."

Berle: "Who's older, you or your brother Larry?"

Santo: "My brother."

Berle: "Who comes after him?"

Santo: "The police."

But by spring training 1971, the Cubs were ready again for baseball.

Or were they? It was a team tailored for another era, perhaps the 1950s, but not the 1970s. One year earlier they had been the only club in the National League with three players hitting more than 25 home runs and 100-plus RBI (Williams, Santo, and Hickman), yet the team had little speed, offensively or defensively, to compete on artificial surfaces.

It was a team suited for Wrigley Field, yet it finished 83–79, tied for third and 14 games behind the Pirates.

"A lot of us no longer understood Leo by then," wrote Fergie Jenkins in his autobiography. "He became more and more withdrawn. He got to the point where he often didn't post the lineup card until 10 minutes before the game. The players didn't know whether they were going to play that day."

"Leo did lose it a little before the end," admits Hank Aguirre. "He called a hit-and-run play in Atlanta, and Kessinger was the hitter. Well, Kess swung at the ball, and Leo chewed him out in the dugout because he fouled off a pitch when the runner had the base stolen. And it had been a hit-and-run play."

"My only beef with Leo then was that he had a style of airing out things in front of other people," says Kessinger. "I always thought stuff like that should be said in private. Other than that, I liked playing for him because he allowed us to be pros."

That was the summer Leo and I were feuding (I was calling him Whatshisname and he was calling me other names), and Durocher loved it. Feuds kept his mind active and blood pumping.

Example: The Cubs were playing an exhibition game in Cooperstown, New York, and we were all invited to a special luncheon, where I found myself seated at a round table next to Joe Pepitone. From another table Leo caught Pepi's eye and motioned for him. When Joe came back he was laughing.

"What's so funny?"

"Leo just offered me $50 to dump a salad on your lap."

"Did you take it?"

"Nahhh, I whipped out $100 and dared him to do it."

That was also the year LEO MUST GO buttons started appearing at Wrigley Field. Somebody also calculated that Leo had already employed 149 players, including 66 pitchers, in six seasons. It was the season Santo was honored at a $50-a-plate dinner by the Diabetes Association and received an expensive-looking jewelry case from teammate Pepitone. Inside the case was a note that said, "It's on the way."

But the gift didn't arrive, and neither did the Cubs' rejuvenation. Badly hurt by Hundley's knee injury and continuing overtones of clubhouse dissension, the Cubs floundered even though others among the superstar lineup were having outstanding individual seasons.

Nineteen seventy-one was the season of one of the worst clubhouse explosions in franchise history, an all-out, screaming, trying-to-strangle confrontation between Durocher and his players, specifically Pepitone, Pappas, and Santo. A festering wound was opened that would never close.

What follows is a recreation of the ugly event, based on graphic accounts from interviewed players, coaches, and Durocher.

It began with pennant-race pressure. The Cubs trailed the Pirates by 4½ games with 37 to play, but Pappas had given up a game-losing base hit on a checked-swing double by Doug Rader of Houston. To Durocher the loss was particularly grating because the hit came on an 0–2 pitch, a pitcher's sin he considered unforgivable. Now on August 23 Leo called for a clubhouse meeting.

It started with the usual. The Cubs weren't hustling, he said. They weren't concentrating. Some of them were lazy. And he took another 0–2 shot at Pappas, whom he would later describe as a "renegade, clubhouse lawyer, and agitator." Then he asked if anyone had anything to say.

Pepitone did. "Why are you always blaming people?" he asked. "Pappas didn't mean to throw that pitch. Santo didn't want to be in a slump. [Santo had skipped batting practice for several days in an attempt to shake a slump, which he had.] All you ever do is criticize players. When I played for Ralph Houk [with the Yankees], he stuck up for his players. That's why we won pennants. The players came first. But all you do is criticize."

Durocher was enraged but listened until Pepitone ran down, then asked, "Are you through?" ("He was purple," recalls Santo. "That's how mad he was.")

Now Durocher stood and started his own speech.

"What are you, a fuckin' clubhouse lawyer?" he screamed at Pepitone.

"I knew I should have kept my mouth shut," responded Pepi.

"You had your say," said Leo, "now I'll have mine," and he proceeded to praise two of his favorites, Williams and Beckert, saying while looking directly at Santo, "Does Beckert ever miss batting practice?"

"What are you trying to say, Leo?" said Santo. "That I don't practice hitting?"

"Well, did you take hitting today?"

"No, and the reason is that I'm out of my slump and I want to keep the feeling I've got. That doesn't mean I don't want to improve myself. If I was hitting .300, Leo, you wouldn't give a shit. But I'm hitting .260, so you're on my ass, and you use my roommate, who's hitting .300, as an example. That's a great example, Leo."

Durocher later wrote in his autobiography, about the meeting, "I had lost control of it. It was out of hand and the players had me backed against a wall, so I hit back."

That's when Leo turned on Santo and said, "I didn't want to bring this up, Ronnie, but I'm going to say it. The only fucking reason that you're having a 'Ron Santo Day' is that Billy and Ernie had one and you asked John Holland for one."

Santo went berserk, nose-to-nose with Durocher, demanding that Holland be called into the clubhouse to refute Leo's accusation.

"I went crazy," recalls Santo. "I wanted to get Leo. I was calling him everything in the book. Guys were holding me and everybody was yelling. Then Leo got on the phone and called Holland, and everything got quiet. A few guys were calling Leo names, and he went up the steps into his office. The rest of us just sat and waited. They put me in a corner, and I just sat there with my head down.

"Then I realize Leo isn't around, and I figure he's up there in his office getting his story straight with Holland, so I went crazy again."

Santo raced up the stairs past the training room and burst into Durocher's office, and, sure enough, there was Leo talking with Holland.

"Get your ass downstairs!" screamed Santo at Holland, and, according to other players, he went for Durocher.

"Somebody grabbed me," says Santo, "but I wasn't going to hit that 66-year-old son of a bitch. No way could I have hit the man. He thought he could handle himself, that's how dumb he was. He wasn't afraid to get hit. That wrinkled bastard wanted to prove he was still playing with the Gashouse Gang or something. But he couldn't have taken a punch. It would have killed him."

Some order was restored, and Santo was screaming for Leo to repeat to Holland what he had said. Everyone else was quiet, and he did. Then Santo, claiming it was a lie, demanded that Holland say so in front of his teammates.

Holland, though, got political.

"He hesitated," recalls Santo, "then said something like, 'Well, Ron, when we talked about a contract we did talk about giving you a Day.'

"But I didn't *ask* for it, John. You offered it. Chrissakes, that was seven months ago anyhow. We were talking about a contract, and you *offered* me a day."

Holland kept hedging ("We talked about a Day for you and decided on it"), and Santo now says, "I could see John was afraid of Leo because Leo had the upper hand with Mr.

Wrigley. Now I didn't know what to do. I had tears in my eyes. I can't hit people. Instead I cry. It's something you have inside that you can't control. So I cried. I cried right there in front of all my teammates."

Now others rejoined the fray.

"I've never seen anything so dirty in my life!" yelled Pepitone to Durocher. Then Jenkins said something, as did others, including Hands and Regan.

"Well, if you guys feel that I'm wrong, then I'm sorry," said Durocher.

"You're so full of shit!" yelled Santo.

"I quit," snarled back Durocher, turning to walk toward his office," and you guys can do it all by yourselves."

But Durocher didn't quit. He and Santo eventually shook hands.

"I shook his hand and walked out," says Santo. "I had to do it."

"I had a cigarette in my hand, and I was shaking so badly I could hardly hold it," recounts Durocher, "but I said, 'Ronnie, I'm not mad at you.' But those other two bastards [Pappas and Pepitone], I was never going to forgive them."

By now it was less than 20 minutes to game time.

Durocher put his uniform back on and walked outside as if nothing had happened.

Santo took two tranquilizers.

"First time up I doubled down the left-field line. Second time up I doubled into left field."

Santo finished with two doubles and a single, and the Cubs won that game but lost seven of their next ten and eventually finished in third place, fourteen games behind the champion Pirates.

Twelve years later, at a banquet celebrating Hundley's first adult baseball camp, Durocher, then 75 and recovering from open-heart surgery, stood at a microphone in front of his former players and apologized to Santo.

"Of course I accepted it," says Santo. "How long can you stay mad at somebody?"

Two weeks after the explosion, which Durocher called the

worst he had ever encountered in baseball, owner Phillip K. Wrigley got into the act. On September 3 Wrigley purchased a full-page advertisement in Chicago papers:

THIS IS FOR CUB FANS
AND ANYONE ELSE WHO IS INTERESTED

It is no secret that in the closing days of a season that held great possibilities the Cub organization is at sixes and sevens and somebody has to do something. So, as head of the corporation, the responsibility falls on me. . . .

Many people seem to have forgotten, but I have not, that after many years of successful seasons, and five league pennants, the Cubs went into the doldrums and for a quarter of a century were perennial dwellers of the second division in spite of everything we could think of to try and do.

We figured out what we thought was needed to make a lot of potential talent into a contending team, and we settled on Leo Durocher, who had the baseball knowledge to build a contender and win pennants, and also knowing he had always been a controversial figure . . . particularly with the press because he just never was cut out to be a diplomat. He accepted the job at less than he was making because he considered it to be a challenge, and Leo thrives on challenges.

In his first year we ended in the cellar, but from then on came steadily up, knocking on the door for the top.

Each near miss has caused more and more criticism, and this year there has been a constant campaign to "Dump Durocher" that has even affected the players, but just as there has to be someone to make final decisions for the corporation, there has to be someone in charge on the field to make the final decisions on the spur of the moment, and right or wrong, that's it.

All this preamble is to say that after . . . consultation with my baseball people, Leo is the team manager and the "Dump Durocher Clique" might as well give up. He is running the team, and if some of the players do not like it and lie down on the job, during the off-season we will see what we can do to find them happier homes.

—Phil Wrigley, President
Chicago National League Ball Club, Inc.

P.S. If only we could find more team players like Ernie Banks.

It was the beginning of the breakup of the 1969 Cubs. Holtzman, who had asked to be traded, now *insisted* on a happier home. Said Holtzman, "Wrigley's suggestion that Ernie Banks was the only team player hit me like a ton of bricks."

Holtzman was traded on November 29, 1971, to the Oakland A's for outfielder Rick Monday, who had yet to save the American flag.

Early in 1972 Callison was traded to the Yankees and said in parting, "I feel sorry for the team, but they're not going to win with Leo."

In March Durocher predicted the Cubs would win the pennant. "This is the best team I've ever managed," said Leo. "We've got speed and versatility."

The 1972 regulars would be: Hundley, catcher; Pepitone, first base; Beckert, second base; Santo, third base; Kessinger, shortstop; Williams, left field; Rick Monday, center field; and Billy North, right field—with Jose Cardenal, Paul Popovich, Carmen Fanzone, and Hickman among those on the bench. The pitching staff would include Jenkins, Hands, Pappas, Burt Hooton, Juan Pizarro, Larry Gura, Bill Bonham, Steve Hamilton, and Regan. Seven of the above-mentioned players had played with the NL All-Star team at least once during the previous three seasons.

"This team could take off and wing it," said Durocher, then 66 years old.

After 90 games into the 1972 season, Durocher was fired. The Cubs, 46–44, finished by winning 39 of their remaining 65 games under new manager Whitey Lockman, but it was too late—not only for 1972 but for the future. This once-great team had been shattered beyond repair.

Lockman's 1973 team sagged badly in August and September to finish in fifth place with a record of 77–84 after being 50–35 in July. The Mets won the division that season with only 81 victories. Even a finishing record of 32–45 would have won the division. Instead the Cubs went 27–48.

That was the end. The future had been written. Holtzman and Durocher were gone. Hands and Regan too. Now
it was time for the rest of the 1969 nucleus to be dismissed
one by one and the payroll reduced. It was end of an era of
incredible frustration, the breakup of a team that teased and
tantalized a city but never really produced.

In order of departure, this is what happened to the best
team that never won:

- Ernie Banks retired at age 40 following the 1971 season,
  without fanfare or official recognition.
- Ken Holtzman was traded on November 29, 1971, to
  Oakland for outfielder Rick Monday.
- Phil Regan was sold on June 2, 1972, to the White Sox for
  cash.
- Bill Hands was traded on November 30, 1972, along with
  pitcher Joe Decker and minor leaguer Bob Maneely, to
  Minnesota for pitcher Dave LaRoche.
- Ron Santo was traded on December 11, 1973, to the White
  Sox for pitchers Steve Stone, Jim Kremmel, and Ken
  Frailing, and catcher Steve Swisher.
- Glenn Beckert was traded on November 3, 1973, along
  with minor league infielder Bobby Fenwick, to the San
  Diego Padres for outfielder Jerry Morales.
- Randy Hundley was traded on December 6, 1973, to the
  Minnesota Twins for catcher George Mitterwald.
- Jim Hickman was traded to St. Louis on March 23, 1974,
  for pitcher Scipio Spinks, who never pitched for the Cubs.
- Billy Williams was traded on October 23, 1974, to Oak-
  land for pitchers Darold Knowles and Bob Locker and
  infielder Manny Trillo.
- Fergie Jenkins was traded on November 17, 1975, to the
  Texas Rangers for infielders Bill Madlock and Vic Harris.
- Don Kessinger was traded on October 28, 1975, to the
  White Sox for pitcher Mike Garman and minor leaguer
  Bobby Hrapmann.

Of the 17 players who came to Chicago in trades for the
prominent '69 Cubs, only Madlock, Morales, Monday, and

Trillo really produced in Wrigley Field. Pitcher Stone found
Cy Young stardom later in Baltimore, and little achievement
was ever recorded in Chicago by Spinks, Harris, Knowles,
Locker, Garman, Hrapmann, Swisher, Kremmel, Frailing,
Fenwick, Mitterwald, or LaRoche.

By December 31, 1969, 475,200 troops were still in Vietnam, with more than 40,000 already killed and another
264,000 wounded. It would be another three years and
18,132 deaths of American young men before the war ended.
Henry Cabot Lodge had resigned as chief U.S. negotiator at
the Paris talks on the Vietnam War, and from over there
came still-unconfirmed reports that 450 villagers had been
massacred by U.S. soldiers.

It was a melancholy autumn of 1969 in Chicago. The
Bears were awful, but compared to what? On November 15,
in the Bears vs. the Falcons game, Chicago running back
Brian Piccolo couldn't stop coughing: four weeks later chest
x-rays showed a shadow.

In late October came the titillating news that Richard
Burton had purchased Elizabeth Taylor a 69.42-carat diamond worth $1 million. Jack Kerouac, novelist and leading
figure of the Beat Generation, died at age 47. The first
Boeing 747 was flown for the public. John Lennon and
Yoko Ono, who had been married in the spring, were
international celebrities.

Cub fans waited for next year.

Cub fans always wait. In March 1972 I received a letter
from a Cubs fan named Dick Knudsen, a 34-year-old machinist from Oak Lawn who said he was spending approximately $1,000 a year on Cubs tickets home and away—
Scottsdale, Cincinnati, St. Louis, etc.

"In 1969 I had to take aspirins every night to get to sleep,"
said Knudsen.

Didn't he believe that was somewhat extreme, even for a
Cub fan?

"I think so, yes. I just want to live long enough to see the
Cubs win the pennant, but I don't think I will."

At the time, curious about Knudsen's commitment, I

asked when he would leave home and perhaps get married.

"Marry? I don't know about that. If I was married how could I afford to go to spring training?"

That was 1972. In late 1988, still curious about Knudsen, I found his name in the Oak Lawn telephone directory and called again. Some things have changed, some haven't. Knudsen didn't marry, but nowadays he's only a weekend –holiday season ticket holder at Wrigley Field.

"I still live and die with the Cubs," says Knudsen, now 50, "but I don't suffer as much. It's a sickness, you know. Once it gets into your blood, you can't get it out. I don't enjoy the players as much today as I did before. We were closer to them then. But I'm still a fan.

"If they lost 161 consecutive games, I guess I'd be there to see number 162."

I cannot explain the human condition of being a Cubs fan. I'm not sure anybody can, although many have tried. It is every person's private heaven or hell. That isn't to say that to qualify one must flaunt membership in the Emil Verban Society, the Die-Hard Cub Fans Club, or whatever. One needn't wear furry caps with red, white, and blue Cs on them, attend a single game in person, or even know what George Will does for a living. You don't have to know that the bleacher walls are 11 feet high, or that fans last sat in center field in 1962, or that a live bear cub attended the very first game played at Wrigley Field in 1916. That's all just trimming and trivia.

If you are a Cub fan I don't have to explain, and if you aren't it doesn't matter.

That the franchise has now gone 43 consecutive seasons without winning a National League pennant *does* matter. It is a record that can never be duplicated, only broken.

Nor is it the intention here to state that everything that happened 20 years ago overshadows what is happening today at Wrigley Field—how foolish that would be. Nostalgia is for dreaming and longing. As somebody once said, the past always looks better than it was; it's only pleasant because it isn't here.

It was foolhardy for Dallas Green to try to eradicate the memory of 1969, an act as arrogant as a KGB man taking down pictures of Joseph Stalin—but it would be just as silly to suggest that what happened in 1984 didn't also leave an indelible imprint.

There was joy at Clark and Addison when Willie Smith opened the 1969 season with a home run. Was there more or less or the same when the Cubs swept the Padres in the opening two games of the 1984 playoffs? The 1969 Cubs won 92 games and broke how many hearts? The 1984 Cubs won 96 games, half a pennant, and broke the same hearts and many new ones.

In 1984 I loaded my entire family plus friends into an RV and headed south from my home in Los Angles to San Diego for the clinching victory to send the Cubs into the World Series. Drinking our Lite beers and Bloody Marys and cooking burgers in the parking lot, we watched those unenlightened Padres fans drive around honking their horns and pulling their teddy bears from ropes behind their cars. How quaint. They were the same folks who cheered for pop flies and stomped their feet between innings.

Then, game by game by game, the Cubs blew the playoffs, and my daughters, too old to cry, cried anyway, and we drove home.

"I tried to warn you," I said. "The Cubs will always break your heart."

It couldn't have been 24 hours later when the first phone call came from Chicago.

"Did you hear about Leon Durham?"

"No, what?"

"He was so despondent that he walked onto the elevated tracks in front of a train."

"No!"

"But it's okay. The train went right between his legs."

The Cubs had gone 15 consecutive seasons without drawing one million fans until the 1968 team attracted 1,043,409. The all-time record was shattered one year later at 1,674,993, and the romance has never really ended. In 21 of the past 22 years the Cubs have drawn more than one million fans, and for four of the last five years, with new marketing expertise and WGN superstation in full voice, the Cubs have drawn more than two million.

Since being purchased by the Tribune Company in 1981, the Cubs have become better managed, better promoted, and better marketed. The old ballpark has lights, and that's OK too, even though many fans are still inclined to agree with Bill Hands about day baseball. It's one man's perverse opinion that if the Cubs had won one pennant—just one—the rest of the National League would have legislated against day baseball, claiming an unfair advantage for the Chicago franchise.

But that didn't happen, and TV advertisers pay more for night games anyway, or was that not a consideration?

There was one major difference between the 1969 team and the 1984 team; they came from different eras. With free agency, agents, long-term/guaranteed/gilt-edged contracts, the disabled list, drug tests, and massive corporate ownership, baseball has changed.

At the conclusion of the 1988 season only two members of the 1984 Cubs remained—Ryne Sandberg and Rick Sutcliffe. It was not a team that was "broken up": this was a one-shot, checkbook aggregation that reached near-utopian heights before degenerating. Had Leon Durham bent his back just a few inches more, Dallas Green would still be in Chicago.

The 1969 Cubs, by comparison, played long together, and somehow, fused by respect for each other and a fierce longing for what almost was, have stayed together.

Forgiven but not forgotten, they move among us, reminders of a glorious yet gaunt summer.

It has been said that in Chicago there are two seasons, winter and construction.

For Cub fans there is only one, and it always comes next year.

Appendix I:
What They Did in '69

Ernie Banks hit .253 with 23 homers and 106 RBI. He led National League first basemen in fielding (.997), was second in games played (155), and led the league in putouts (1,419) and total chances accepted (1,510). He appeared in his 13th All-Star Game. That winter he was voted Chicagoan of the Year by the Chicago Press Club, an honor seldom bestowed on a sports figure.

Glenn Beckert hit .291 with one homer and 37 RBI. For the fourth straight year he was the "toughest to strike out" in the National League with only 22 whiffs in 543 at-bats. He was the only Cub to have five hits in one game. He missed 30-plus games with major injuries, and he made first All-Star Game appearance.

Bill Hands was 20–14 with a 2.49 ERA and was voted Chicago Player of the Year by baseball writers. He pitched 300 innings for the best season of his career, was a consistent stopper of losing streaks, and when he won his 20th game on September 28 in Pittsburgh he ended an 11-game Cub losing streak in Forbes Field dating back to 1968. He struck out 181 and walked 73.

Jim Hickman hit .237 with 21 homers and 54 RBI. In 27 games in August he had 10 homers and 25 RBI, averaging .301. He had 14 of 21 homers and 31 of 54 RBI in the last two months, and his RBI per time at bat (338) were topped only by Banks's and Santo's.

Ken Holtzman was 17-13 with a 3.59 ERA for the best season of his young career. Pitched a no-hitter on August 19 at Wrigley Field. He had a string of 33 consecutive scoreless innings early in season. He struck out 176, walked 93.

Randy Hundley hit .255 with 18 homers and 64 RBI. He led the league with fewest errors by a catcher (9) and the most double plays (17). He tied for lead in the most appearances (151) and the most assists (79), was second in putouts (978) and total chances (1,065), and finished third in overall defense (.992). He made his first appearance in All-Star Game.

Fergie Jenkins was 21-15 with a 3.21 ERA and started 42 games, completing 23. He was also the best hitter among the pitchers with 15 hits, 1 HR, and a RBI. He established the club record for strikeouts for the third straight year with 273, which also led the National League, and he walked only 71. In his third consecutive 20-win season, he had seven shutouts.

Don Kessinger hit .273 with four homers and 53 RBI. He won a Gold Glove award, leading National League short-stops in the most games played (157) and every defensive category—fielding percentage (.976), fewest errors (20), total chances (828), and most double plays (101). He reached base safely in each of the first 41 games and led Cubs in runs scored with 109. He was second in the National League in doubles (38).

Phil Regan was 12–6 with a 3.70 ERA and 17 saves in 71 appearances. He finished 49 games. He had his best success against the Mets: a 2–0 record, 2 saves, and a 0.90 ERA.

Ron Santo hit .289 with 29 homers and 123 RBI (second in the National League to Willie McCovey's 126). He was second in fielding among third basemen (.947), tied for the league lead in games (160), led in putouts (144), was second in assists (334), and was second in total chances (505). He tied the league record for most years leading the league in putouts (7) and led the Cubs in home runs and runs batted in. He made his sixth All-Star appearance.

Billy Williams hit .293 with 21 homers and 95 RBI. He was the only Cub to play 163 games. He tied two major league records with most two-base hits one game (4) and making all of his team's hits in one game (4). He led the Cubs in batting average, hits (188), total bases (304), and triples (10).

Appendix II:
Assorted Stats from '69

SCORES OF CHICAGO CUBS' 1969 GAMES

APRIL

			Winner	Loser
8—Phila.	W	7–6§	Regan	Lersch
9—Phila.	W	11–3	Hands	Wise
10—Phila.	W	6–2	Holtzman	Fryman
11—Montreal	W	1–0x	Abernathy	Sembera
12—Montreal	L	3–7	Grant	Jenkins
13—Montreal	W	7–6	Regan	Stoneman
14—Pitts.	W	4–0	Holtzman	Veale
15—Pitts.	W	7–4	Aguirre	Ellis
16—At St. L.	W	1–0	Jenkins	Carlton
17—At St. L.	W	3–0	Hands	Giusti
19—At Mon.	W	6–5§	Regan	Shaw
20—At Mon.	W	6–3	Jenkins	Morton
20—At Mon.	L	2–4	Wegener	Niekro
22—At Pitts.	L	5–7	Hartenstein	Hands
22—At Pitts.	L	5–6	Dal Canton	Nye
24—St. Louis	L	2–3	Giusti	Holtzman
25—At N. Y.	W	3–1	Jenkins	Seaver
26—At N. Y.	W	9–3	Hands	Cardwell
27—At N. Y.	W	8–6	Regan	Koonce
27—At N. Y.	L	0–3	McGraw	Nye

28—At Phila.	W	2–1‡	Abernathy	Wise
29—At Phila.	W	10–0	Jenkins	Jackson
30—At Phila.	L	1–3	Fryman	Hands

MAY

			Winner	Loser
2—N. York	W	6–4	Holtzman	Gentry
3—N. York	W	3–2	Regan	Koonce
4—N. York	L	2–3	Seaver	Hands
4—N. York	L	2–3	McGraw	Selma
6—Los Ang.	W	7–1	Holtzman	Sutton
7—Los Ang.	L	2–4x	Brewer	Jenkins
9—S. Fran.	L	1–11	Bolin	Hands
11—S. Fran.	W	8–0	Holtzman	Sadecki
12—S. Diego	W	2–0	Jenkins	Ross
13—S. Diego	W	19–0	Selma	Kelley
14—S. Diego	W	3–2	Nottebart	Podres
16—At Hous.	W	11–0	Holtzman	Dierker
17—At Hous.	L	4–5	Wilson	Nottebart
18—At Hous.	L	5–6	Ray	Regan
20—At L. A.	W	7–0	Holtzman	Sutton
21—At L. A.	L	1–3	Osteen	Hands
22—At L. A.	W	3–0	Jenkins	Singer
23—At S. D.	W	6–0	Selma	Ross
24—At S. D.	W	7–5	Abernathy	Kelley
25—At S. D.	L	2–10	Podres	Nye
25—At S. D.	W	1–0	Abernathy	Niekro
27—At S. F.	L	4–5	Linzy	Regan
28—At S. F.	W	9–8	Holtzman	Robertson
30—Atlanta	W	2–0	Hands	Reed
31—Atlanta	W	3–2	Jenkins	Niekro

JUNE

			Winner	Loser
1—Atlanta	W	13–4	Selma	Jarvis
3—Houston	W	4–2	Hands	Lemaster
4—Houston	W	5–4	Jenkins	Griffin
6—Cinn.	W	14–8	Holtzman	Cloninger
7—Cinn.	T	5–5†	—	—
9—Cinn.	L	1–4	Culver	Jenkins
10—At Atl.	W	3–1	Holtzman	Reed
11—At Atl.	L	1–5	Niekro	Hands

12—At Atl.	W	12–6	Selma	Hill
13—At Cinn.	W	14–8‡	Regan	Pena
14—At Cinn.	W	9–8‡	Regan	Granger
15—At Cinn.	L	6–7	Carroll	Regan
15—At Cinn.	W	5–4y	Nye	Arrigo
16—At Pitts.	L	8–9	Dal Canton	Regan
17—At Pitts.	L	0–1	Veale	Jenkins
17—At Pitts.	L	3–4	Blass	Abernathy
18—At Pitts.	L	2–3‡	Gibbon	Regan
20—Montreal	W	2–0	Hands	Robertson
21—Montreal	L	2–3	Reed	Jenkins
22—Montreal	W	7–6	Selma	Shaw
22—Montreal	L	4–5*	Face	Reynolds
23—Pitts.	W	5–4	Regan	Dal Canton
24—Pitts.	W	3–2	Hands	Bunning
25—Pitts.	W	5–2	Jenkins	Veale
26—Pitts.	W	7–5‡	Regan	Dal Canton
27—St. Louis	L	1–3	Carlton	Holtzman
28—St. Louis	W	3–1	Hands	Giusti
29—St. Louis	W	3–1	Jenkins	Gibson
29—St. Louis	W	12–1	Selma	Grant
30—At Mon.	L	2–5	Reed	Lemonds

JULY

			Winner	Loser
1—At Mon.	L	4–11	Renko	Holtzman
2—At Mon.	W	4–2	Hands	Stoneman
3—At Mon.	W	8–4	Selma	Wegener
4—At St. L.	W	3–1‡	Jenkins	Gibson
5—At St. L.	L	1–5	Briles	Holtzman
6—At St. L.	L	2–4	Carlton	Hands
6—At St. L.	L	3–6	Taylor	Nye
8—At N. Y.	L	3–4	Koosman	Jenkins
9—At N. Y.	L	0–4	Seaver	Holtzman
10—At N. Y.	W	6–2	Hands	Gentry
11—Phila.	L	5–7	Boozer	Abernathy
12—Phila.	W	7–4	Jenkins	Wise
13—Phila.	W	6–0	Holtzman	Fryman
13—Phila.	W	6–4	Colborn	Palmer
14—N. York	W	1–0	Hands	Seaver
15—N. York	L	4–5	Gentry	Selma
16—N. York	L	5–9	Koonce	Jenkins
18—At Phila.	W	9–5	Regan	Wilson
19—At Phila.	L	3–5	Wise	Hands

20—At Phila.	W	1–0	Jenkins	Jackson
20—At Phila.	W	6–1	Selma	Champion
24—Los Ang.	W	5–3	Holtzman	Sutton
25—Los Ang.	L	2–4	Osteen	Jenkins
26—Los Ang.	W	3–2§	Regan	Brewer
27—Los Ang.	L	2–6	Drysdale	Jenkins
28—S. Fran.	W	4–3‡	Nye	Marichal
29—S. Fran.	L	2–4	Linzy	Abernathy
30—S. Fran.	L	3–6	Perry	Nye
31—S. Fran.	W	12–2	Jenkins	Bolin

AUGUST

			Winner	Loser
1—S. Diego	W	5–2	Hands	Kirby
2—S. Diego	W	4–1	Holtzman	Santorini
3—S. Diego	W	4–3	Selma	Niekro
4—At Hous.	W	9–3	Jenkins	Griffin
5—At Hous.	W	5–2	Hands	Lemaster
6—At Hous.	W	5–4	Nye	Billingham
8—At L. A.	L	0–5	Singer	Jenkins
9—At L. A.	W	4–0	Hands	Foster
10—At L. A.	L	2–4	Sutton	Holtzman
12—At S. D.	W	4–0	Jenkins	Santorini
13—At S. D.	W	4–2	Hands	Niekro
15—At S. F.	L	0–3	Marichal	Holtzman
16—At S. F.	W	3–0	Jenkins	Perry
17—At S. F.	L	3–5	Linzy	Hands
17—At S. F.	W	3–1	Selma	Bryant
19—Atlanta	W	3–0	Holtzman	Niekro
20—Atlanta	L	2–6	Reed	Jenkins
21—Atlanta	L	1–3	Britton	Hands
22—Houston	L	2–8	Dierker	Selma
23—Houston	W	11–5	Holtzman	Gladding
24—Houston	W	10–9	Regan	Gladding
24—Houston	L	2–3	Wilson	Johnson
25—Cinn.	L	8–9	Nolan	Hands
26—Cinn.	L	7–8	Merritt	Selma
27—Cinn.	L	3–6	Cloninger	Holtzman
28—Cinn.	W	3–1	Jenkins	Arrigo
29—At Atl.	W	2–1	Hands	Jarvis
30—At Atl.	W	5–4	Johnson	Reed
31—At Atl.	W	8–4	Holtzman	Niekro

SEPTEMBER

			Winner	Loser
2—At Cinn.	W	8-2	Jenkins	Cloninger
3—At Cinn.	L	0-2	Maloney	Hands
5—Pitts.	L	2-9	Blass	Holtzman
6—Pitts.	L	4-13	Veale	Jenkins
7—Pitts.	L	5-7§	Dal Canton	Johnson
8—At N. Y.	L	2-3	Koosman	Hands
9—At N. Y.	L	1-7	Seaver	Jenkins
10—At Phila.	L	2-6	Wise	Holtzman
11—At Phila.	L	3-4	James	Selma
12—At St. L.	W	5-1	Hands	Taylor
13—At St. L.	L	4-7	Grant	Jenkins
14—At St. L.	L	1-2‡	Gibson	Holtzman
15—At Mon.	L	2-8	Wegener	Selma
16—At Mon.	W	5-4	Hands	Robertson
17—Phila.	W	9-7	Jenkins	Champion
18—Phila.	L	3-5	Jackson	Regan
19—St. Louis	W	2-1‡	Holtzman	Gibson
19—St. Louis	L	2-7	Torrez	Selma
20—St. Louis	L	1-4	Carlton	Hands
21—St. Louis	W	4-3	Jenkins	Taylor
23—Montreal	L	3-7	Stoneman	Holtzman
24—Montreal	W	6-3	Hands	Renko
26—At Pitts.	L	0-2	Ellis	Jenkins
27—At Pitts.	L	1-4	Blass	Holtzman
28—At Pitts.	W	3-1	Hands	Veale

OCTOBER

			Winner	Loser
1—N. York	L	5-6x	Taylor	Selma
2—N. York	W	5-3	Decker	Cardwell

* 6 innings.
† Game halted by rain with two outs in top of ninth.
‡ 10 innings.
§ 11 innings.
x 12 innings.
y Suspended game, completed September 2.

'69 ROSTER

Manager: Leo Durocher

Won 92 Lost 70 Pct. .568 2nd

POS	Player	B	G	AB	H	2B	3B	HR	HR%	R	RBI	BB	SO	SB	Pinch Hit AB	Pinch Hit H	BA	SA
Regulars																		
1B	Ernie Banks	R	155	565	143	19	2	23	4.1	60	106	42	101	0	2	2	.253	.416
2B	Glenn Beckert	R	131	543	158	22	1	1	0.2	69	37	24	24	6	1	0	.291	.341
SS	Don Kessinger	B	158	664	181	38	6	4	0.6	109	53	61	70	11	1	0	.273	.366
3B	Ron Santo	R	160	575	166	18	4	29	5.0	97	123	96	97	1	1	0	.289	.485
RF	Jim Hickman	R	134	338	80	11	2	21	6.2	38	54	47	74	2	18	5	.237	.467
CF	Don Young	R	101	272	65	12	3	6	2.2	36	27	38	74	1	0	0	.239	.371
LF	Billy Williams	L	163	642	188	33	10	21	3.3	103	95	59	70	3	2	0	.293	.474
C	Randy Hundley	R	151	522	133	15	1	18	3.4	67	64	61	90	2	1	0	.255	.391
Substitutes																		
UT	Paul Popovich	R	60	154	48	6	0	1	0.6	26	14	18	14	0	22	7	.312	.370
2B	Nate Oliver	R	44	44	7	3	0	1	2.3	15	4	1	10	0	3	0	.159	.295
1B	Rick Bladt	R	10	13	2	0	0	0	0.0	1	1	0	5	0	1	0	.154	.154
OF	Al Spangler	L	82	213	45	8	1	4	1.9	23	23	21	16	0	26	1	.211	.315
OF	Willie Smith	L	103	195	48	9	1	9	4.6	21	25	25	49	1	40	12	.246	.441
OF	Jim Qualls	B	43	120	30	5	3	0	0.0	12	9	2	14	2	4	2	.250	.342
OF	Oscar Gamble	L	24	71	16	1	1	1	1.4	6	5	10	12	0	0	0	.225	.310
OF	Adolfo Phillips	R	28	49	11	3	1	0	0.0	5	1	16	15	1	1	0	.224	.327
OF	Jimmie Hall	L	11	24	5	1	0	0	0.0	1	1	1	5	0	1	1	.208	.250
CO	Ken Rudolph	R	27	34	7	1	0	1	2.9	7	6	6	11	0	10	3	.206	.324

| | | | | | | | | | | | | | | | Pinch Hit | | | |
POS	Player	B	G	AB	H	2B	3B	HR	HR%	R	RBI	BB	SO	SB	AB	H	BA	SA
C	Bill Heath	L	27	32	5	0	1	0	0.0	1	1	12	4	0	12	2	.156	.219
C	Gene Oliver	R	23	27	6	3	0	0	0.0	0	0	1	9	0	14	4	.222	.333
CO	John Hairston	R	3	4	1	0	0	0	0.0	0	0	0	2	0	1	1	.250	.250
C	Randy Bobb	R	3	2	0	0	0	0	0.0	0	0	0	1	0	0	0	.000	.000
PH	Manny Jimenez	L	6	6	1	0	0	0	0.0	0	0	0	2	0	6	1	.167	.167
PH	Charley Smith	R	2	2	0	0	0	0	0.0	0	0	0	0	0	2	0	.000	.000

Pitchers

| | | | | | | | | | | | | | | | Pinch Hit | | | |
POS	Player	B	G	AB	H	2B	3B	HR	HR%	R	RBI	BB	SO	SB	AB	H	BA	SA
P	Ferguson Jenkins	R	43	108	15	2	1	1	0.9	6	9	6	42	0	0	0	.139	.204
P	Ken Holtzman	R	39	100	15	1	1	1	1.0	5	7	2	32	0	0	0	.150	.210
P	Bill Hands	R	41	98	9	0	0	0	0.0	5	3	4	45	0	0	0	.092	.092
P	Dick Selma	R	36	52	8	1	1	0	0.0	3	0	1	17	0	0	0	.154	.212
P	Rich Nye	L	36	16	1	0	0	0	0.0	1	0	0	7	0	0	0	.063	.063
P	Phil Regan	R	71	15	2	1	0	0	0.0	0	0	2	2	0	0	0	.133	.133
P	Ted Abernathy	R	56	8	2	0	0	0	0.0	1	1	2	2	0	0	0	.250	.375
P	Hank Aguirre	R	41	5	1	1	0	0	0.0	2	0	0	1	0	0	0	.400	.400
P	Joe Niekro	R	4	5	1	0	0	0	0.0	0	2	0	1	0	0	0	.200	.400
P	Ken Johnson	R	9	4	0	0	0	0	0.0	0	0	0	4	0	0	0	.000	.000
P	Jim Colborn	R	6	3	0	0	0	0	0.0	0	0	0	2	0	0	0	.000	.000
P	Joe Decker	R	4	2	0	0	0	0	0.0	0	0	0	1	0	0	0	.000	.000
P	Don Nottebart	R	16	1	0	0	0	0	0.0	0	0	1	1	0	0	0	.000	.000
P	Archie Reynolds	R	2	1	0	0	0	0	0.0	0	0	2	1	0	0	0	.000	.000
P	Dave Lemonds	L	2	1	0	0	0	0	0.0	0	0	0	0	0	0	0	.000	.000
P	Gary Ross	R	2	0	0	0	0	0	—	0	0	0	0	0	0	0	—	—
P	Alec Distaso	R	2	0	0	0	0	0	—	0	0	0	0	0	0	0	—	—
Team Total				5530	1400	215	40	142	2.6	72	671	559	928	30	169	41	.253	.384

INDIVIDUAL PITCHING

Pitcher	T	W	L	PCT	ERA	SV	G	GS	CG	IP	H	BB	SO	R	ER	ShO	H/9	BB/9	SO/9
Ferguson Jenkins	R	21	15	.583	3.21	1	43	42	23	311	284	71	273	122	111	7	8.22	2.05	7.90
Bill Hands	R	20	14	.588	2.49	0	41	41	18	300	268	73	181	102	83	3	8.04	2.19	5.43
Ken Holtzman	L	17	13	.567	3.59	0	39	39	12	261	248	93	176	117	104	6	8.55	3.21	6.07
Dick Selma	R	10	8	.556	3.63	1	36	25	4	168.2	137	72	161	74	68	2	7.31	3.84	8.59
Phil Regan	R	12	6	.667	3.70	17	71	0	0	112	120	35	56	49	46	0	9.64	2.81	4.50
Ted Abernathy	R	4	3	.571	3.18	3	56	0	0	85	75	42	55	38	30	0	7.94	4.45	5.82
Rich Nye	L	3	5	.375	5.09	3	34	5	1	69	72	21	39	43	39	0	9.39	2.74	5.09
Hank Aguirre	L	1	0	1.000	2.60	1	41	0	0	45	45	12	19	13	13	0	9.00	2.40	3.80
Joe Niekro	R	0	1	.000	3.72	0	4	3	0	19.1	24	6	7	9	8	0	11.17	2.79	3.26
Ken Johnson	R	1	2	.333	2.84	1	9	1	0	19	17	13	18	8	6	0	8.05	6.16	8.53
Don Nottebart	R	1	1	.500	7.00	0	16	0	0	8	28	7	8	14	14	0	14.00	3.50	4.00
Jim Colborn	R	1	0	1.000	3.00	0	6	2	0	15	15	9	4	6	5	0	9.00	5.40	2.40
Joe Decker	R	1	0	1.000	3.00	0	4	1	0	12	10	6	3	4	4	0	7.50	4.50	9.75
Archie Reynolds	R	0	0	.000	2.57	0	2	2	0	7	11	7	4	5	2	0	14.14	9.00	5.14
Alec Distaso	R	0	0	—	3.60	0	2	0	0	5	6	1	1	2	2	0	10.80	1.80	1.80
Dave Lemonds	L	0	1	.000	3.60	0	2	1	0	5	5	5	0	2	2	0	7.00	9.00	0.00
Gary Ross	R	0	0	.000	13.50	0	2	1	0	2	1	2	2	3	3	0	4.50	9.00	9.00
Team Total		92	70	.568	3.34	27	408	163	58	1454.0	1366	475	1007	611	540	8	8.46	2.94	6.30

INDIVIDUAL FIELDING

POS	Player	T	G	PO	A	E	DP	TC/G	FA
1B	E. Banks	R	153	1419	87	4	116	9.9	.997
	W. Smith	L	24	159	9	1	14	7.0	.994
	R. Bladt	R	7	12	1	0	0	1.9	1.000
2B	G. Beckert	R	129	262	401	24	71	5.3	.965
	P. Popovich	R	25	50	64	3	13	4.7	.974
	N. Oliver	R	13	22	31	0	9	4.1	1.000
	J. Qualls	R	4	7	4	0	2	2.8	1.000
SS	D. Kessinger	R	157	266	542	20	101	5.3	.976
	P. Popovich	R	7	13	23	0	7	5.1	1.000
3B	R. Santo	R	160	144	334	27	23	3.2	.947
	P. Popovich	R	6	2	9	1	1	2.0	.917
OF	B. Williams	R	159	250	15	12	2	1.7	.957
	D. Young	R	100	191	4	5	0	2.0	.975
	J. Hickman	R	125	153	6	3	0	1.3	.981
	A. Spangler	L	58	75	1	4	0	1.4	.950
	J. Qualls	R	35	55	1	0	0	1.6	1.000
	O. Gamble	R	24	41	1	4	0	1.9	.913
	A. Phillips	R	25	43	0	2	0	1.8	.956
	W. Smith	L	33	26	0	2	0	0.8	.929
	J. Hairston	R	1	0	0	0	0	0.0	.000
	J. Hall	R	5	5	0	0	0	1.0	1.000
	K. Rudolph	R	3	2	0	0	0	0.7	1.000
	P. Popovich	R	1	1	0	0	0	1.0	1.000
C	R. Hundley	R	151	978	79	8	17	7.1	.992
	B. Heath	R	9	44	3	1	1	5.3	.979
	K. Rudolph	R	11	39	3	1	0	3.9	.977
	G. Oliver	R	6	28	2	0	1	5.0	1.000
	J. Hairston	R	1	3	1	0	0	4.0	1.000
	R. Bobb	R	2	4	0	0	0	2.0	1.000

Appendix III:
What Became of the Class of '69

THE REGULARS

Ernie Banks, first base

Executive vice president, corporate sales, New World Van Lines, Inc., Compton, California

Glenn Beckert, second base

Commodities trader, Shatkin Trading Company, the Chicago Board of Trade, Chicago

Don Kessinger, shortstop

Securities broker; partner with Kyle Rote, Jr., in Athletic Resource Management, a company that represents athletes, Memphis, Tennessee

Ron Santo, third base

Partner, Unipoint Corporation, Chicago (a company that builds diesel fuel facilities); co-owner of four Kentucky Fried Chicken franchises

Jim Hickman, right field	Minor league hitting instructor, the Cincinnati Reds
Don Young, center field	Unknown
Billy Williams, left field	Coordinator, speakers' bureau, marketing department, the Chicago Cubs
Randy Hundley, catcher	Owner and originator, Randy Hundley's Official Big League Baseball Camps

THE BENCH

Paul Popovich, infielder	The Bench Coach, the Vero Beach (Florida) Dodgers (Class A)
Nate Oliver, infielder	Manager, the Reno (Nevada) Silver Sox (Class A); station manager, Bay Area Rapid Transit, Oakland, California
Rick Bladt, outfielder	Carpenter, Mount Angel, Oregon
Al Spangler, outfielder	Algebra teacher, baseball coach, and athletic director, Hargrave High School, Huffman, Texas
Willie Smith, outfielder	Foreman, Magic Chef, Inc., a microwave company, Anniston, Alabama
Jimmy Qualls, outfielder	Farmer, near Quincy, Illinois

Oscar Gamble, outfielder	Hitting coach, Auburn University at Montgomery, Alabama
Adolfo Phillips, outfielder	Baseball coach, the Panamanian government, Panama City, Panama
Jimmie Hall, outfielder	Employee, a trucking company, Wilson, North Carolina
Ken Rudolph, catcher	Operations manager, United Parcel Service, Tempe, Arizona
Bill Heath, catcher	President, CEO, the Center for Financial Planning, Houston, Texas
Gene Oliver, catcher	Car salesman, Quad Cities area; coach, Hundley baseball camps
John Hairston, catcher	School teacher, Portland, Oregon
Randy Bobb, catcher	Deceased
Manny Jimenez, pinch hitter	Unknown, New York, New York
Charley Smith, pinch hitter	Senior maintenance man, city of Sparks, Nevada

THE PITCHERS

Fergie Jenkins	Minor league pitching coach, the Texas Rangers
Ken Holtzman	Insurance executive, Chicago
Bill Hands	Co-owner, Hands Fuel Company and Joe's Garage, Orient, New York

Dick Selma	Merchandiser, Fleming Foods, Fresno, California
Dr. Rich Nye	Veterinarian, specializing in exotic birds, Westchester, Illinois; trader, Chicago Mercantile Exchange, Chicago
Phil Regan	Major league scout, the Los Angeles Dodgers
Ted Abernathy	Receiving man, Summey Products, a module home company, Dallas, North Carolina
Hank Aguirre	Founder and owner, Mexican Industries in Michigan, Inc., Detroit, Michigan
Joe Niekro	Pitching coach, the Portland (Oregon) Beavers
Ken Johnson	Assistant baseball coach, Louisiana College, Pineville, Louisiana
Jim Colborn	Minor league coordinator, the Chicago Cubs, Chicago
Joe Decker	Northwest sales representative, a videocassette company, Boise, Idaho
Don Nottebart	Owner, two carpet retail stores, Houston, Texas
Archie Reynolds	Owner, Archie's (a nightclub), Azle, Texas

Dave Lemonds	Regional sales manager, Marion Laboratories, Charlotte, North Carolina
Gary Ross	Owner, liquor store, Encinitas, California
Alec Distaso	Detective, Rampart Division, Los Angeles Police Department, Los Angeles, California

THE MANAGER AND HIS COACHES

Leo Durocher, manager	Retired, Palm Springs, California
Joey Amalfitano, coach	Coach, the Los Angeles Dodgers
Joe Becker, pitching coach	Retired, Vero Beach, Florida
Pete Reiser, coach	Deceased
Verlon (Rube) Walker, coach	Deceased

Index